I Believe in Preaching

D1390979

Also by John Stott:

Men with a Message
Basic Christianity
Your Confirmation
What Christ Thinks of the Church
The Preacher's Portrait
Confess Your Sins
The Epistles of John (Tyndale New Testament
    Commentary)
The Canticles and Selected Psalms
Men Made New
Our Guilty Silence
Only One Way
One People
Christ the Controversialist
Understanding the Bible
Guard the Gospel
Balanced Christianity
Christian Mission in the Modern World
Baptism and Fullness
The Lausanne Covenant (an exposition and commentary)
Christian Counter-Culture
Focus on Christ
God's New Society

I Believe in Preaching

John Stott

Hodder & Stoughton

LONDON SYDNEY AUCKLAND TORONTO

British Library Cataloguing in Publication Data

Stott, John R. W.
  I believe in preaching.
  1. Preaching
  I. Title
  251   BV4211.2

  ISBN 0 340 48882 4

Contents

Editor's Preface

The aim of this *I Believe* series has been to take a fresh, biblical, positive look at some of the important areas of Christian belief and practice which have been neglected or minimized in modern times. Few areas so need that new look as preaching.

The standard of preaching in the modern world is deplorable. There are few great preachers. Many clergy do not seem to believe in it any more as a powerful way in which to proclaim the gospel and change the life. This is the age of the sermonette: and sermonettes make Christianettes.[1] Much of the current uncertainty about the gospel and the mission of the Church must be due to a generation of preachers which has lost confidence in the Word of God, and no longer takes the trouble to study it in depth and to proclaim it without fear or favour.

John Stott is one of the few great preachers in Britain today. He has, moreover, been released into a ministry of writing and travel which takes him all over the world. It is, therefore, particularly gratifying that he has allowed himself to be persuaded to write this book which will take its place as one of the major treatments of the subject. It takes a preacher to write effectively about preaching, and that is what we have in this book.

A glance at the Contents will indicate the scope of this remarkable book. He shows the glorious heritage and the mighty effect of preaching over the centuries, and incidentally throughout this book displays an astonishing breadth and depth in his own reading on the subject. He faces head-on the objections to preaching; he marshals encouragement to preaching, and he shows how one foot of the preacher must always be anchored in the Bible and the other in the contemporary world. The chapters on the study and the preparation which make for effective preaching are full of wisdom and helpful advice, and will be both a challenge and an inspiration to preachers. But expertise by itself is not enough. The preacher must live his message and must by his humility and passion allow the Holy Spirit to work through him, and expect such preaching in the power of the Spirit to change lives.

The opening five words of this book aptly summarize its theme. 'Preaching is indispensable to Christianity.' *It is just that*. And because he knows the truth, and feels it deeply, and has experienced its power all over the world, Dr. John Stott has produced a book which, like a good sermon, is addressed both to the head and to the heart; a book which aims to go through both head and heart to the will. For this book seeks to encourage and challenge all preachers to give themselves more wholeheartedly to their calling, to make known God's way of salvation to a world that has lost its way. There is no higher vocation than that.

There are signs today in many parts of the world of a significant growth in the Christian Church. What is now needed is a revival of confident, intelligent, relevant, biblical preaching which will further that growth and build up mature disciples of Jesus Christ. If any book can stimulate such a revival in preaching, this is it.

MICHAEL GREEN
Easter, 1981

Note

1 cf. p. 294

Author's Introduction

It is a rash and foolhardy enterprise for any preacher to preach to other preachers about preaching. I certainly do not claim to be an expert myself. On the contrary, I confess that in the pulpit I am often seized with 'communication frustration', for a message burns within me, but I am unable to convey to others what I am thinking, let alone feeling. And seldom if ever do I leave the pulpit without a sense of partial failure, a mood of penitence, a cry to God for forgiveness, and a resolve to look to him for grace to do better in the future.

At the same time, I confess to being – for reasons which will emerge in the following chapters – an impenitent believer in the indispensable necessity of preaching both for evangelism and for the healthy growth of the Church. The contemporary situation makes preaching more difficult; it does not make it any less necessary.

A countless number of books have been written on preaching. I myself have read nearly a hundred books on homiletics, communication and related themes. How then can yet another be justified? If anything is distinctive about *I Believe in Preaching*, I think it is that I have tried to bring together several complementary aspects of the topic, which have often been kept apart. Thus, in the opening historical survey I hope readers will feel, as I do, that there is a certain 'glory' in the preaching ministry, which prepares us to face with integrity in the second chapter the problems which beset it today. Although in Chapters Five and Six I seek to give practical advice both on study and on sermon preparation, I say little about such matters as delivery, elocution and gesture. This is partly because these matters are best learned by being 'apprenticed' to an experienced preacher, by trial and error, and by friendly critics. It is more because

I want to put first things first, and because I believe that by far the most important secrets of preaching are not technical but theological and personal. Hence Chapter Three on 'Theological Foundations for Preaching' and Chapters Seven and Eight on such personal characteristics of the preacher as sincerity, earnestness, courage and humility. Another particular emphasis I have made, born of growing experience and conviction, is on 'Preaching as Bridge-building' (Chapter Four). A true sermon bridges the gulf between the biblical and the modern worlds, and must be equally earthed in both.

All preachers are aware of the painful tension between ideals and reality. Some readers will feel not only that I have included a plethora of quotations, but that too many of these come from authors who belong to a bygone age remote from our situation. As for quotations in general, I have simply wanted to share with others the fruits of my reading. Although I have also written with freedom and frankness out of my own experience, it would have been arrogant to confine myself to this. Preaching has an unbroken tradition in the Church of nearly twenty centuries. We have very much to learn from the great preachers of the past whose ministry God has so signally blessed. The fact that our reality differs from theirs seems to me no reason why we should not share their ideals.

Other readers will find me too idealistic in a different sense, namely that I do not take sufficient account of the problems under which many clergy labour today. They are overworked and underpaid. They are exposed to unrelenting intellectual, social, moral and spiritual pressures, of which our forefathers knew nothing. Their morale is low. Many suffer from loneliness, discouragement and depression. Some have several village congregations to care for (I think of a presbyter of the Church of South India who has thirty, with only a bicycle on which to visit them). Others are struggling in a decayed and neglected inner city area, with a handful of members and as yet no leaders. Do I not set impossibly high standards of study and preparation, which may be appropriate for a long-established urban or suburban church but not for a pioneer, church-planting situation? Yes, it is true both that my own experience has been largely limited to All Souls Church in London and to similar churches elsewhere, and that I have had such churches mostly in mind while writing. Nevertheless, I have done my best to remember other situations.

The ideals I have unfolded I believe to be universally true, although of course they need to be adapted to each particular reality. Whether the preacher is addressing a large congregation in a modern town church, or occupies an ancient pulpit in an ancient European village church, or is huddled with a tiny remnant in the draughty corner of a dilapidated old edifice which has long since outgrown its usefulness, or is talking to a crowd of peasants in a hut in Latin America or under some trees in Africa, or is sitting informally in a western home with a small group gathered round him – yet, with all these diversities, very much remains the same. We have the same Word of God, and the same human beings, and the same fallible preacher called by the same living God to study both the Word and the world in order to relate the one to the other with honesty, conviction, courage and meekness.

The privilege of preaching is given to an increasing number of different people today. Although I have written with full-time stipendiary pastors mainly in view, I believe strongly in the rightness and helpfulness of a team ministry, and I have remembered both the auxiliary pastors and the lay preachers who may belong to it. Also, although I address myself to preachers, I have not forgotten their listeners. In nearly every church closer and more cordial relations between pastors and people, preachers and listeners, would be beneficial. There is need for more cooperation between them in the preparing of sermons, and more candour in evaluating them. The average congregation can have a far greater influence than it realizes on the standard of preaching it receives, by asking for more biblical and contemporary sermons, by setting their pastors

11

free from administration so that they may have more time to study and prepare, and by their expressions of appreciation and encouragement when their pastors take their preaching responsibility seriously.

Finally, I want to thank some of the many people who have helped in the writing of this book. I begin with the Rev. E. J. H. Nash, who showed me the way to Christ when I was almost seventeen, nurtured me and prayed for me with astonishing faithfulness, developed my appetite for the Word of God, and gave me my first taste of the joys of expounding it.

Next, I thank the long-suffering congregation of All Souls Church, who have been the anvil on which I have forged whatever preaching skills I have, and the church family who have surrounded me with their love, encouragement and prayers. With them I thank Michael Baughen, who came to All Souls as Vicar in 1970 and succeeded me as Rector in 1975, and who has given me the privilege of being a member of his pastoral team and of continuing to preach.

I express my special gratitude to Frances Whitehead who this month has completed twenty-five years as my secretary, whose industry and efficiency are proverbial, and who has laboriously deciphered the scribble into which my handwriting degenerates when the heavenly muse descends upon me. She has now typed – or shared in the typing of – about twenty books.

I thank Ted Schroder, who was born in New Zealand and now ministers in the United States, and who during his four-year curacy at All Souls kept challenging me to relate the gospel to the modern world. I also thank innumerable pastors at conferences, seminars and workshops on preaching in all six continents; and the students of Trinity Evangelical Divinity School, Gordon-Conwell seminary, Fuller Theological Seminary and the Theological Students' Fellowship, who have listened to me lecturing on this topic. These pastors and students have stimulated me by their questions.

I am grateful to Roy McCloughry, Tom Cooper and

Mark Labberton, who one after the other have helped me as part-time study assistants, especially to Mark who in addition read the manuscript of this book three times and made helpful suggestions, not least from the perspective of seminarians. I thank my friends Dick and Rosemary Bird who for many years have accompanied me to my Welsh cottage, the Hookses, and unselfishly created the conditions in which I could write in peace and without distraction. I also thank numerous people who have answered questions put to them in writing, especially Bishop Lesslie Newbigin, Professor James Stewart, Malcolm Muggeridge, Iain Murray, Leith Samuel, Oliver Barclay, Bishop John Reid and Bishop Timothy Dudley-Smith.

Special thanks are due to Os Guinness, Andrew Kirk, Michael Baughen and Rob Warner for making time to read the MS and to send me their comments. Michael Green, editor of this *I Believe* series, also read it, in spite of an attack of bronchitis, and to him I am additionally indebted for the generous terms in which he has written his Preface.

JOHN STOTT
Easter 1981

Abbreviations and Versions of the Bible

AG   Arndt, William F. and Gingrich, F. Wilbur, A Greek–
        English Lexicon of the New Testament and other
        Early Christian Literature (University of Chicago
        Press and Cambridge University Press, 1957).
AV   Authorized Version of the Bible, 1611 ('King James').
LXX   The Old Testament in Greek according to the Septua-
        gint.
NASB   New American Standard Bible.
NEB   New English Bible (New Testament 1961, second
        edition 1970; Old Testament 1970).
NIV   New International Version of the Bible (Hodder &
        Stoughton, New Testament 1974, Old Testament
        1979).
RSV   Revised Standard Version of the Bible (New Testa-
        ment 1946, second edition 1971; Old Testament
        1952).

Unless otherwise stated, biblical quotations are taken from the
Revised Standard Version.

CHAPTER ONE

The Glory of Preaching: A Historical Sketch

Preaching is indispensable to Christianity. Without preaching a necessary part of its authenticity has been lost. For Christianity is, in its very essence, a religion of the Word of God. No attempt to understand Christianity can succeed which overlooks or denies the truth that the living God has taken the initiative to reveal himself savingly to fallen humanity; or that his self-revelation has been given by the most straightforward means of communication known to us, namely by a word and words; or that he calls upon those who have heard his Word to speak it to others.

First, God spoke through the prophets, interpreting to them the significance of his actions in the history of Israel, and simultaneously instructing them to convey his message to his people either by speech or by writing or both. Next, and supremely, he spoke in his Son, his 'Word . . . made flesh', and in his Word's words, whether spoken directly or through his apostles. Thirdly, he speaks through his Spirit, who himself bears witness to Christ and to Scripture, and makes both living to the people of God today. This Trinitarian statement of a speaking Father, Son and Holy Spirit, and so of a Word of God that is scriptural, incarnate and contemporary, is fundamental to the Christian religion. And it is God's speech which makes our speech necessary. We must speak what he has spoken. Hence the paramount obligation to preach.

This emphasis is, moreover, unique to Christianity. Of course every religion has its accredited teachers, whether Hindu gurus or Jewish rabbis or Moslem mullahs. Yet these instructors in religion and ethics, even if endowed with official authority and personal charisma, are essentially the expositors of an ancient tradition. Only Christian preachers claim to be heralds of good news from God, and dare to think of themselves as his ambassadors or representatives who actually utter 'oracles of God' (1 Pet. 4:11). 'Preaching is an essential part and a distinguishing feature of Christianity,' wrote E. C. Dargan in his two-volume *History of Preaching*. Again, 'Preaching is distinctively a Christian institution.'[1]

That preaching is central and distinctive to Christianity has been recognized throughout the Church's long and colourful story, even from the beginning. So before we weigh the objections to preaching, and consider how we should respond to them, it seems to me both healthy and helpful to set the contemporary argument in the context of Church history. To be sure, neither time-honoured opinions of the past nor influential voices of the present are infallible. Yet the impressive unanimity of their conviction about the primacy and power of preaching (and I shall deliberately draw from a broad spectrum of ecclesiastical tradition) will give us a good perspective from which to view the opposing position, and put us in a good mood to do so.

Jesus, the Apostles and the Fathers

The only place to begin is with Jesus himself. 'The Founder of Christianity was himself the first of its preachers; but he was preceded by his forerunner and followed by his apostles, and in the preaching of these the proclamation and teaching of God's Word by public address was made an essential and permanent feature of the Christian religion.'[2] Certainly the evangelists present Jesus as having been first and foremost an itinerant preacher. 'Jesus came . . . preaching,' Mark announces, as he introduces the public ministry (Mark 1:14, cf. Matt. 4:17). So it was entirely legitimate for George Buttrick, later chaplain of Harvard, to take these three words as the title of his 1931 Lyman Beecher lectures at Yale. The synoptic evangelists sum-

16

marize his Galilean ministry in these terms, 'Jesus went about all the cities and villages, teaching in their synagogues and preaching the gospel of the kingdom.' (Matt. 9:35, cf. 4:23 and Mark 1:39.) Indeed, this was Jesus' own understanding of his mission at that period. He claimed in the Nazareth synagogue that, in fulfilment of the prophecy of Isaiah 61, the Spirit of the Lord had anointed him to preach his liberating message. Consequently, he 'must' do so. It was 'for this purpose', he explained, that he had been 'sent' (Luke 4:18, 43, cf. Mark 1:38 'for that is why I came out'). John's witness to Jesus' self-conscious mission as preacher and teacher is similar. He accepted the title 'Rabbi', he claimed to have 'spoken openly to the world' and to have 'said nothing secretly', and he told Pilate he had come into the world 'to bear witness to the truth' (John 13:13; 18:20, 37).

That the apostles after Pentecost gave priority to the ministry of preaching is specifically stated in Acts 6. They resisted the temptation to get involved in other forms of service, in order to devote themselves 'to prayer and to the ministry of the word' (v.4). For it was to this that Jesus had primarily called them. During his lifetime he had sent them out to preach (Mark 3:14), although temporarily restricting their ministry to 'the lost sheep of the house of Israel' (Matt. 10:5–7). After his resurrection, however, he had solemnly commissioned them to take the gospel to the nations (e.g. Matt. 28:19; Luke 24:47). According to the longer ending of Mark, 'they went forth and preached everywhere.' (16:20) They proclaimed in the power of the Holy Spirit the good news of the death and resurrection, or the sufferings and glory, of the Christ (1 Pet. 1:12). In the Acts we watch them doing so, first Peter and the other Jerusalem apostles who 'spoke the word of God with boldness' (4:31), and then Luke's hero Paul in his three missionary expeditions, until Luke leaves him in Rome under house arrest, yet 'preaching the kingdom of God and teaching about the Lord Jesus Christ quite openly and unhindered' (28:31). In this Luke is faithfully reflecting Paul's

17

own perception of his ministry. Christ had sent him to preach the gospel, he wrote, not to baptize; so he felt a certain 'necessity' or compulsion to do so. Besides, preaching was God's appointed way by which sinners would hear of the Saviour and so call on him for salvation, for 'how are they to hear without a preacher?' (1 Cor. 1:17; 9;16; Rom. 10:14, 15). Then at the end of his life, knowing that he had fought his fight and finished his race, he passed the commission on to his young lieutenant Timothy. In the presence of God, and in anticipation of the return of Christ to judge and to reign, he solemnly charged him, 'Preach the word, be urgent in season and out of season, convince, rebuke, and exhort, be unfailing in patience and in teaching.' (2 Tim. 4:1, 2)

So prominent was the place of preaching and teaching in the ministry of Jesus and his apostles that it is hardly surprising to find the same emphasis on it among the early church fathers.

The Didache, or 'Teaching of the Lord through the Twelve Apostles', dating probably from near the beginning of the second century, is a church manual on ethics, the sacraments, the ministry and the second coming of Jesus. It refers to a variety of teaching ministries, to 'bishops and deacons' on the one hand and to itinerant 'teachers, apostles and prophets' on the other. Travelling teachers are to be welcomed, but practical tests are given by which their genuineness may be assessed. If a teacher contradicts the apostolic faith, if he stays more than two days and/or asks for money, and if he fails to practise what he preaches, then he is a false prophet (11:1–2 and 12:1–5). If he is genuine, however, he must be listened to with humility. 'Be long-suffering and pitiful and guileless and gentle and good and always trembling at the words which thou hast heard.' Again, 'My child, him that speaketh to thee the Word of God remember night and day; and thou shalt honour him as the Lord.' (3:8; 4:1)[3]

About the middle of the second century Justin Martyr's *First Apology* was published. He addressed it to the Emperor, defended Christianity against misrepresentations, and argued that it is true because the Christ who died and rose was the embodiment of truth and the Saviour of mankind. Towards the end he gave an account of 'the weekly worship of the Christians'. It is notable both for the prominence given to the reading and preaching of the Scriptures, and for the combination of Word and sacrament:

> And on the day called Sunday, all who live in cities or in the country gather together to one place, and the memoirs of the apostles or the writings of the prophets are read, as long as time permits; then, when the reader has ceased, the president verbally instructs, and exhorts to the imitation of these good things. Then we all rise together and pray, and, as we before said, when our prayer is ended, bread and wine and water are brought, and the president in like manner offers prayers and thanksgivings, according to his ability, and the people assent, saying Amen.[4]

At the end of the second century the Latin father Tertullian wrote his *Apology* in order to clear Christians of false accusations and demonstrate the injustice of the persecutions they were having to endure. Writing of 'the peculiarities of the Christian society', he emphasized the love and unity which knit them together, and then described their meetings:

> We assemble to read our sacred writings . . . With the sacred words we nourish our faith, we animate our hope, we make our confidence more steadfast, and no less by inculcations of God's precepts we confirm good habits. In the same place also exhortations are made, rebukes and sacred censures are administered . . .[5]

Tertullian's contemporary, the Greek father Irenæus, Bishop of Lyons, stressed the responsibility of the presbyters to adhere to the apostles' teaching:

These also preserve this faith of ours in one God, who accomplished such marvellous dispensations for our sake; and they expound the Scriptures to us without danger, neither blaspheming God, nor dishonouring the patriarchs, nor despising the prophets.[6]

Eusebius, Bishop of Caesarea at the beginning of the fourth century and the father of Church history, was able to sum up the first two hundred years of the Christian era in terms of the work of preachers and teachers:

They set out on journeys from home and performed the work of evangelists, making it their aim to preach to such as had not yet heard the word of faith at all, and to give them the book of the divine Gospels. But they were content to lay the foundation only of the Faith in some foreign places, appointing others as pastors to whom they entrusted the care of those lately brought in; then they would depart to other lands and nations, with the grace and cooperation of God.[7]

From the later patristic period I will take only one example, indeed the most notable, namely John Chrysostom, who preached for twelve years in the Cathedral in Antioch before becoming Bishop of Constantinople in A.D. 398. In an exposition of Ephesians 6:13 ('take the whole armour of God . . .'), he voiced his conviction about the unique importance of preaching. Like our human body, he said, the Body of Christ is subject to many diseases. Medicines, correct diet, suitable climate and adequate sleep all help to restore our physical health. But how shall Christ's Body be healed?

One only means and one way of cure has been given us . . . and that is teaching of the Word. This is the best instrument, this the best diet and climate; this serves instead of medicine, this serves instead of cautery and cutting; whether it be needful to burn or to amputate, this one method must be used; and without it nothing else will avail.[8]

It was more than a century after his death that his greatness as a preacher came to be recognized and he was nicknamed *Chrysostomos*, 'golden-mouthed': 'he is generally and justly regarded as the greatest pulpit orator of the Greek church. Nor has he any superior or equal among the Latin Fathers. He remains to this day a model for preachers in large cities.'[9]

Four chief characteristics of his preaching may be mentioned. First, he was biblical. Not only did he preach systematically through several books, but his sermons are full of biblical quotations and allusions. Secondly, his interpretation of the Scriptures was simple and straightforward. He followed the Antiochene school of 'literal' exegesis, in contrast to fanciful Alexandrian allegorizations. Thirdly, his moral applications were down to earth. Reading his sermons today, one can imagine without difficulty the pomp of the imperial court, the luxuries of the aristocracy, the wild races of the hippodrome, in fact the whole life of an oriental city at the end of the fourth century. Fourthly, he was fearless in his condemnations. In fact, 'he was a martyr of the pulpit, for it was chiefly his faithful preaching that caused his exile.'[10]

The Friars and the Reformers

We jump now, in this brief sketch, more than five hundred years to the founding of the medieval Mendicant Orders. For 'the Age of Preaching', wrote Charles Smyth, 'dates from the coming of the Friars. . . . The history of the pulpit as we know it begins with the Preaching Friars. They met, and stimulated, a growing popular demand for sermons. They revolutionized the technique. They magnified the office.'[11] Although Francis of Assisi (1182–1226) was a man more of compassionate service than of learning, and insisted that 'our acting and teaching must go together', he was nevertheless 'as committed to preaching as to poverty: "Unless you preach everywhere you go", said Francis, "there is no use to go anywhere to preach." From the very beginning of his ministry, that had been his motto.'[12] His contemporary Dominic (1170–1221) laid even greater emphasis on preaching. Combining personal austerity with evangelistic zeal, he travelled widely in the cause of the gospel, especially in Italy, France and Spain, and organized his 'black frairs' into an Order of Preachers. A century later Humbert de Romans (died 1277), one of the finest of Dominican Ministers General, said: 'Christ only once heard Mass . . . but he laid great stress on prayer and preaching, especially on preaching.'[13] And a century later still, the great Franciscan preacher St Bernardino of Siena (1380–1444) made this unexpected statement: 'If of these two things you can do only one – either hear the mass or hear the sermon – you should let the mass go, rather than the sermon. . . . There is less peril for your soul in not hearing mass than in not hearing the sermon.'[14]

From this surprising assertion of the primacy of the Word by Franciscans and Dominicans it is not a big step to that great forerunner or 'morning star' of the Reformation, John Wycliffe (1329–1384). Associated all his life with Oxford University, and a prolific writer, his keen intellect gradually broke away from medieval scholasticism, and he proclaimed Holy Scripture as the supreme authority in faith and life. Responsible for instigating the first complete English Bible (translated from the Vulgate), and probably sharing in some of the translating himself, he was a diligent biblical preacher, and from the Scriptures attacked the papacy, indulgences, transubstantiation and the Church's wealth. He had no doubt that the chief vocation of the clergy was to preach:

The highest service that men may attain to on earth is to preach the Word of God. This service falls peculiarly to priests, and therefore God more straightly demands it of them. . . . And for this cause, Jesus Christ left other

22

works and occupied himself mostly in preaching, and
thus did his apostles, and for this, God loved them. . . .
The Church, however, is honoured most by the preaching of God's Word, and hence this is the best service that
priests may render unto God. . . . And thus, if our
bishops preach not in their own persons, and hinder true
priests from preaching, they are in the sins of the bishops
who killed the Lord Jesus Christ.[15]

The Renaissance not only preceded the Reformation,
but paved the way for it. Beginning in fourteenth-century
Italy, with brilliant scholars like Petrarch, whose 'hu-
manism' expressed itself in the study of classical Greek
and Roman texts, it gained a more Christian flavour when it
moved in the following century into Northern Europe. For
the preoccupation of the 'Christian humanists' like
Erasmus and Thomas More was the study of the Christian
classics, both biblical and patristic. As a result, they were
critical of corruption in the Church, called for reform according to the Word of God, and recognized the key role of
preachers in securing this reform.

The most important function of the priest is teaching
(wrote Erasmus), by which he may instruct, admonish,
chide and console. A layman can baptize. All the people
can pray. The priest does not always baptize, he does not
always absolve, but he should always teach. What good is
it to be baptized if one has not been catechized, what
good to go to the Lord's Table if one does not know what
it means?[16]

So the old adage that 'Erasmus laid the egg that Luther
hatched' seems to be true. Certainly Erasmus' insistence on
the supremacy of Word over sacrament, because the sacraments depend for their efficacy on their interpretation by
the Word, was endorsed and amplified by Luther. 'The
Reformation gave centrality to the sermon. The pulpit was
higher than the altar, for Luther held that salvation is

through the Word, and without the Word the elements are devoid of sacramental quality, but the Word is sterile unless it is spoken.'[17] In all his writings Luther lost no opportunity to magnify the liberating and sustaining power of the Word of God. Thus, 'the Church owes its life to the Word of promise, and is nourished and preserved by this same Word – the promises of God make the Church, not the Church the promises of God.'[18] Moreover, there are only two authentic sacraments, 'Baptism and Bread', because 'only in these two do we find both the divinely instituted sign and the promise of the forgiveness of sins.'[19] God's Word is therefore indispensable for our spiritual life. 'The soul can do without all things except the Word of God . . . if it has the Word it is rich and lacks nothing, since this Word is the Word of life, of truth, of light, of peace, of righteousness, of salvation, of joy, of liberty.' This is so because the Word centres on Christ. Hence the necessity of preaching Christ from the Word, 'for to preach Christ means to feed the soul, to make it righteous, to set it free and to save it, if it believe the preaching.'[20]

Since the health of the Christian and of the Church depends on the Word of God, the preaching and teaching of it is both 'the most important part of divine service'[21] and the 'highest and only duty and obligation' of every bishop, pastor and preacher.[22] It is also such a weighty responsibility that it is extremely demanding. Luther gives nine 'properties and virtues' of a good preacher. The first seven are fairly predictable. He should, of course, 'teach systematically, . . . have a ready wit, . . . be eloquent, . . . have a good voice and . . . a good memory'. Next, 'he should know when to make an end', and, one might add, how to make a beginning, for he 'should be sure of his doctrine'. Then, 'eighthly, he should venture and engage body and blood, wealth and honour, in the Word' and 'ninthly, he should suffer himself to be mocked and jeered of every one.'[23] The risk of ridicule, the risk of losing life, wealth and name – these according to Luther were the ultimate tests of 'a good preacher'.

Such a statement was no mere academic theory; Luther lived by it himself, notably during the greatest crisis of his life. Excommunicated by papal bull in January 1521, he was summoned in April to appear before the Diet of Worms, over which the Emperor Charles V presided. He refused to recant unless both the testimony of the Scriptures and obvious reason proved him wrong, for, he said, 'I am bound in conscience and held fast to the Word of God.' During the following days he was granted a hearing by a bench of learned judges. But in reality he had been condemned before the trial began. It ended with his ultimatum: 'Even if I were to lose my body and my life on account of it, I cannot depart from the true Word of God.' It was the preaching of this divine Word, not political intrigue or the power of the sword, which established the Reformation in Germany. Luther put it later, 'I simply taught, preached, wrote God's Word: otherwise I did nothing. And when, while I slept, or drank Wittenberg beer with my Philip and my Amsdorf, the Word so greatly weakened the papacy that never a Prince or Emperor inflicted such damage upon it. I did nothing. The Word did it all.'[24]

As Calvin wrote his Institutes in the comparative peace of Geneva, he too exalted the Word of God. In particular, he emphasized that the first and major mark of a true Church was the faithful preaching of the Word. 'Wherever we see the Word of God purely preached and heard', he wrote, 'and the sacraments administered according to Christ's institution, there, it is not to be doubted, a Church of God exists.' In fact, this ministry of Word and sacrament, the audible and visible proclaimation of the gospel, must be adjudged 'a perpetual token by which to distinguish the Church'.[25]

The English Reformers were strongly influenced by Calvin. To a great extent they accepted his teaching that the sacraments derive their efficacy from the Word and lack efficacy without it, that Word and sacraments are indispensable marks of the Church, and that the priesthood is essentially a ministry of the Word. Thus, Anglican Article XIX declared that 'the visible church of Christ is a congregation of faithful (i.e. believing) men, in which the pure Word of God is preached, and the sacraments be duly ministered according to Christ's ordinance. . . .' And the Bishop, while ordaining candidates to the presbyterate, not only gave a Bible to each as a symbol of his office, but exhorted him to be 'studious . . . in reading and learning the Scriptures' and authorized him by the power of the Holy Spirit 'to preach the Word of God and to minister the holy sacraments in the congregation'.

No reformer took this sacred task more seriously than Hugh Latimer, the popular preacher of the English Reformation. Born about 1485 as the son of a yeoman farmer in Leicestershire, and consecrated Bishop of Worcester in 1535, he never became prelatical or lost his homely, rustic touch. Instead, 'He spoke *from* the heart, and his words . . . went *to* the heart.'[26]

His great burden was that the people of England were still lost in spiritual darkness, and that the clergy were to blame for this because they neglected the ministry of the Word. Specially blameworthy were the bishops. They were so taken up, he said, with 'ruffling in their rents, dancing in their dominions . . . munching in their mangers, and moiling in their gay manors and mansions' that they had no time for preaching.[27]

Latimer's best known – and perhaps most powerful – address is known as 'The Sermon of the Plough', and was preached in St Paul's Cathedral on 18 January 1548, soon after he had been released from his incarceration in the Tower of London. His theme was that 'God's Word is seed to be sown in God's field' and that 'the preacher is the sower.' As he developed it, he drew on his personal experience of farming on his father's Leicestershire estate. The preacher, he argued, should be like the ploughman, because he should 'labour at all seasons of the year'. But he bewailed the fact that instead the clergy spent their time meddling in business and pleasure. As a result, 'by the lording and loitering, preaching and ploughing is clean gone.' Then Latimer kept his hearers in suspense by this famous passage:

And now I would ask you a strange question; who is the most diligent bishop and prelate in all England; that passes all the rest in doing his office? I can tell, for I know who it is; I know him well. But now I think I see you listening and hearkening that I should name him. There is one that passes all the other, and is the most diligent prelate and preacher in all England. And will ye know who it is? I will tell you – it is the Devil. He is the most diligent preacher of all others; he is never out of his diocese; he is never from his cure; you shall never find him unoccupied; he is ever in his parish; he keeps residence at all times; you shall never find him out of the way; call for him when you will, he is ever at home. He is the most diligent preacher in all the realm; he is ever at his plough; no lording or loitering can hinder him; he is ever applying his business; you shall never find him idle, I warrant you . . . Where the devil is resident, and has his plough going, there away with books and up with candles; away with bibles and up with beads; away with the light of the gospel and up with the light of candles, yea, at noonday; . . . up with man's traditions and his laws, down with God's traditions and his most holy word; . . . Oh that our prelates would be as diligent to sow the corn of good doctrine as Satan is to sow cockle and darnel! . . . There was never such a preacher in England as he is.

The conclusion of the sermon went like this:

The prelates . . . are lords, and no labourers; but the devil is diligent at his plough. He is no unpreaching prelate; he is no lordly loiterer from his cure; but a busy ploughman . . . Therefore, ye unpreaching prelates, learn of the devil: to be diligent in doing of your office

. . . If you will not learn of God, nor good men, to be diligent in your office, learn of the devil.[28]

I have referred to Luther and Calvin for the Continental Reformation, and to Latimer for the English. They were preachers, and they believed in preaching. Yet they were only leading examples of a widespread conviction and practice. Here is E. C. Dargan's comment:

The great events and achievements of that mighty revolution were largely the work of preachers and preaching; for it was by the Word of God, through the ministry of earnest men who believed, loved and taught it, that the best and most enduring work of the Reformation was done. And, conversely, the events and principles of the movement powerfully reacted on preaching itself, giving it new spirit, new power, new forms, so that the relation between the Reformation and preaching may be succinctly described as one of mutual dependence, aid and guidance.[29]

The Puritans and the Evangelicals

The prominence which was given to preaching by the early Reformers continued to be given in the latter part of the sixteenth century and in the seventeenth by the Puritans. They have been described by many names, some rude, others not so rude. But 'the name which best sums up their character', writes Irvonwy Morgan, 'is the "Godly Preachers".' He goes on to explain why:

The essential thing in understanding the Puritans was that they were preachers before they were anything else, and preachers with a particular emphasis that could be distinguished from other preachers by those who heard them . . . What bound them together, undergirded their striving, and gave them the dynamic to persist was their consciousness that they were called to preach the

28

Gospel. 'Woe is me if I preach not the Gospel' was their inspiration and justification. Puritan tradition in the first and last resort must be assessed in terms of the pulpit, and the words of the ex-Dominican Friar Thomas Sampson, one of the leaders and first sufferers of the Puritan Movement . . . can stand as their slogan: 'Let others be Bishops', he says, 'I will undertake the office of preacher or none at all.'[30]

Among the seventeenth-century Puritans Richard Baxter, author of *The Reformed Pastor* (1656), stands out as consistently exemplifying the ideals which the Puritan tradition and his own book set forth. He felt oppressed by the ignorance, laziness and licentiousness of the clergy, which had been exposed by a parliamentary committee in their report *The First Century of Scandalous Malignant Priests* (1643), which supplied one hundred shocking case histories. So Baxter addressed his *Reformed Pastor* to his fellow clergy, especially the members of his Worcestershire Ministerial Association, and shared with them the principles which directed his own pastoral work in the parish of Kidderminster. 'In a word', he wrote, 'we must teach them, as much as we can, of the *word* and *works* of God. O what two volumes are these for a minister to preach upon! How great, how excellent, how wonderful and mysterious! All Christians are disciples or scholars of Christ; the Church is his school, we are his ushers; the Bible is his grammar; this is it that we must be daily teaching them.'[31]

Baxter's methods of teaching were twofold. On the one hand, he pioneered the practice of catechizing families. Since there were about 800 families in his parish, and since he desired to enquire into their spiritual progress at least once a year, he and his colleague between them invited to their homes fifteen or sixteen families every week. Each family would come alone and stay one hour. They would be asked to recite the catechism, be helped to understand it, and be questioned about their personal experience of its truths. This catechizing would occupy Baxter two whole days a week, and was one essential part of his work. But the other part, 'and that the most excellent because it tendeth to work on many', was 'the public preaching of the Word'. It was a work, he insisted, 'that requireth greater skill and especially greater life and zeal, than any of us bring to it. It is no small matter to stand up in the face of a congregation and deliver a message as from the living God, in the name of our Redeemer.'[32]

It would be quite mistaken to suppose, however, that the importance of preaching was recognized in the seventeenth century only by the Puritans. Just four years before Baxter wrote *The Reformed Pastor*, George Herbert wrote his *A Priest to the Temple* (alternatively entitled *The Country Parson, his Character and Rule of Holy Life*), although it was not published for another twenty years. There is evidence that the two men knew and respected one another. Certainly Baxter applauded Herbert's poetry and piety, although Herbert has been described as an early Anglo-Catholic. Yet he laid an essentially 'Puritan' emphasis on preaching. His seventh chapter, entitled 'The Parson Preaching', begins: 'The Country Parson preacheth constantly, the pulpit is his joy and his throne.' Moreover, he draws his message from 'the book of books, the storehouse and magazine of life and comfort, the holy Scriptures', for 'there he sucks, and lives'. His main characteristic is not that he is 'witty, or learned, or eloquent, but holy', and so earnest is he in his desire to communicate, that he even interrupts his own sermon with 'many Apostrophes to God as "Oh, Lord, bless my people, and teach them this point".'[33]

On the other side of the Atlantic, and a few years later, Cotton Mather, the American Puritan, was exercizing in Boston a ministry whose influence was being felt on both sides of the ocean. Fellow of Harvard, scholarly theologian and prolific writer, he provided in his book *Student and Preacher* what he termed 'Directions for a Candidate of the Ministry'. His view of the Christian minister in general, and of the preacher in particular, was extremely exalted. His preface begins:

> The office of the Christian ministry, rightly understood, is the most honourable, and important, that any man in the whole world can ever sustain; and it will be one of the wonders and employments of eternity to consider the reasons why the wisdom and goodness of God assigned this office to imperfect and guilty man! . . . The great design and intention of the office of a Christian preacher are to restore the throne and dominion of God in the souls of men; to display in the most lively colours, and proclaim in the clearest language, the wonderful perfections, offices and grace of the Son of God; and to attract the souls of men into a state of everlasting friendship with him . . . It is a work which an angel might wish for, as an honour to his character; yea, an office which every angel in heaven might covet to be employed in for a thousand years to come. It is such an honourable, important and useful office, that if a man be put into it by God, and made faithful and successful through life, he may look down with disdain upon a crown, and shed a tear of pity on the brightest monarch on earth.[34]

Cotton Mather died in 1728. Just a decade later, newly returned from two years in Georgia, disillusioned because in his own judgment unconverted, John Wesley was granted his 'heart-warming' experience in which, he said, he put his 'trust in Christ, in Christ only for salvation', and an assurance was given to him that his sins had been taken away, even his, and that Christ had saved him from the law of sin and death. At once he began to preach the free salvation he had just received. True, influenced by his reading of Richard Baxter, he encouraged a house-to-house ministry and a catechizing of converts. But preaching was his own characteristic ministry. In churches and church yards, on village greens, in fields and in natural amphitheatres, he proclaimed the gospel and 'offered Christ' to the vast crowds who gathered to listen to him. 'I do indeed live by preaching', he commented in his Journal on 28 August 1757. All the time his textbook was the Bible, for he knew that its overriding purpose was to point to Christ and enlighten its readers for salvation. In his preface to the *Standard Sermons* he wrote:

I am a spirit come from God, and returning to God: just hovering over a great gulf; till, a few moments hence, I am no more seen; I drop into an unchangeable eternity! I want to know one thing – the way to heaven: . . . God himself has condescended to teach the way: for this very end he came from heaven. He hath written it down in a book. O give me that book! At any price, give me the book of God! I have it: here is knowledge enough for me. Let me be *homo unius libri* (a man of one Book). Here then I am, far from the busy ways of men. I sit down alone: only God is here. In his presence I open, I read his book; for this end, to find the way to heaven.[35]

And out of his biblical meditations John Wesley preached, sharing with others what he had found, and pointing the way both to heaven and to holiness.

Although John Wesley has become better known to the public than his younger contemporary George Whitefield (probably because of the world-wide Christian denomination which bears Wesley's name), Whitefield was almost certainly the more powerful preacher. In Britain and America (which he visited seven times), indoors and out of doors, he averaged about twenty sermons a week for thirty-four years. Eloquent, zealous, dogmatic, passionate, he enlivened his preaching with vivid metaphors, homely illustrations and dramatic gestures. By these he would hold his audiences spellbound, as he either addressed direct questions to them or begged them earnestly to be reconciled with God. He had complete confidence in the authority of his message, and was determined that it should receive the respect it deserved as God's Word. Once in a New Jersey meeting-house he 'noticed an old man settling down for his accustomed, sermon-time nap', writes John Pollock, one of his biographers. Whitefield began his sermon quietly, without disturbing the gentleman's slumbers. But then 'in measured, deliberate words' he said:

If I had come to speak to you in my own name, you might rest your elbows upon your knees and your heads on your hands, and go to sleep! . . . But I have come to you in the name of the Lord God of hosts, and (he clapped his hands and stamped his foot) I *must* and I *will* be heard.' The old man woke up startled.[36]

The Nineteenth Century

Charles Simeon was born in 1759, the same year as William Wilberforce, who became his lifelong friend. His career overlapped just over ten years with Whitefield's and thirty-two years with Wesley's. Having been converted while an undergraduate at Cambridge, he longed to have the opportunity to preach the gospel there. Walking past Holy Trinity Church in the heart of the university campus, he used to say to himself, 'How should I rejoice if God were to give me that church, that I might preach his gospel there, and be a herald for him in the midst of the university.'[37] God answered his prayer, and in 1782 he became the church's vicar. At first, however, he met with the most violent opposition. The seat-holders boycotted the services and locked the doors to their pews, so that for more than ten years the congregation had to stand, and often there were rowdy scenes. But Simeon persevered, and gradually won the respect of both town and gown. For fifty-four years he occupied the pulpit of Holy Trinity Church, systematically opening up the Scriptures, and determined without compromise, as his memorial stone in the chancel reads, 'to know nothing except Jesus Christ and him crucified'.

Simeon's lofty understanding of preaching arose from his concept of the minister as an ambassador. He wrote to John Venn on the occasion of his ordination in 1782, some four months after his own:

My dearest Friend, I most sincerely congratulate you not on a permission to receive £40 or £50 a year, nor on the title of Reverend, but on your accession to the most valuable, most honourable, most important, and most glorious office in the world – to that of an ambassador of the Lord Jesus Christ.[38]

This is certainly how he viewed his own ministry. He once expounded the text containing Jesus' injunction 'Take heed therefore how ye hear' (Lk. 8:18) in such a way as to give 'Directions How to Hear Sermons'. One of the reasons why Jesus gave this caution, he argued, was 'because God himself speaks to us by the preacher'. He went on:

Ministers are ambassadors for God, and speak in Christ's stead. If they preach what is founded on the Scriptures, their word, as far as it is agreeable to the mind of God, is to be considered as God's. This is asserted by our Lord and his apostles. We ought therefore to receive the preacher's word as the word of God himself. With what humility, then, ought we to attend to it! What judgments may we not expect, if we slight it![39]

Throughout the nineteenth century, in spite of the assaults of the higher criticism on the Bible (associated with the name of Julius Wellhausen, his contemporaries and successors), and in spite of the evolutionary theories of Charles Darwin, the pulpit maintained its prestige in England. People flocked to hear the great preachers of the day and read their printed sermons with eagerness. There was John Henry Newman (1801–1890) at the University Church in Oxford, Canon H. P. Liddon (1829–1890) at St. Paul's Cathedral, F. W. Robertson (1816–1853) in Brighton, and, most eminent of all, Charles Haddon Spurgeon (1834–1892) in his Metropolitan Tabernacle in London.

Let that eminent Victorian Scot, Thomas Carlyle (1795–1881), sum up for us the unique influence of the preacher.

His witness is the more impressive because he was to some extent an outsider, for he wrote as a historian and was an outspoken critic of churches and their creeds. Yet fourth on his list of 'heroes' or 'great men', who exercize leadership in the community, he named the 'priest', by whom he evidently meant the 'preacher', 'the spiritual Captain of the people'. As models he selected Luther and Knox: 'these two men we will account our best priests, inasmuch as they were our best reformers.' What Carlyle admired in them was their lonely courage. At the Diet of Worms Luther was undaunted by the most imposing dignitaries of Church and State. On the one side sits 'the world's pomp and power'; on the other, there 'stands up for God's truth one man, the poor miner Hans Luther's son.' 'Here I stand', he said, 'I can do no other. God help me!' In Carlyle's opinion it was 'the greatest moment in the modern history of men'. Indeed, the vast work of human liberation in the following centuries, in both Europe and America, began then; 'the germ of it all lay there.' Scotland's debt to John Knox, 'the bravest of all Scotchmen', was similar: 'This that Knox did for his nation, I say, we may really call a resurrection as from death . . . The people began to *live*.' Such is the power of the preached Word.[40]

The respect, almost the awe, in which the pulpit was held by many during the Victorian era, is well illustrated in Herman Melville's *Moby Dick* (1851). He gives a graphic account of the naval chaplain's sermon in New Bedford, southern Massachusetts, which deserves to be quoted in full. On a stormy December Sunday, Ishmael was waiting to board a whaler, in order to sail south. Being, as he later explained, 'a good Christian, born and bred in the bosom of the infallible Presbyterian Church',[41] he attended divine service in a little 'whaleman's chapel'. Inside he found 'a small scattered congregation of sailors, and sailors' wives and widows', their 'muffled silence' contrasting with 'the shrieks of the storm outside'. Soon the chaplain entered, an old man named Father Mapple. Having himself been a harpooner in his youth, he retained his love for the sea and his nautical vocabulary. The lofty pulpit was reached not by steps but by a perpendicular ship's ladder. Hand over hand, with an old sailor's skill, Father Mapple mounted the preaching place, and then to Ishmael's astonishment hauled the ladder up after him 'till the whole was deposited within, leaving him impregnable in his little Quebec'. Melville goes on to describe the pulpit's panelled front as being 'in the likeness of a ship's bluff bows', while 'the Holy Bible rested on a projecting piece of scroll work, fashioned after a ship's fiddle-headed beak.' 'What could be more full of meaning?' he asks.

> For the pulpit is ever this earth's foremost part; all the rest comes in its rear; the pulpit leads the world. From thence it is [that] the storm of God's wrath is first descried, and the bow must bear the earliest brunt. From thence it is [that] the God of breezes fair and foul is first invoked for favorable winds. Yes, the world's a ship on its passage out, and not a voyage complete; and the pulpit is its prow.[42]

The Chapter which follows is entitled 'The Sermon' and supplies a striking example of pulpit-power. Father Mapple, addressing his congregation as 'shipmates', preached from the story of Jonah. Although this book, he explained, was 'one of the smallest strands in the mighty cable of the Scriptures', it yet contained 'a two-stranded lesson, a lesson to us all as sinful men, and a lesson to me as a pilot of the living God'. To fugitives from God Jonah was a model of true repentance. But he was also a fearful warning to every pilot-preacher who shirks his Gospel duty and, 'as the great Pilot Paul has it, while preaching to others is himself a castaway!'[43]

'The pulpit leads the world.' Few would dare to advance this claim today, but it would not have sounded an exaggeration in the last century. At the same time, those who discerned the privilege of preaching were distressed by those who did not. One example of this distress was Dr.

James W. Alexander, son of Archibald Alexander the first professor in the new Princeton Theological Seminary in 1812, and himself a professor there from 1849 to 1851. For twenty years he had been a pastor, however, for, as Charles Hodge said of him, 'the pulpit was his appropriate sphere.'

> I fear none of us apprehend as we ought to do the value of the preacher's office. Our young men do not gird themselves for it with the spirit of those who are on the eve of a great conflict; nor do they prepare as those who are to lay hands upon the springs of the mightiest passions, and stir up to their depths the ocean of human feelings. Where this estimate of the work prevails, men even of inferior training accomplish much . . . The pulpit will still remain the grand means of effecting the mass of men. It is God's own method, and he will honour it . . . In every age, great reformers have been great preachers . . .[44]

Preaching is not only influential in the lives of others, Alexander later argued; it is also very fulfilling for the preacher:

> There is happiness in preaching. It may be so performed as to be as dull to the speaker as it is to the hearers; but in favoured instances it furnishes the purest and noblest excitements, and in these is happiness. Nowhere are experienced, more than in the pulpit, the clear, heavenward soaring of the intellect, the daring flight of imagination, or the sweet agitations of holy passion.[45]

Because of this power and this pleasure, small wonder that Alexander Whyte of Edinburgh, just after the turn of the century, could admonish a discouraged Methodist minister with these words: 'Never think of giving up preaching! The angels around the throne envy you your great work.'[46] That was in 1908. The previous year saw the publication of the Congregational theologian P. T. Forsyth's book *Positive*

Preaching and the Modern Mind. These are its opening words: 'It is, perhaps, an overbold beginning, but I will venture to say that with its preaching Christianity stands or falls.'[47]

The Twentieth Century

Our century began in a mood of euphoria. Expectations – at least of the favoured, educated minority of the west – were of a period of political stability, scientific progress and material wealth. No clouds darkened the world's horizons. The Church shared in the general sense of bonhomie. It was still a respectable social institution, and the occupants of its pulpits were shown esteem, even deference.

The best example I have come across from this period of unbounded confidence in the beneficent effects of preaching is that of the Reverend Charles Silvester Horne, who delivered the 1914 Beecher Lectures on Preaching at Yale, and called them *The Romance of Preaching.* He died only days later on the boat which was bringing him home. He must have prepared the lectures in 1913, for they betray no apprehensions of approaching war. Horne was both a Congregational minister and a member of the British parliament. He had a reputation for eloquence in the House of Commons, and for passion in the pulpit. H. H. Asquith often went to hear him preach because, he said, 'he had a fire in his belly'. Being both a politician and a preacher, he was able from personal experience to compare the two vocations, and he had no doubt which was the more influential:

The preacher, who is the messenger of God, is the real master of society; not elected by society to be its ruler, but elect of God to form its ideals and through them to guide and rule its life. Show me the man who, in the midst of a community however secularized in manners, can compel it to think with him, can kindle its enthusiasm, revive its faith, cleanse its passions, purify its ambitions, and give steadfastness to its will, and I will show you the real master of society, no matter what party may nominally hold the reins of government, no matter what figurehead may occupy the ostensible place of authority.[48]

He was well aware of the preacher's competitors in the art and business of communication. He spoke of the dramatist, the journalist, the socialist agitator, the novelist, the statesman, the poet and the playwright. To this list we would today add the television writer and producer. He knew, as we do, that people's ears were besieged by rival voices. Yet still he accorded the first place in the hierarchy of moral and social power to the preacher:

The real romance of history is this romance of the preacher: the sublime miracle of the God-intoxicated soul with vision of an eternal Will, and sense of an Empire to which all continents, tongues, races belong. This man stands serene amid the clash of arms and the foolish braggadocio of Force, asking only for the sword named Truth, for the harness of Righteousness, and the spirit of Peace. This is the world's unconquerable and irresistible Hero. All its most enduring victories are his.[49]

So then, Horne continued, 'who should be proud of their calling if not we? What other history has ever equalled ours? Think of the procession of preachers! . . . Gradually before their message ancient pagan empires tottered, heathen despots bowed the head.'[50] He specially mentioned Savonarola, Calvin and Knox as 'supreme examples of the power which the man of the Gospel can exercize in shaping the civil and national life of free peoples.'[51]

Another man, also a Congregational minister, who considered preaching more powerful than politics was Dr. J. D. Jones (died 1917), who for nearly forty years was minister of Richmond Hill Congregational Church in

Bournemouth. Urged by the leader of a political party to stand as a parliamentary candidate, he declined, and quoted as his reason Nehemiah's answer to Sanballat and Tobiah when they tried to stop him building Jerusalem's walls. 'I am doing a great work', he had said to them, 'so that I cannot come down.' J. D. Jones emphasized the last two words. 'It would have been a "come down" to forsake the pulpit for the political arena,' he declared. 'I do not disparage the work that Parliament can do in the way of bettering human conditions, but the ultimate healing of the world's hurt is not to be effected by legislation but by the redeeming grace of God, and the proclamation of that redeeming grace is the highest work to which any man can be called.'[52]

The optimism of the century's early years was shattered first by the outbreak of World War I and then by the horrors of mud and blood in the trenches. Europe emerged from those four years in a chastened mood, which was soon made worse by the years of economic depression. The utterances of churchmen became more sober. Yet confidence in the privilege and power of the pulpit ministry survived. Indeed, perceptive theologians like Karl Barth, whose former liberal optimism had been destroyed by the war and replaced by a new realism about mankind and a new faith in God, expressed their conviction that preaching had gained an even greater importance than before.

It is simply a truism [declared Barth in 1928], that there is nothing more important, more urgent, more helpful, more redemptive and more salutary, there is nothing, from the viewpoint of heaven and earth, more relevant to the real situation than the speaking and the hearing of the Word of God in the originative and regulative power of its truth, in its all-eradicating and all-reconciling earnestness, in the light that it casts not only upon *time* and time's confusions but also beyond, towards the brightness of *eternity*, revealing time and eternity

40

through each other and *in* each other – the Word, the Logos, of the Living God.'[53]

It stands to reason that every recovery of confidence in the Word of God, and so in a living God who spoke and speaks, however this truth may be defined, is bound to result in a recovery of preaching. This must be why so many great preachers have belonged to the reformed tradition. Another example is James Black of Edinburgh, who in his 1923 Warrack Lectures in Scotland and Sprunt Lectures in America issued a stirring exhortation to his student audiences to take their preaching seriously: 'Ours is a great and magnificent service,' he said, 'and deserves the consecration of any gift we possess . . . May I ask you, therefore, to resolve early to make your preaching the big business of your life.'[54] Again, 'Our work is big enough for us to use all the preparation and all the talent we can bring to its discharge . . . Yours will be the care and shepherding of souls. Bring to it all the enthusiasm and passion of your own rich life.'[55]

Much more surprising is the priority given to preaching by a man of such theologically liberal views as Bishop Hensley Henson. Yet in 1927, in his sermons and ordination charges published under the title *Church and Parson in England*, he deplored 'the spectacle, alas but too common, of a congregation settling down in sorrowful resignation, if not in shameless slumber, to the infliction of the sermon'.[56] In contrast to this scorn for the pulpit he declared his own conviction: 'of all the actions of the Christian ministry preaching is the highest, and the test of our reverence for our profession is our performance of the preacher's duty.'[57] Consequently he exhorted his fellow clergy: 'Never allow yourself to take a mean view of your duty as preacher . . . In a sense we may say truly that all the activities of the pastorate are gathered up in the ministry of preaching.'[58]

The life and work of Dietrich Bonhoeffer are still being evaluated. While the courage with which he went to his execution in the Flossenburg concentration camp in 1945 is universally admired, scholars continue to debate what he meant by some of his theological statements. Those who knew him best, like his friend Eberhard Bethge, assure us that in his 'non-religious' interpretation of Christianity he never intended to dispense with the true worship of the gathered community. On the contrary, this is essential precisely because it is the occasion on which the call of Christ may be heard:

> If we would hear his call to follow, we must listen where he is to be found, that is, in the church through the ministry of word and sacrament. The preaching of the church and the administration of the sacraments is the place where Jesus Christ is present. If you would hear the call of Jesus, you need no personal revelation; all you have to do is hear the sermon and receive the sacrament, that is, to hear the gospel of Christ crucified and risen.[59]

In one of his lectures on preaching delivered before the outbreak of the war, Bonhoeffer stressed even more strongly the central importance of preaching:

> For the sake of the proclaimed word the world exists with all of its words. In the sermon the foundation for a new world is laid. Here the original word becomes audible. There is no evading or getting away from the spoken word of the sermon, nothing releases us from the necessity of this witness, not even cult or liturgy . . . The preacher should be assured that Christ enters the congregation through those words which he proclaims from the Scripture.[60]

Even the Second World War, although it accelerated the process of secularization in Europe, did not quench preaching. During and after it three distinguished Methodist ministers occupied London pulpits and drew large crowds – Leslie Weatherhead at the City Temple, Donald Soper at Kingsway Hall (and also in the open air at Marble Arch and on Tower Hill), and Will Sangster at Westminster Central Hall. A wit once remarked that they could best be distinguished from one another by their three loves, since 'Sangster loved the Lord, Weatherhead loved his people, while Soper loved an argument.' Of the three Sangster was probably the most eloquent preacher. Born a cockney, and leaving school at the age of fifteen to work as an office boy in the City, he yet became a Methodist local preacher when he was eighteen, and in 1950 was elected President of the Methodist Conference in Britain. In his well-known book *The Craft of the Sermon* (1954) he could scarcely find words lofty enough to describe the preacher's task. Near the beginning he wrote:

> Called to preach! . . . Commissioned of God to teach the word! A herald of the great King! A witness of the Eternal Gospel! Could any work be more high and holy? To this supreme task God sent his only begotten Son. In all the frustration and confusion of the times, is it possible to imagine a work comparable in importance with that of proclaiming the will of God to wayward men?[61]
>
> Not by accident, nor yet by the thrustful egotism of men, was the pulpit given the central place in the Reformed Churches. It is there of design and devotion. It is there by the logic of things. It is there as *the throne of the Word of God*.[62]

Then towards the end of the book he expressed his personal conviction that 'preaching the Good News of Jesus Christ is the highest, holiest activity to which a man can give himself: a task which angels might envy and for which archangels might forsake the court of Heaven.'[63] As Andrew Blackwood similarly commented, 'preaching should rank as the noblest work on earth.'[64]

So we come to the 1960s, 70s and 80s. The tide of preaching ebbed, and the ebb is still low today. At least in the western world the decline of preaching is a symptom of the decline of the Church. An era of scepticism is not conducive to the recovery of confident proclamation. Yet there are not wanting voices which both declare its vital import- ance and call for its renewal. We hear these voices in virtually all the Churches. I have chosen a sample from the Roman Catholic, Anglican and Free Churches.

Some Roman Catholic writers are very concerned about the low level of contemporary preaching. According to the elderly Jesuit theologian Karl Rahner, one of the burning questions of the day concerns what he terms 'the trouble with preaching'. This is the failure to relate the Christian message to the everyday world. 'Many leave the Church because the language flowing from the pulpit has no mean- ing for them; it has no connection with their own life and simply bypasses many threatening and unavoidable issues . . . "The trouble with preaching" is becoming even more troublesome.'[65]

But this should not be so for those who have read the documents which emanated from the Second Vatican Council. The sixth chapter of the 'Dogmatic Constitution on Divine Revelation', entitled 'Sacred Scripture in the Life of the Church', contains strong assertions about the duty to study and apply the Scriptures:

> Catholic exegetes . . . and other students of sacred theol- ogy, working diligently together and using appropriate means, should devote their energies, under the watchful care of the sacred teaching office of the Church, to an exploration and exposition of the divine writings. This task should be done in such a way that as many ministers of the divine word as possible will be able effectively to provide the nourishment of the Scriptures for the people of God, thereby enlightening their minds, strengthening their wills, and setting men's hearts on fire with the love of God . . .[66]

> Therefore, all the clergy must hold fast to the sacred Scriptures through diligent sacred reading and careful study . . . This cultivation of Scripture is required lest any of them become 'an empty preacher of the word of

God outwardly, who is not a listener to it inwardly'
(Augustine), since they must share the abundant wealth
of the divine word with the faithful committed to
them . . .[67]

Christian people, the text continues, must also read the
Scriptures for themselves. 'In this way, therefore, through
the reading and study of the sacred books, let "the word of
the Lord run and be glorified" (2 Thess. 3:1), and let the
treasure of revelation entrusted to the Church increasingly
fill the hearts of men.'[68]

The 'Decree on the Ministry and Life of Priests' returns
to this theme, and summons the Roman clergy to preach
the gospel:

ᶜince no one can be saved who has not first believed,
priests, as co-workers with their bishops, have as their
primary duty the proclamation of the gospel of God to all
. . . The task of priests is not to teach their own wisdom
but God's Word, and to summon all men urgently to
conversion and to holiness . . . Such preaching must not
present God's Word in a general and abstract fashion
only, but it must apply the perennial truth of the gospel
to the concrete circumstances of life.[69]

The Anglican church, as we have seen, has been adorned
by a long succession of gifted preachers. In recent years,
however, no Church leader has done more to stimulate the
recovery of preaching in the Church of England than
Donald Coggan, Archbishop of Canterbury from 1974 to
1980. An able preacher, who has described himself as having been for half a century 'under the joyful tyranny of
being a minister of the Word',[70] it was largely by his initiative that the College of Preachers (already well established
in Washington D.C.) was founded in England. In his first
book on preaching, *Stewards of Grace* (1958), he expressed
his conviction about the indispensability of preaching in
these terms:

Here is the miracle of the divine economy, that between the forgiveness of God and the sin of man stands – *the preacher*! That between the provision of God and the need of man stands – *the preacher*! That between the truth of God and the quest of man stands – *the preacher*! It is his task to link human sin to forgiveness, human need to divine omnipotence, human search to divine revelation . . .[71]

My Free-Church example is Dr. Martyn Lloyd-Jones who from 1938 to 1968 exercized an extremely influential ministry at Westminster Chapel in London. Never out of his own pulpit on Sundays (except during vacations), his message reached to the furthest corners of the earth. His medical training and early practice as a physician, his unshakeable commitment to the authority of Scripture and to the Christ of Scripture, his keen analytical mind, his penetrating insight into the human heart, and his passionate Welsh fire, combined to make him the most powerful British preacher of the fifties and sixties. In *Preaching and Preachers* (1971), first delivered as lectures at Westminster Theological Seminary in Philadelphia, he shares with us his strongest convictions. His opening chapter is entitled 'The Primacy of Preaching'. In it he declares, 'To me the work of preaching is the highest and the greatest and the most glorious calling to which anyone can ever be called. If you want something in addition to that I would say without any hesitation that the most urgent need in the Christian Church today is true preaching.'[72] Then, towards the end of the book he writes of 'the romance of preaching': 'There is nothing like it. It is the greatest work in the world, the most thrilling, the most exciting, the most rewarding, and the most wonderful.'[73]

With those superlatives I conclude my brief historical sketch. It is far from complete. It lays no claim to being a comprehensive 'history of preaching'. Instead, it is a very subjective selection of witnesses. Nevertheless, it has at least a double value.

First, it demonstrates how long and broad the Christian tradition is which accords great importance to preaching. It spans nearly twenty centuries, beginning with Jesus and his apostles, continuing through the early fathers and the great post-Nicene theologian-preachers like Chrysostom in the East and Augustine in the West, going on through the medieval preaching friars Francis and Dominic, the Reformers and the Puritans, Wesley and Whitefield, and culminating in modern churchmen of the nineteenth and twentieth centuries. Secondly, this long and broad tradition is consistent. Without doubt there have been exceptions, who neglected and even denigrated preaching, and whom I have omitted from my story. But they have been exceptions, deplorable deviations from the norm. The Christian consensus down the centuries has been to magnify the importance of preaching, and to resort to the same arguments and vocabulary in order to do so. We can hardly fail to be inspired by this common testimony.

Here, then, is a tradition which cannot lightly be set aside. Certainly, it may be scrutinized and assessed. Certainly, it is challenged today by the social revolution of our era. Certainly, the challenges have to be met with openness and integrity, as we shall seek to do in the next chapter. Yet we shall be able to evaluate them with greater impartiality, and feel less threatened by the attack and less dazzled by the arguments, now that we have looked back over Church history and glimpsed the glory of preaching through the eyes of its champions in every century.

Notes

1 Dargan, Vol. I, pp. 12 and 552.
2 Dargan, Vol. II, p. 7.
3 *The Didache*, in *Ante-Nicene Fathers*, Vol. VII, p. 378.
4 Justin Martyr, Chapter LXVII, in *Ante-Nicene Fathers*, Vol. I, p. 186.
5 Tertullian, Chapter XXXIX, in *Ante-Nicene Fathers*, Vol. III, p. 46.
6 Irenaeus, *Adversus Haereses*, in *Ante-Nicene Fathers*, Vol. I, p. 498.

7 Eusebius, III. 37.2.
8 Fant and Pinson, Vol. I, pp. 108–9.
9 Schaff, Vol. IX, p. 22.
10 ibid.
11 Smyth, *The Art*, p. 13.
12 Fant and Pinson, Vol. I, pp. 174–5.
13 Smyth, op. cit., p. 16.
14 ibid., pp. 15, 16.
15 *Contra Fratres*, in Fant and Pinson, Vol. I, p. 234.
16 Erasmus' treatise *On Preaching*, in Bainton, *Erasmus*, p. 324.
17 Bainton, *Erasmus*, p. 348.
18 Luther, *A Prelude on the Babylonian Captivity of the Church*, in Rupp, pp. 85–6.
19 ibid.
20 Luther, *Of the Liberty of a Christian Man*, in Rupp, p. 87.
21 *Luther's Works*, ed. Lehmann, Vol. 53, p. 68.
22 Luther, *Treatise on Good Works*, in *Luther's Works*, ed. Lehmann, Vol. 44, p. 58.
23 *Luther's Table-Talk*, 'Of Preachers and Preaching', para. cccc.
24 Rupp, pp. 96–9.
25 Calvin, IV, I. 9 and 2.1, pp. 1023 and 1041.
26 From the 'Brief Account' of Latimer's life which introduces *Select Sermons*, p. 10.
27 Moorman, p. 183.
28 *Works of Hugh Latimer*, Vol. I, pp. 59–78.
29 Dargan, Vol. I, pp. 366–7.
30 Morgan, I., *Godly Preachers*, pp. 10, 11.
31 Baxter, *Reformed Pastor*, p. 75.
32 ibid., p. 81.
33 Herbert, pp. 20–4.
34 Mather, pp. iii–v.
35 Wesley, *Sermons* p. vi.
36 Pollock, *George Whitefield*, p. 248.
37 Carus, p. 41.
38 ibid., p. 28.
39 Simeon, *Wisdom* pp. 188–9.
40 Carlyle, Chapter 4, 'The Hero as Priest', pp. 181–241.
41 Melville, p. 147.
42 ibid., pp. 128–34.
43 ibid., pp. 135–43.
44 Alexander, pp. 9–10.

45 ibid., p. 117.
46 Barbour, p. 307.
47 Forsyth, p. 1.
48 Horne, p. 15.
49 ibid., p. 19.
50 ibid., pp. 37–8.
51 ibid., p. 178.
52 Gammie, p. 169.
53 Barth, pp. 123–4.
54 Black, p. 4.
55 ibid., pp. 168–9.
56 Henson, *Church and Parson*, p. 143.
57 ibid., p. 153.
58 ibid., p. 138.
59 From *The Cost of Discipleship*, 1937, in Fant, *Bonhoeffer*, p. 28.
60 Fant, *Bonhoeffer*, p. 130.
61 Sangster, *The Craft*, pp. 14–15.
62 ibid., p. 7.
63 ibid., p. 297.
64 Blackwood, p. 13.
65 Rahner, p. 1.
66 Abbott, para. 23.
67 ibid., para. 25
68 ibid., para. 26, pp. 126–8.
69 ibid., para. 4, pp. 539–40.
70 Coggan, *On Preaching*, p. 3.
71 Coggan, *Stewards*, p. 18.
72 Lloyd-Jones, *Preaching*, p. 9.
73 ibid., p. 297.

CHAPTER TWO

Contemporary Objections to Preaching

The prophets of doom in today's Church are confidently predicting that the day of preaching is over. It is a dying art, they say, an outmoded form of communication, 'an echo from an abandoned past'.[1] Not only have modern media superseded it, but it is incompatible with the modern mood. Consequently, the sermon no longer enjoys the honour which used to be accorded to it and which was expressed in the quotations collected in Chapter One. Even 'sermon-tasting', a reprehensible kind of ecclesiastical pub-crawling, which involves erratic churchgoing merely with a view to sampling and subsequently comparing the eminent preachers of the day, has gone out of vogue. Books of sermons, once popular, have become a risky publishing venture. In some churches the sermon is reduced to an apologetic five minutes; in others it has been replaced by either a 'dialogue' or a 'happening'. According to Dr. Howard Williams' outspoken verdict, 'the sermon is out.'[2]

Equally outspoken is Dr. Donald Coggan's opposing statement that this view of preaching is 'a specious lie', perpetrated by 'Our Father Below' (as C. S. Lewis called the devil), as a result of which he has won a strategic victory. Not only has he effectively silenced some preachers, but he has also demoralized those who continue to preach. They go to their pulpits 'as men who have lost their battle before they start; the ground of conviction has slipped from under their feet'.[3]

My purpose in this chapter is to try to uncover the roots of the contemporary disenchantment with preaching. I want to look at the three main arguments which are being advanced against preaching – the anti-authority mood, the cybernetics revolution and the loss of confidence in the gospel – and at the same time make a preliminary response to them.

The Anti-authority Mood

Seldom if ever in its long history has the world witnessed such a self-conscious revolt against authority. Not that the phenomenon of protest and rebellion is new. Ever since the fall of man human nature has been rebellious, 'hostile to God and unwilling, even unable, to 'submit to God's law'. (Rom. 8:7) And this basic fact about the human condition has had a thousand ugly manifestations. What seems new today, however, is both the world-wide scale of the revolt and the philosophical arguments with which it is sometimes buttressed. There can be no doubt that the twentieth century has been caught up in a global revolution, epitomized in the two World Wars. The old order is giving place to a new. All the accepted authorities (family, school, university, State, Church, Bible, Pope, God) are being challenged. Anything which savours of 'establishment', that is, of entrenched privilege or unassailable power, is being scrutinized and opposed. A 'radical' is precisely somebody who asks awkward and irreverent questions of some 'establishment' which previously regarded itself as immune to criticism.

It would be very insensitive to react to the whole current rebellion negatively or to give it a blanket condemnation as devilish. For some of it is responsible, mature and in the fullest sense Christian. It arises from the Christian doctrine of mankind made in the image of God, and therefore protests against all forms of dehumanization. It sets itself against the social injustices which insult God the Creator, seeks to protect human beings from oppression, and longs to liberate them into the enjoyment of their God-intended freedom. In politics it protests against every authoritarian regime, whether of the left or of the right, which discriminates against minorities, denies people their civil rights,

51

forbids the free expression of opinions or imprisons people for their views alone. In economics it protests against the exploitation of the poor and against the new social servitude, slavery to the consumer market and to the machine. In industry it protests against the class confrontation between management and unions, and calls for a greater measure of responsible participation for the workers. In education it protests against indoctrination, the misuse of the classroom to bend the malleable minds of the young into predetermined shapes, and calls instead for an educational process which stimulates children and young people to develop their own personal potential.

When the rebellion is expressed in such terms as these, far from opposing it, Christians should be in the vanguard of those who promote it. For its inspiration is the glory of God in the humanization of Godlike human beings. It is when the advocates of change go beyond this, and announce their determination to abolish the democratic process itself, and with it all forms of censorship by consent, and proclaim that there are no longer any objective standards of truth or goodness, that we are obliged to part company with them. For Christians distinguish between true and false authority, that is, between the tyranny which crushes our humanity and the rational, benevolent authority under which we find our authentic human freedom.

While the current mood prevails, both those making a reckless bid for anarchy and those seeking true freedom tend to view the pulpit as a symbol of authority against which they are rebelling. Equality of educational opportunity, at least in the West, has sharpened people's critical faculties. Now everybody has his own opinions and his own convictions, and considers them just as good as the preacher's. 'Who does he think he is', people ask – silently if not aloud – 'that he should presume to lay down the law to me?' Common usage of pulpit words reflects this distortion. 'To preach' has come to mean 'to give advice in an offensive, tedious or obtrusive manner',[4] while to be 'sermonic' is to inflict on someone a patronizing harangue.

Although this resistance to authoritative pulpit pronouncements has become widespread in our century, it
began at least with the Enlightenment in the eighteenth
century and grew more vocal in the nineteenth. No more
vigorous (or humorous) expression of it has been given
than by Anthony Trollope in *Barchester Towers*, which was
first published in 1857. The novel's main character is the
Rev. Obadiah Slope, domestic chaplain to the hen-pecked
Bishop Proudie of Barchester. Trollope makes no secret of
his active dislike for him. He describes him in the most
unflattering terms:

> His hair is lank, and of a dull pale reddish hue. It is always
> formed into three straight lumpy masses . . . His face is
> nearly of the same colour as his hair, though perhaps a
> little redder: it is not unlike beef – beef, however, one
> would say, of a bad quality . . . His nose, however, is his
> redeeming feature: it is pronounced straight and well
> formed; though I myself should have liked it better did it
> not possess a somewhat spongy, porous appearance, as
> though it had been cleverly formed out of a red coloured
> cork.[5]

Having thus aroused his readers' distaste for Mr. Slope's
appearance ('the damp, sandy-haired, saucer-eyed, red-
fisted Mr. Slope'),[6] Trollope is ready to arouse their hostility to his preaching. Although the Barchester clergy
belonged to 'the high and dry church', Obadiah Slope (a
low churchman) had no respect for their sensitivities and
proceeded in his first sermon in the cathedral to anathe-
matize all those opinions and habits which they held most
dear. This gives Trollope the excuse he wants to inveigh
against preaching and preachers:

> There is, perhaps, no greater hardship at present in-
> flicted on mankind in civilized and free countries, than
> the necessity of listening to sermons. No-one but a
> preaching clergyman has, in these realms, the power of

compelling an audience to sit silent, and be tormented. No-one but a preaching clergyman can revel in platitudes, truisms and untruisms, and yet receive, as his undisputed privilege, the same respectful demeanour as though words of impassioned eloquence, or persuasive logic, fell from his lips. Let a professor of law or physic find his place in a lecture room, and there pour forth jejune words and useless empty phrases, and he will pour them forth to empty benches. Let a barrister attempt to talk without talking well, and he will talk but seldom. A judge's charge need be listened to perforce by none but the jury, prisoner or gaoler. A member of Parliament can be coughed down or counted out. Town councillors can be tabooed. But no-one can rid himself of the preaching clergyman. He is the bore of the age, . . . the nightmare that disturbs our Sunday's rest, the incubus that overloads our religion and makes God's service distasteful. We are not forced into church! No: but we desire more than that. We desire not to be forced to stay away. We desire, nay, we are resolute, to enjoy the comfort of public worship; but we desire also that we may do so without an amount of tedium which ordinary human nature cannot endure with patience; that we may be able to leave the house of God, without that anxious longing for escape, which is the common consequence of common sermons.[7]

Trollope's antipathy to sermons was not just that they induced boredom, but that they seemed to him an improper exercise of authority, especially when the preacher was young. When the Rev. Francis Arabin, formerly Professor of Poetry at Oxford University, had been installed as Vicar of St. Ewold's Church, Ullathorne, he was extremely nervous while preaching his first sermon. Trollope expressed his astonishment that 'even very young men' who are 'little more than boys' can muster courage to preach and 'ascend a rostrum high above the heads of the submissive crowd'. 'It seems strange to us', he adds, 'that they are not stricken dumb by the new and awful solemnity of their position . . . Clergymen who could not preach would be such blessings that they would be bribed to adhere to their incompetence.'[8]

Today, more than a century later, we are conscious of the same hatred of authority figures. What has changed is that the resistance is much more widespread, open and strident. As for the churches, many have a preponderance of the middle-aged and elderly, who have grown out of the protest phase and can be relied on to be comparatively docile. In many cases, however, the young vote with their feet and steer clear of such archaic institutions. The anti-authority mood reached maximum heat and exploded in the 1960s. The Berkeley campus of the University of California became the battleground of the Free Speech Movement, and in Paris the students joined the workers in taking to the streets and the barricades. Now, after a lapse of a decade and more, at least some governments and some universities have learned some lessons. There is less censorship and more freedom. So the target for the hostility of the young has shifted from institutions (since that battle has been partly won) to ideas, and specially the ideas which old, discredited institutions persist in trying to impose on others. Charlie Watts of the Rolling Stones expresses this attitude perfectly, 'I'm against any form of organized thought. I'm against . . . organized religion like the church. I don't see how you can organize ten million minds to believe one thing.'[9] Others went further and opposed thought altogether; the 70s were the decade of the non-rational.

Thus, minds cannot be organized and thoughts cannot be forced on people. No institution, however venerable, has the right to impose an idea upon us by the weight of its own authority. Nor even can any idea impose itself upon us all. For there is no such thing as a truth which is absolute and therefore universal. On the contrary, everything is relative and subjective. Before I can believe any idea, it has to authenticate itself to me personally; and before you can be expected to believe it, it must become self-authenticating to you. Until this happens, we neither should nor can believe.

A Christian Response

How, then, should preachers react to the anti-authority spirit of today? What distinctively Christian critique and response may be made? We should not allow ourselves to be stampeded into abandoning preaching. Nor should we make the opposite mistake of a greater dogmatism so that, whenever our beliefs and statements are challenged, we merely repeat them in a louder voice. Is it possible, in place of these extremes, to maintain our loyalty to the historic Christian faith, while at the same time recognizing and respecting the modern mood of doubt and denial? I think it is. Let me suggest certain truths we shall be wise to remember and certain attitudes we shall be wise to cultivate.

First, we need to remember *the nature of human beings* in Christian understanding. According to the first two chapters of Genesis, God created mankind male and female to be both morally responsible (receiving commandments) and free (invited but not coerced into loving obedience). We cannot therefore acquiesce either in licence (which denies responsibility) or in slavery (which denies freedom). Christians know from both Scripture and experience that human fulfilment is impossible outside some context of authority. Freedom unlimited is an illusion. The mind is free only under the authority of truth, and the will under the authority of righteousness. It is under Christ's yoke that we find the rest he promises, not in discarding it. (Matt. 11:29, 30) Similarly, citizens can enjoy freedom only within an ordered society. Parents with teenaged children also know the truth of this principle. For adolescents who are rebelling against parental authority are wanting not only to experience greater freedom but also to discover the limits of their freedom. As they push against the fence, they devoutly hope it will not collapse. As with adolescents so with adults; we need what P. T. Forsyth called 'that authority which men at once resent and crave'.[10]

Secondly, we need to remember *the doctrine of revelation*. It is a basic tenet of the Christian religion that we believe what we believe not because human beings have invented it but because God has revealed it. In consequence, there is an authority inherent in Christianity which can never be destroyed. Preachers who share this assurance see themselves as trustees of divine revelation, or, as the apostle Paul expressed it, 'stewards of the mysteries of God' (1 Cor. 4:1), that is, of the secrets which he has disclosed. This conviction need not lead us into an obnoxious kind of dogmatism – cocksure, inflexible and arrogant – but it will enable us to proclaim the gospel with quiet confidence as good news from God.

Theodore Parker Ferris, who lectured in homiletics at the Episcopal Theological School and later became Rector of Trinity Church, Boston, made this one of the major emphases of his 1950 inaugural series of the George Craig Stewart Lectures on Preaching, which were subsequently published with the title *Go Tell the People*. The purpose of a sermon, he urged, is to declare, to disclose, to reveal something. Too many sermons are written 'in the imperative mode', whereas the religion of the Bible 'is written largely in the revealing language of the indicative mode'. 'Listen to some of the great declarations of the Bible,' he went on, and quoted Old Testament verses like 'In the beginning God created the heavens and the earth,' 'The Lord is my light and my salvation,' and 'they who wait for the Lord shall renew their strength.' (Gen. 1:1; Ps. 27:1; Isa. 40:31) 'These are not arguments or exhortations or speculations. They are simple, forthright statements about the nature of things which have been revealed to men . . . The power of the religion of the Bible is to be found in its affirmations.' The same is true, he continued, of the great proclamations of the New Testament like 'I am the way, the truth and the life' or 'God was in Christ reconciling the world to himself.' (John 14:6; 2 Cor. 5:19)[11] 'This book on

57

preaching', Dr. Ferris summed up, 'has but a single theme. The theme is this. A sermon is by its very nature a revelation, not an exhortation.'[12]

Thirdly, we need to remember *the locus of authority*. Consider again the affirmations T. P. Ferris quoted, and many others in the Bible like them. Wherein lies their authority? It resides only in the God who made them, and not at all in us who quote them today. There is something inherently horrid about human beings who claim and attempt to wield a personal authority they do not possess. It is particularly inappropriate in the pulpit. When a preacher pontificates like a tinpot demagogue, or boasts of his power and glory as Nebuchadnezzar did on the roof of his royal palace in Babylon (Dan. 4:28, 29), he deserves the judgment which fell on that dictator: he was driven from his palace mad, 'ate grass like an ox, . . . till his hair grew as long as eagles' feathers, and his nails were like birds' claws'. For 'those who walk in pride God is able to abase.' (Dan. 4:33, 37)

But suppose in our preaching we are careful to demonstrate that the authority with which we preach inheres neither in us as individuals, nor primarily in our office as clergy or preachers, nor even in the church whose members and accredited pastors we may be, but supremely in the Word of God which we expound? Then the people should be willing to hear, particularly if we put the matter beyond doubt by showing that we desire to live under this authority ourselves. As Donald Coggan has put it, in order 'to preach, a man must know the authority of being under Authority.'[13] It is for this reason that we shall be wise neither to say 'Thus says the Lord' (since we do not have the authority of an inspired Old Testament prophet) nor to declare 'I say to you' (since we do not have the authority of Jesus Christ and his apostles), but rather, at least most of the time, to use the 'we' form of address. For then it will be clear that we preach nothing to others which we do not also and first preach to ourselves, and that authority and humility are not mutually exclusive. 'It is authority that the world chiefly needs and the preaching of the hour lacks,' wrote P. T. Forsyth, in 1907, 'an authoritative Gospel in a humble personality.'[14]

Fourthly, we need to remember *the relevance of the gospel*. A major reason for the contemptuous dismissal of some sermons is that people perceive them to be unrelated to real life as they know it. The fact that they are preached with authority makes them all the more distasteful. But when the preached message rings true, and is seen to relate to human reality, it carries its own authority, and authenticates itself. So then, it is not enough for us to make pronouncements of authority; we have to argue the reasonableness and demonstrate the relevance of what we declare. Then people will listen respectively.

This is the point which Dr. Clement Welsh, since 1963 Director of Studies and Warden of the American College of Preachers in Washington D.C., is at pains to make in his book *Preaching in a New Key* (1974). He says he cannot accept Karl Barth's statement that 'preaching is the Word of God which he himself has spoken' because this 'high' doctrine 'is haunted by the ghosts of many unanswered questions concerning the authority of scriptures' and 'raises worrisome questions about mistaking man's voice for God's voice.'[15] So he suggests that we begin at the other end, with the listener not the preacher, with creation not redemption. For the listener lives in the created world and, being 'the most fantastic processor of information the world has ever seen',[16] wants to make sense of the complexity of his human experiences. In order to help him do so, the preacher 'must give to the creation (i.e. to the phenomena of human life) the same exegetical care that he would give a passage of scripture'.[17] In fact, Dr. Welsh urges 'a combination of these two homiletical doctrines, the one stressing revelation and scripture, and the other stressing apologetics and reason'.[18] I do not think he is denying the place of any 'word of authority', although sometimes he seems to come perilously close to this; rather is he rejecting that kind of *ex cathedra* preaching which is divorced from worldly reality, answers the wrong questions, and discourages responsible thinking in the congregation. Even authoritative sermons will commend themselves if they are preached 'in a new key', by addressing the ultimate questions of human life meaningfully.[19]

Dialogical Preaching

Fifthly, we need to remember *the dialogical character of preaching*. That is, a true sermon is not the monologue which it appears to be. 'Monotonous ministerial monologue' is the expression sometimes used. The Rev. R. E. O. White, Principal of the Baptist Theological College of Scotland, quotes an even ruder definition, 'a monstrous monologue by a moron to mutes'.[20] But I want to argue that true preaching is always dialogical. Not in the sense of 'dialogue sermons', in which two preachers debate an issue, or one interviews and quizzes the other (an excellent arrangement for an after-church or mid-week meeting but, it seems to me, out of place in the context of public worship). Nor am I suggesting that we encourage hecklers, although, to be sure, some unscripted interruptions would enliven the proceedings in most Western churches and put us preachers on our mettle.

Vocal dialogue between preacher and congregation is, however, commonplace in the Black worship of North America. It is vividly described by Dr. Henry H. Mitchell, Founding Director of the Ecumenical Center for Black Church Studies, Los Angeles, in his books *Black Preaching* (1970) and *The Recovery of Preaching* (1977). The latter has a chapter entitled 'Preaching as Dialogue'. 'Unhampered by the Teutonic captivity of white theology', as he puts it, and 'unscathed by the proud abstractions of the Western world', American Blacks have been free in their worship to express authentic Black selfhood. Black religion is 'soul religion', unafraid of emotion and ecstasy.[21] 'They have had call-and-response in Africa for centuries, and in Black Christian worship in America from the very start – three centuries ago.'[22] In particular, 'the Black worshipper does not merely acknowledge the Word delivered by the preacher; he talks back! Sometimes he may shout. The day is not far past, if indeed it has passed at all, when the Black worshipper would consider a worship service a failure if there were no shouting.'[23] Dr. Mitchell concedes that this kind of audible talk-back or 'raucous reverence of real people'[24] (cries of 'Amen!', 'Tell it!', 'That's right!', 'Sho' 'nough!', 'Yes sir!', 'So true!' etc.) is at times no more than a cultural habit or convention, and that at other times 'so much noise is, in actuality, a substitute for action.'[25] Yet, generally speaking, it is a genuine expression of audience participation and a great support and stimulation to the preacher. Indeed, when a Black congregation's heart and mind are gripped by the sermon, 'the ensuing dialogue between preacher and people is the epitome of creative worship.'[26]

In other contexts, however, the kind of dialogical preaching I am recommending is different. It refers to the silent dialogue which should be developing between the preacher and his hearers. For what he says provokes questions in their minds which he then proceeds to answer. His answer raises further questions, to which again he replies. One of the greatest gifts a preacher needs is such a sensitive understanding of people and their problems that he can anticipate their reactions to each part of his sermon and respond to them. Preaching is rather like playing chess, in that the expert chess player keeps several moves ahead of his opponent, and is always ready to respond, whatever piece he decides to move next.

I remember reading an amusing article in the *Guardian Weekly* by Peter Fiddick[27] on 'the difficult art of being an audience'. It was entitled 'None shall sleep.' He confessed to the problem he had in keeping awake during concerts. His earliest recollection of falling asleep in public, he said, was at the Methodist Central Hall in Slough, when he was about seven years old. He nodded off during the sermon, and 'woke up, mortified, in the middle of the next hymn.'

Later, however, he learned to beat 'the sermon problem by having mental debates with the preacher', a technique which failed in a Chopin recital 'since waltzes are not susceptible to argument'. Peter Fiddick probably imagines that preachers would be furious if they thought their listeners were having 'mental debates' with them. But surely, on the contrary, we should be delighted. We have no wish to encourage passivity in the congregation. We want to provoke people to think, to answer us and argue with us in their minds, and we should maintain such a lively (though silent) dialogue with them that they find it impossible to fall asleep.

It is particularly important to do this when our topic is at all controversial. Our tendency is naturally to express our own convictions, in which case we may overlook the problems which these raise in other people's minds, whether the believers (or half-believers) in church or the unbelievers they will meet in their office or shop the following day. For example, we could not preach on 'the whole earth is full of his glory' (Isa. 6:3) and ignore the fact that the earth is plagued with earthquake, predation and famine as well as with order, plenty and loveliness. Nor could we preach on the providence of God who 'in everything . . . works for good with those who love him' (Rom. 8:28), without showing an awareness of evil and pain.

I could multiply examples. We should not preach on marriage and forget the single people in the congregation, or on Christian joy and forget the sorrows and tragedies which some will be experiencing. We cannot expound Christ's promise to answer prayer without remembering that some prayers remain unanswered, or his command not to be anxious without acknowledging that people have good reasons for anxiety. To anticipate people's objections is to cover our flanks against counter-attack.

A dialogue between speaker and listeners, or between writer and readers, often develops in Scripture. In the Old Testament we find it in the Book of Malachi. '"I have loved you", says the Lord. But you say "How hast thou loved us?"' (1:12) Again, 'You have wearied the Lord with your words. Yet you say "How have we wearied him?"' (2:17) And again, '"Will man rob God? Yet you are robbing me. But you say 'How are we robbing thee?' In your tithes and offerings."' (3:8)

In the New Testament Jesus himself often used a similar method. Several of his parables ended with a question, and probably in this case he expected the people to reply audibly. He engaged them in a dialogue. For instance, 'Which of these three, do you think, proved neighbour to the man who fell among the robbers?' And 'When therefore the owner of the vineyard comes, what will he do to those tenants?' (Luke 10:36; Matt. 21:40) Or after he had washed the apostles' feet, he asked them, 'Do you know what I have done to you?' (John 13:12)

The past master at this art, however, was the apostle Paul, and the best example is his letter to the Romans. Throughout its early chapters, as he dictates to Tertius, he is conscious of Jewish objections to his argument. Many times he voices their objection and answers it. Take this dialogue, for instance:

> Then what advantage has the Jew? Or what is the value of circumcision?
> Much in every way. To begin with, the Jews are entrusted with the oracles of God.
> What if some were unfaithful? Does their faithlessness nullify the faithfulness of God?
> By no means! Let God be true, though every man be false . . .
> But if our wickedness serves to show the justice of God, what shall we say? That God is unjust to inflict wrath on us? (I speak in a human way.)
> By no means! For then how could God judge the world?
> (Rom. 3:1–6; cf. vv. 27–31)

It may well be, as a number of scholars have pointed out, that Paul was deliberately copying the Stoic 'diatribes', whose 'salient features', in the words of Professor James Stewart, 'were their rhetorical questions, their preference for short disconnected sentences, their use of the device of an imaginary objector, their flinging backwards and forwards of challenge and rejoinder . . .'[28] It is a device of preachers rather than writers, but is found in authors who are preachers too. Thus Luther, whose commentaries were first given as lectures, not infrequently interjected, 'Do I hear somebody saying . . .?' or 'You do not imagine, do you, that . . .?', while Billy Graham constantly says, 'But, Billy, you may ask . . .' and expresses the problem which he imagines a non-Christian in his audience may have.

In his autobiographical sketch *Crowded Canvas* (1974) Canon Max Warren, formerly General Secretary of the Church Missionary Society, defined communication as a special ability:

> to out-do the Communist technique of 'double-think' and do a Christian 'quadruple-think'. 'Quadruple-thinking' is thinking out what I have to say, then thinking out how the other man will understand what I say, and then re-thinking what I have to say, so that, when I say it, he will think what I am thinking! . . . 'Quadruple-thinking' involves mental pain and great spiritual sensitivity.[29]

Painful as it is, it is of the essence of dialogical preaching and lessens the offence which authoritative preaching would otherwise give.

The Cybernetics Revolution

'Cybernetics' (from *kybernētēs*, a steersman) is the study of the mechanisms of communication, both human and electronic, that is to say, in both brains and computers. And the 'cybernetics revolution' refers to radical changes in communication as a result of the development of complex electronic equipment.

The high priest of the cybernetics revolution was that remarkable Canadian Roman Catholic, Professor Marshall McLuhan, founder of the Centre for Culture and Technology at the University of Toronto in 1963, and its director for fourteen years, who died on the last day of 1980. He was at the height of his influence in the sixties. The first of his books to attract widespread public attention, *The Gutenberg Galaxy: The Making of Typographic Man*, was published in 1962, and his best-known book *Understanding Media: The Extensions of Man* in 1964. During the seventies his popularity waned, and his whole scheme has been subjected to severe, even hostile, criticism. He was certainly guilty of wild exaggeration. Nevertheless, one of his fiercest critics, Dr. Jonathan Miller, who does not hesitate to characterize his conclusions as 'bizarre', 'absurd', 'incoherent' and even 'nonsensical', yet acknowledges 'the intense excitement' with which he first read him and the fact that 'he has successfully convened a debate on a subject which has been neglected too long.'[30]

When the dust of controversy has settled, it seems certain that Marshall McLuhan's name will be included among the pioneers of communication theory. History is not likely to forget expressions like 'the global village', 'the medium is the message' (as well as 'the massage'), and 'hot' and 'cool' communication, which he has added to our vocabulary. It would be foolish, therefore, to regard his theories as passé; we need to come to grips with them.

We begin with his reading of history. He depicted primitive man as enjoying a harmonious existence through the balanced, simultaneous use of his five senses. As the tribal chieftains sat round the camp fire, they would communicate with one another in a 'cool' or casual manner, absorbing information and impressions by sight, sound, touch, taste and smell. This idyllic situation was, however, shattered by two disastrous inventions. The first was the phonetic alphabet. Previously, ancient pictographic writing (in China) and hieroglyphic writing (in Babylonia), because they had a visual meaning, preserved a link between the ear and the eye. But in the phonetic alphabet 'semantically meaningless letters are used to correspond to semantically meaningless sounds,' causing a 'sudden breach between the auditory and the visual experience of man'.[31] In consequence, the phonetic alphabet upset mankind's sensory equilibrium by making the eye the dominant sense and in effect turning the reader's ear into an eye.

The second disastrous occurrence (in the McLuhan scheme) was the invention of movable type in the fifteenth century by Johann Gutenberg (died 1468), the main villain of his story. Typography brought tribalism to an end. It broke up the collective unity of primitive human society. It turned each human being into an individualist and a specialist, for 'literacy . . . takes him out of his collective tribal world and beaches him in individual isolation.'[32] Now he is able to sit in a corner by himself, with his back to the world, reading a book. Moreover, as he reads and his eye follows each line of print, he finds himself locked into linear logic, thereby losing the magic of multi-sensual learning. He also becomes a literalist, for his imagination atrophies.

But in 1844 a third invention (that of the telegraph by Samuel Morse) heralded the dawn of a new age, namely the electronic age. Whereas alphabet and print had increasingly alienated human beings from one another, 'the tendency of electric media is to create a kind of organic interdependence among all the institutions of society.'[33] Human beings who had been detribalized by print, are now through our increasingly sophisticated electronic gadgetry becoming retribalized. 'The simultaneity of electric communication . . . makes each of us present and accessible to every other person in the world.'[34] The whole world has thus become a 'global village'.[35]

In this social revolution television has exercized a major role. McLuhan argued that it has reversed the harmful processes initiated by the phonetic alphabet and the printing press, for it has reintroduced to human life the benefits of 'cool' communication. 'A hot medium,' he wrote, 'is one that extends one single sense in "high definition"' (i.e. in a state that is 'well filled with data'). A 'cool' medium, on the other hand, instead of bombarding one sense with much information, permits the gradual gleaning of information by several senses together. The crucial difference lies in the amount of information provided by the medium and the corresponding amount which needs to be provided by the listener or viewer. 'Hot media are . . . low in participation, and cool media are high in participation or completion by the audience.'[36] Now both television and the spoken word are 'cool', because both demand audience participation. In consequence, 'TV will not work as background. It engages you. You have to be *with* it.'[37]

Is television, then, a serious rival to preaching as a means of communication? Has the box in the lounge replaced the pulpit in the church? Marshall McLuhan did not answer this question, for he never asked it. But if asked, his answer would seem to me to have been necessarily ambivalent. For on the one hand he approved of the spoken word (his number-one enemy was 'print'), since the spoken word is a cool medium and 'involves all of the senses dramatically'.[38] Thus, when two people are talking to one another, they are not only listening to each other, but watching each other's facial expressions and gestures, perhaps touching or holding each other, and even smelling each other's characteristic smell. These have their equivalents in the preacher–congregation relationship; most churches even have a recognizable smell! On the other hand, the future of language is imperilled by electronic technology, since the latter has no need of words. 'Electricity points the way to an extension of the process of consciousness itself, on a world scale, and without any verbalization whatever.' McLuhan appeared to welcome such a development, hailing it as the destruction of the Tower of Babel, and even as 'a Pentecostal condition of universal understanding and unity'. Languages would be bypassed altogether in favour of 'a general cosmic consciousness' and 'the condition of speechlessness that could confer a perpetuity of collective harmony and peace'.[39]

Although Marshall McLuhan dreamed his dreams about the comparative blessings of speech and speechlessness, for myself I believe the faculty of speech to be a distinctively human gift, a marvellously versatile means of communication, and a reflection of the divine image we bear. For though doves can coo, donkeys bray, monkeys squeal and pigs grunt, only human beings can speak. According to the Bible, the living God himself is a speaking God. He has communicated with us by speech, and he means us to communicate with one another in the same way. To decline to do so would immeasurably impoverish us, and diminish our dignity to that of birds and beasts.

Since Marshall McLuhan's heyday, the invention of the transistor, which uses silicone crystals as powerful electronic amplifiers, has further transformed computer science. Transistorized computers, or micro-processors, whose first models were marketed only in 1975, have already made their cumbersome ancestors of the 1950s look as archaic as dinosaurs. They are not only so small as to be readily portable, and much cheaper to produce and to operate, but will soon have such a vastly improved memory as to store a whole encyclopaedia on a single chip, and reach such a speed as to have a switching potential of about a trillion a second.

Social seers are trying to assess the consequences of the chip revolution. They forecast that, in some respects at least, the world may be a safer place, since a universal credit-card system will render money-based crime obsolete, while danger-protecting devices will make cars collision-proof. At the same time, people may travel less. Commuting will diminish, because industry will be operated by robots, hours of employment will decrease, and business will be decentralized; 'office and home will be combined, the public transport system will give way to giant data communications networks, and the business motor-car will be traded in for the latest video conference system.'[40]

The computer revolution relates chiefly to data processing, that is, its storage, retrieval, sorting and communication. All current forms of communication are bound, therefore, to be affected by it. One chapter of Christopher Evans' book *The Mighty Micro* (1979) is entitled 'The Death of the Printed Word'.[41] Having pointed out that both books and computers are essentially 'devices for storing information', he goes on to argue that computers are 'vastly superior' to books, not only because they are becoming increasingly smaller and cheaper, but also because 'electronic books' will be 'dynamic', able to collect, sift and present material. Moreover, their powers of presentation will include both the visual (on the television screen) and the aural (by that strange synthetic speech called 'computaspeak').

It is difficult to imagine the world in the year A.D. 2000, by which time versatile micro-processors are likely to be as common as simple calculators are today. We should certainly welcome the fact that the silicon chip will transcend human brain-power, as the machine has transcended human muscle-power. Much less welcome will be the probable reduction of human contact as the new electronic network renders personal relationships ever less necessary. In such a dehumanized society the fellowship of the local church will become increasingly important, whose members meet one another, and talk and listen to one another in person rather than on screen. In this human context of mutual love the speaking and hearing of the Word of God is also likely to become more necessary for the preservation of our humanness, not less.

The Influence of Television

I come back, then, to the rivalry between the box and the pulpit. Certainly television is a major factor in all our lives. In Britain 98% of homes have at least one TV set, and the average household has it switched on for between 30 and 35 hours a week. Actual viewing time for an adult is between 16 and 18 hours a week, which means that he spends the best part of 8 whole years of his life before a TV screen.[42]

American statistics are higher. According to surveys conducted in 1970 and 1971, the weekly average viewing time for adults was 23.3 hours.[43]

It is extremely difficult to make a balanced estimate of the social effects of television. Without doubt the positive benefits have been enormous. TV enables people to share in events and experiences from which otherwise – through lack of time, privilege, money or health – they would be excluded. They can take part in great occasions of national celebration or mourning (a wedding or funeral, a monarch's coronation or president's installation, or the visit of a Head of State from another country). They can travel to outlandish places which they could never afford to visit personally, and be introduced to some of the wonders of nature. They can view films, plays and sporting events. They can keep abreast of world news, and be stimulated to grasp the political, social and moral issues being debated at the time. All this is great gain.

Nevertheless, there is another side, which particularly relates to the preaching and hearing of sermons. Television makes it harder for people to listen attentively and responsively, and therefore for preachers to hold a congregation's attention, let alone secure an appropriate response. Why is this? I will try to summarize the five deleterious tendencies of television.

First, TV tends to make people *physically lazy*. It offers them home-based entertainment at the turn of a knob. So why not relax in a comfortable arm chair, and even do their 'worshipping' before the screen? Why bother to turn out for church? Television-conditioned people are more reluctant to go out, and more resentful of intrusions, than others. Although the so-called 'electronic Church' of the United States, which has an enormous viewing audience, has brought great blessing to people confined to their homes through old age or sickness, it is very doubtful whether able-bodied people should ever regard it as a substitute for local church membership. The screen inhibits full personal participation in fellowship, sacrament and congregational worship, let alone active service and witness.

Secondly, TV tends to make people *intellectually uncritical*. Of course it need not, and most channels include programmes designed to provoke thought. Yet I think Marshall McLuhan exaggerated the 'participation' element which TV demands. Many people flop down before the box precisely because after a hard day's work they want to be entertained, not to be made to participate, least of all to think. So the disease known as 'spectatoritis' spreads. People can no longer listen without looking. TV offers them more pictures than arguments.

Now of course McLuhan knew this. Believing in 1968 that Richard Nixon had lost the 1960 Presidential Election because of John F. Kennedy's better television image, the preoccupation of Nixon's Republican advisers in 1968 was how to get him to 'project electronically',[44] that is, how to convert his screen image from that of a dry, humourless lawyer into a warm, animated human being. So they hired Marshall McLuhan as consultant and circulated to their entourage suitable extracts from his *Understanding Media*. He wrote to them, 'Policies and issues are useless for election purposes . . . The shaping of a candidate's integral image has taken the place of discussing conflicting points of view.'[45] William Gavin, one of Nixon's chief aides, urged as a policy, 'Break away from linear logic: present a barrage of impressions.'[46] He then summed up his approach in the words, 'get the voters to like the guy, and the battle's two-thirds won.'[47] There is no need for us to disagree that images are more powerful than issues, and pictures than arguments. But to substitute the one for the other is to surrender human dignity to human frailty. Christians should not acquiesce in anything which blunts people's critical faculties.

Thirdly, TV tends to make people *emotionally insensitive*. In one way the opposite is the case. TV has had the welcome effect of bringing visually into our homes and on to our consciences scenes which otherwise we could never

71

have witnessed. The horrors of war, the deprivations of famine and poverty, the devastations of earthquake, flood and hurricane, and the plight of refugees – these things are forced upon our attention (as they should be) as never before. We cannot shut our eyes to them any longer. And yet we can and do. Indeed, understandably so. For there is a limit to the volume of pain and tragedy which our emotions can bear. After a while, when the burden becomes too heavy, we either cross the room in order to turn to another channel or switch off the set, or we continue to watch without feeling, having switched off our emotions inside. We become skilled in emotional self-defence. At this point appeals become counter-productive; we have no feeling left to respond to them; I sometimes wonder if we are breeding a new 'gospel-hardened' generation because they have been subjected *ad nauseam* not to glib stereotypes of the good news but to television pictures which have permanently damaged their mechanisms of emotional reaction.

Fourthly, TV tends to make people *psychologically confused*. For television belongs to the realm of the artificial and the contrived. Most of the programmes we see on the screen were not filmed in real life, but in a studio. To borrow one of those McLuhan puns which make his critics wince, they belong like movies not to the real world but to 'the reel world'.[48] Programmes filmed outside a studio also lack a measure of authenticity either because, since the filming, they have been edited (e.g. news and documentaries) or because, if relayed live, we are being given a vicarious experience and participating only at second hand. True, we can actually watch a football game (though on the screen) and hear the crowds yelling (though through a speaker), yet there is no way in which we can feel the wind of that tornado or smell the odours of that slum.

It was this element of unreality in television which Malcolm Muggeridge emphasized in his 1976 'London Lectures in Contemporary Christianity' entitled *Christ and the Media*. He was 'contrasting the fantasy of the media with the reality of Christ'.[49] He expressed his personal longing 'to stay . . . with the reality of Christ' and to persuade others to do so, 'to lash themselves to it, as in the old days of sail sailors would lash themselves to the mast when storms blew up and the seas were rough.'[50] The questions which this contrast raises in my mind are these: how easily can people switch from the one world to the other? Do they recognize, when they hear God's Word and worship him, that now at last they are in touch with ultimate reality? Or do they, as I fear, move from one unreal situation to another, somnambulating as in a dream, because television has introduced them to a world of fantasy from which they never entirely escape?

Fifthly, TV tends to make people *morally disordered*. I do not mean that viewers automatically imitate the sexual or violent behaviour they see on the screen. The 1977 Home Office study *Screen Violence and Film Censorship*, while confessing that the social research had been inadequate, concluded that screen violence 'is unlikely in itself to impel ordinary viewers to behave in ways they would otherwise not have done'.[51] The Annan Report on *The Future of Broadcasting* (1977) reached a similar conclusion, although it added that there was real public concern about violence on television, and that the public have a case which the broadcasters must answer.[52]

The morally 'disordering' influence of television to which I am referring is more subtle and insidious than direct incitement. What happens to all of us, unless our powers of moral judgment are acute and alert, is that our understanding of what is 'normal' begins to be modified. Under the impression that 'everybody does it', and that nobody nowadays believes much in God or in absolutes of truth and goodness, our defences are lowered and our values imperceptibly altered. We begin to assume that physical violence (when we are provoked), sexual promiscuity (when we are aroused) and extravagant consumer expenditure (when we are tempted) are the accepted norms of Western society at the end of the twentieth century. We have been conned.

The most vulnerable members of the population, of course, are children. Yet they are the greatest TV addicts. In Britain 'two children in every three are watching television between 3 and 5 hours a day (21 to 35 hours a week).'[53] In the United States pre-school children constitute the largest television audience, and their weekly average viewing time is at least 30.4 hours.[54] 'By the age of seventeen the average American child has logged 15,000 hours watching TV – the equivalent of almost two years day and night.'[55]

Marie Winn has documented the effects of television on American children in her disturbing book *The Plug-In Drug* (1977). Her thesis is that the damage children suffer is due not so much to the content of television programmes as to the television-watching experience itself. It inhibits homework and outdoor play. It hinders the child's development in language, imagination, perception, learning, self-direction and relationships. It encourages passivity and diminishes creativity. And it disrupts natural family life. Worst of all, it induces what has been called 'the television trance'. It 'has not merely blurred the distinctions between the real and unreal for steady viewers, but . . . by doing so it has dulled their sensitivities to real events.'[56]

To sum up, physical laziness, intellectual flabbiness, emotional exhaustion, psychological confusion and moral disorientation: all these are increased by lengthy exposure to television. And children are the ones who suffer most harm.

How should we react to this negative critique of the effects of contemporary television? I am not advocating that we all sell or smash our sets, or that we try to put the clock back to the pre-television era. Such reactionary behaviour is as unnecessary as it is impossible. Most of the damaging tendencies I have described are due more to the poor quality of some programmes and to uncritical, obsessional viewing than to the medium itself. On balance, as a medium, television offers more blessings than curses. What is needed, then?

First, Christian parents need to exert greater discipline over their children's access to the 'box'. In Britain 79% of children 'say their parents exercize no control over the number of hours they spend watching television per day or week.'[57] Yet indiscriminate television viewing exposes the next generation to 'consensus-propaganda', to what Peter Abbs calls 'mass-culture'. His thesis is that man is 'the most imitative creature in the world and learns by imitation' (Aristotle), that children absorb accepted cultural value-symbols, and that in our society these are being created by the commercial elites.[58]

Secondly, Christians should seek to penetrate the world of the mass media, and equip themselves as television script writers, producers and performers. We can hardly complain of the low standard of many current programmes if we take no constructive initiatives to provide alternatives which are not only technically equal if not better, but more wholesome as well. In previous eras, as each new medium of communication has been developed (writing, painting, music, drama, print, film, radio), Christians have been among the first to discern its potential and to press it into the service of worship and evangelism. It must be the same with television. Indeed, in some parts of the world, it already is.

Thirdly, preachers have to reckon with a TV-conditioned congregation. We have a colossal task on our hands if we hope to counteract the baneful tendencies of much modern television. We can no longer assume that people either want to listen to sermons, or indeed are able to listen. When they are accustomed to the swiftly moving images of the screen, how can we expect them to give their attention to one person talking, with no frills, no light relief and nothing else to look at? Is it not beyond them? In consequence, when the sermon begins, they switch off. You can almost hear the click. I do not think this is reason enough to give up preaching, for (as I shall argue shortly) there is something unique and irreplaceable about it. But we shall certainly have to fight for people's attention.

Whatever is dull, drab, dowdy, slow or monotonous cannot compete in the television age. Television challenges preachers to make our presentation of the truth attractive through variety, colour, illustration, humour and fast-flowing movement. And in addition, although nothing can supplant preaching, it definitely needs to be supplemented.

The Learning Process
There are four ways in which human beings learn: by listening, discussing, watching and discovering. One might call these audition, conversation, observation and participation. The first is the most direct, mouth to ear, speaker to hearer, and of course includes preaching. But it is not by any means always the most effective. 'Most people find it difficult to understand purely verbal concepts. They *suspect* the ear; they don't trust it. In general, we feel more secure when things are *visible*, when we can "see for ourselves".'[59] So the other three aspects of the learning process should find a place in each local church's Christian Education programme.

Dialegesthai, to 'reason' or 'argue', is a verb frequently used by Luke to describe the evangelistic preaching of Paul. 'He argued with them out of the scriptures,' particularly with Jewish people. Presumably it was a vocal dialogue in which he presented his case, some questioned it, others contradicted it, and he replied to their questions and criticisms. We need not doubt that he employed a similar method in *catechēsis*, the instruction of converts. So today just as in a university the lecture is supplemented by seminars or tutorials (with close contact between tutor and students), so in the church the sermon should be supplemented by a variety of classes for study and groups for discussion.

A friend of mine, who is a university lecturer, has shared with me very frankly the frustrations he has felt in relation to the preaching in his own church. 'I have squirmed for months, even years,' he told me, 'and have longed for an opportunity to respond.' In his conviction, the lay leaders of the church should be involved with the pastor in deciding sermon themes and should sometimes preach themselves, if they have the gift and training. But his major concern was the contrast in teaching method between university and church. 'In a university class there is an *immediate* opportunity to respond, to interrupt, to ask questions; and it is encouraged, since the class is a forum for discussion.' In his church, however, no similar opportunity was given; indeed any kind of come-back was discouraged.

We have tried in London to encourage various forms of response. In addition to 'Beginners' Groups' for new Christians and 'Fellowship Groups' for more established Christians, 'Agnostics Anonymous' encourages enquirers to raise their problems and voice their doubts, with no holds barred. 'Talk-back' opportunities are sometimes provided after church. Following a morning sermon on a current issue, we have invited people to bring a sandwich lunch, stay behind and join in discussion of the theme. More general question-times are held, particularly after a series of sermons, and we have occasionally organized a longer 'teach-in'.

One of our preachers recently gave the congregation three separate opportunities to respond to questions which he put to them on the basis of his text. This was Philippians 1:12–19 in which Paul refers both to the Christians who had become 'much more bold' in their witness as a result of his example and to the varied motives for which they were preaching Christ. First, he asked us to write down specific ways in which we could either encourage others to be bolder in their witness or imitate their bold witness ourselves. Secondly, he invited us to discuss with people sitting near us in church the factors in our situation which either hindered or helped our witness. And thirdly, he used the overhead projector to screen a list of eight mixed motives in evangelism, and urged us silently to confess whichever of these may have motivated us. Each session lasted three minutes. I thought it was a very worthwhile experiment; it involved people willy-nilly in the dialogue and obliged us in a very practical way to face the challenge of the text. In the more informal atmosphere of a smaller congregation I see no reason why – at least sometimes – questions relating to the sermon should not be encouraged immediately it is over.

'Observation' introduces us to a wide range of visual aids. Of course the two sacraments of Baptism and the Lord's Supper are divinely provided visual aids, 'visible words' dramatizing the grace of God in salvation through Christ. Some preachers use either blackboard or overhead projector to great effect, while others use film or slides, and soon video-cassettes will be readily available. Brief dramatic presentations, which illustrate some truth of lesson or sermon, can make a powerful impact. There is biblical precedent for them in the acted parables of Ezekiel. Some churches are also reintroducing liturgical 'dance', although I think 'mime' would be a more accurate word, since the action is a silent expression of worship. It always needs a musical accompaniment. Better still, the 'dance' should accompany and seek to interpret the words of a hymn or psalm. When drama, dance and dialogue are combined, one might almost refer to '3-D worship'.

Then there are two other visual aids which God himself has designed. First, he means the pastor to be a visual aid to the congregation. Titus was told, 'Show yourself in all respects a model of good deeds.' And Timothy similarly was to 'set the believers an example in speech and conduct, in love, in faith, in purity'. (Titus 2:7; 1 Tim. 4:12) In both texts the noun is *tupos*, a 'type' or 'pattern', a word used also of Old Testament characters, whose example can be either a warning or an encouragement to us. We preachers cannot expect to communicate verbally from the pulpit if visually out of it we contradict ourselves.

Secondly, God means the congregation to be a visual aid to the world. If we want our gospel to be credible, we must embody it. Unfortunately, as Gavin Reid has rightly written, 'whether the church likes it or not, it is – in nonverbal modes – communicating all the time, and much of what it is "saying" is inimical to its true message.'[60]

The fourth way human beings learn is by discovering and doing. Of course people have always taught themselves this way. A child learns to swim by swimming, and to ride a bicycle by riding it. Apprenticeships have from time immemorial been accepted as the best way to learn a trade. But today 'participation' – in political decision-making and in the process of learning – is being stressed more than ever. School children are encouraged to undertake projects of their own, especially in maths and science, and to find things out by themselves. This is 'child-centred' education or the 'heuristic' method of learning.

For adults the best example is travel. Take the Holy Land. We can listen to lectures, read books, see films and slides, and talk to travellers. But nothing can compare with actually going there ourselves. Then we can absorb impressions by all five senses. We see the Lake of Galilee and the undulating hills of Samaria with our own eyes. We hear the noise of bargaining in the market-place and the bleating of a mixed flock of sheep and goats. We touch an old, gnarled olive tree, or let the waters of the River Jordan trickle through our fingers. We taste the juice of the grapes of Israel, or the sweetness of a fig or orange or pomegranate. We smell the scent of the flowers of the field. And the whole Bible comes alive! We have 'discovered' the land for ourselves.

The same principle should operate in the local church. Biblical preaching and teaching on such topics as prayer and evangelism I take to be indispensable. But in such practical activities a grasp of the theory is not enough. We can learn to pray only by praying, especially in a prayer group. And we can learn to evangelize only by going out with a more experienced Christian either to witness on the street corner or to visit in some homes. Moreover, it is by active membership of the Body of Christ that we learn the meaning of the Church which is described in the New Testament. A fellowship meeting is a happening in which the individual is accepted, welcomed and loved. Then abstract concepts of forgiveness, reconciliation and fellowship take on a concrete form, and preached truth comes to life.

So the way we learn is a rich and diverse process. We are assimilating knowledge and experience all the time, directly and indirectly, consciously and unconsciously, by words and images, by listening and looking, by discussing and discovering, by passive absorption and by participating in the action ourselves.

How, then, can a special case be made out for preaching? Let me try. The elements of the fairly new science of 'communication theory' are now well known. As my example I will take David K. Berlo's introduction *The Process of Communication* (1960). Building on the trio 'speaker, audience and speech' which Aristotle gave in his *Rhetoric*, Dr. Berlo elaborates as follows. First, there is a 'source' (the person desiring to communicate), together with the 'message' he has to communicate. Secondly, he has to 'encode' it in symbols (words or images) and, thirdly, select a 'channel' or medium by which to convey it (if by words, they can be spoken, written, telephoned, or radioed; if by images, they can be drawn, painted, acted, or filmed). Finally, there is the 'receiver' who is the target of the communication and must 'decode' or interpret it. Dr. Berlo sums up: 'Communication requires six basic ingredients: a source, an encoder, a message, a channel, a decoder, and a receiver. The source encodes a message. The encoded message is transmitted in some channel. The message is decoded, and interpreted by the receiver.'[61]

Since the source and the encoder are usually the same person, and the receiver and the decoder, I prefer to simplify this model to four ingredients, namely the source (who communicates), the message (what he has to communicate), the code and channel (how he communicates) and the receiver (to whom the communication is addressed). My contention is that, although preaching as a means of communication conforms to all other means, it is nevertheless *sui generis*. There is no other form of communication which resembles it and therefore could replace it. All its four ingredients are special, and in combination they are unique. Let me explain.

The source, more often than not, is a pastor (though could be a lay preacher) who believes himself called by God to preach, and whose call has been recognized by the Church, which therefore authorizes him by a solemn commissioning to exercize his ministry, and prays that God will confirm his call by empowering him with the Holy Spirit. This, then, is no ordinary communication 'source'. At least in the ideal this preaching person stands in the pulpit, divinely called, commissioned and empowered, a servant of God, an ambassador of Christ, a Spirit-filled witness to Christ.

The 'receivers' (or 'receptors') are a Christian congregation (for I am not now thinking of evangelistic preaching) who have gathered deliberately on the Lord's Day 'to set forth his most worthy praise' and 'to hear his most holy word'. There is, therefore, a profound empathy between preacher and congregation, arising from their common faith. The shepherd is commissioned to feed the flock, the steward to dispense to the household. Both sides know this. It is partly for this purpose that they have assembled. Expectation is in the air. So the pulpit prayer before the sermon begins is (or should be) no empty formality. It is rather a vital opportunity for preacher and people to pray for one another, put themselves into the hand of God, humble themselves before him, and pray that his voice may be heard and his glory seen.

The 'message' is God's own Word. For the people have not gathered to hear a human being, but to meet with God. They desire like Mary of Bethany to sit at the feet of Jesus and listen to his teaching. They are spiritually hungry. The bread they desire is the Word of God.

What, then, are the code and channel of the communication? Obviously the code is words and the channel speech. Yet the communication is to be understood neither in physical terms (from pulpit to pew), nor even in human terms (one mouth speaking, many ears listening), but in divine terms (God speaking through his minister to his people).

It is this total context which makes preaching unique. For here are God's people assembled in God's presence to hear God's Word from God's minister.

That is what I mean when I claim that, even in this age that is saturated with the most elaborate media of communication, preaching remains *sui generis*. No film or play, no drama or dialogue, no seminar or lecture, no Sunday School or discussion group has all these elements in combination. What is unique is not an ideal or an atmosphere, but a reality. The living God is present, according to his covenant pledge, in the midst of his worshipping people, and has promised to make himself known to them through Word and sacrament. Nothing could ever replace this.

Although in the rather flowery language of a century ago, Matthew Simpson gave an admirable summary of the uniqueness of the sermon event. He wrote of the preacher:

> His throne is the pulpit; he stands in Christ's stead; his message is the word of God; around him are immortal souls; the Saviour, unseen, is beside him; the Holy Spirit broods over the congregation; angels gaze upon the scene, and heaven and hell await the issue. What associations, and what vast responsibility![62]

Thus Word and worship belong indissolubly to each other. All worship is an intelligent and loving response to the revelation of God, because it is the adoration of his Name. Therefore acceptable worship is impossible without preaching. For preaching is making known the Name of the Lord, and worship is praising the Name of the Lord made known. Far from being an alien intrusion into worship, the reading and preaching of the Word are actually indispensable to it. The two cannot be divorced. Indeed, it is their unnatural divorce which accounts for the low level of so much contemporary worship. Our worship is poor because our knowledge of God is poor, and our knowledge of God is poor because our preaching is poor. But when the Word of God is expounded in its fulness, and the congregation begin to glimpse the glory of the living God, they bow down in solemn awe and joyful wonder before his throne. It is preaching which accomplishes this, the proclamation of the Word of God in the power of the Spirit of God. That is why preaching is unique and irreplaceable.

The Church's Loss of Confidence in the Gospel

The contemporary loss of confidence in the gospel is the most basic of all hindrances to preaching. For to 'preach' (*kērussein*) is to assume the role of a herald or town crier and publicly to proclaim a message, while to 'evangelize' (*euangelizesthai*) is to spread good news. Both metaphors presuppose that we have been given something to say: *kērussein* depends on the *kērygma* (the proclamation or announcement) and *euangelizesthai* on the *euangelion* (the evangel or gospel). Without a clear and confident message preaching is impossible. Yet it is precisely this that the Church seems nowadays to lack.

Not that this phenomenon is altogether new. Throughout Church history the pendulum has swung between eras of faith and eras of doubt. In 1882, for example, Macmillan published an essay by Sir John Pentland Mahaffy entitled *The Decay of Modern Preaching*. And at the beginning of this century Canon J. G. Simpson of Manchester bemoaned the absence of authoritative preaching in England: 'Not only does the race of great preachers seem for the time to be extinct, but the power of the pulpit has declined . . . The pulpit of the present day has no clear, ringing and definite message.' Small wonder that a child, wearied by a preacher's boring utterance, appealed 'Mother, pay the man, and let us go home.'[63]

Yet as we approach the end of the twentieth century we are conscious that the erosion of Christian faith in the West has continued. Relativity has been applied to doctrine and ethics, and absolutes have disappeared. Darwin has convinced many that religion is an evolutionary phase, Marx that it is a sociological phenomenon, and Freud that it is a neurosis. Biblical authority has for many been undermined by biblical criticism. The comparative study of religions has tended to downgrade Christianity to one religion among many, and has encouraged the growth of syncretism. Existentialism severs our historical roots, insisting that nothing matters but the encounter and decision of the moment. Then there are the blatant denials of radical or secular theology, denials of the infinite, loving personality of God and of the essential deity of Jesus. These things have contributed to a loss of nerve among preachers. Some frankly confess that they see their function as sharing their doubts with their congregation.

Others are assuming a false modesty by insisting that the 'Christian presence' in the world needs to be not only a serving but a silent presence. Or if they have an active role at all, they understand it in terms of dialogue rather than proclamation; they need, they say, to sit down humbly alongside secular man and let him teach them. I remember vividly how at the Fourth Assembly of the World Council of Churches at Uppsala, Sweden, in 1968, one of the Geneva secretariat proposed to the section on 'mission' that they include this sentence in their report, 'In this dialogue Christ speaks through the brother, correcting our distorted image of the truth.' At first hearing it sounded innocuous, until you realized that 'the brother' meant the non-Christian partner in the dialogue. If this sentence had been accepted, it would have been the only reference in the section report to Christ speaking, and it would have up-ended evangelism into a proclamation of the gospel by the non-Christian to the Christian!

This may be an extreme case, but it exemplifies the vogue of false humility, which declines to claim any uniqueness or finality for our Lord Jesus Christ. The whole Church seems to be caught in a crisis of identity, in which it is unsure of itself and confused about its message and mission. Michael Green sums it up with his customary forthrightness in his preface to *The Truth of God Incarnate*, the riposte he edited to *The Myth of God Incarnate*. His preface is entitled 'Scepticism in the Church'. In it he writes, 'During the past forty-five years . . . we have seen an increasing reluctance to accept traditional full-blooded Christianity, complete with an inspired Bible and an incarnate Christ, and a growing tendency to accommodate Christianity to the spirit of the age.'[64]

Now there is no chance of a recovery of preaching without a prior recovery of conviction. We need to regain our confidence in the truth, relevance and power of the gospel, and begin to get excited about it again. Is the gospel good news from God, or not? Campbell Morgan, the gifted expositor who for two separate periods earlier in this century was minister of Westminster Chapel in London, was quite clear about this:

Preaching is not the proclamation of a theory, or the discussion of a doubt. A man has a perfect right to proclaim a theory of any sort, or to discuss his doubts. But that is not preaching. 'Give me the benefit of your convictions, if you have any. Keep your doubts to yourself; I have enough of my own,' said Geothe. We are never preaching when we are hazarding speculations. Of course we do so. We are bound to speculate sometimes. I sometimes say: 'I am speculating; stop taking notes.' Speculation is not preaching. Neither is the declaration of negations preaching. Preaching is the proclamation of the Word, the truth as the truth has been revealed.[65]

The Recovery of Christian Morale
How, then, might we expect a recovery of Christian morale to take place? Will we ever be able to echo Paul's affirmations as he contemplated, unabashed, his visit to imperial Rome? 'I am under obligation both to Greeks and to barbarians, both to the wise and to the unwise. So I am eager to

preach the gospel to you also who are in Rome. For I am not ashamed of the gospel: it is the power of God for salvation to everyone who has faith, to the Jew first and also to the Greeks.' (Rom. 1:14–16) At present the Church's attitude to evangelism might be summarized in exactly contrary terms: 'no enthusiasm, little sense of obligation, and considerable embarrassment'. How could this be reversed into the apostolic 'I am under obligation . . . I am eager . . . I am not ashamed'?

First, we need to distinguish between superficially similar words like assurance, conviction, presumption and bigotry. Conviction is the state of being convinced, and assurance of being sure, by adequate evidence or argument, that something is true. Presumption is a premature assumption of its truth, a confidence resting on inadequate or unexamined premises. Bigotry is both blind and obstinate; the bigot closes his eyes to the data and clings to his opinions regardless. Presumption and bigotry are incompatible with any serious concern for truth and with worship of the God of truth. At least some degree of Christian conviction and assurance, however, is both compatible and reasonable, for it is grounded on good historical evidence or, as the New Testament writers call it, 'witness'. The verbs to 'know' and 'believe' and 'be persuaded' are liberally sprinkled throughout the New Testament. Faith and confidence are regarded as norms of Christian experience, not as exceptions. Indeed, the apostles and evangelists not infrequently tell their readers that the purpose of what they are writing (whether their personal testimony to Jesus or that of other eye-witnesses) is 'that you may know' or 'that you may believe' (e.g. Luke 1:1–4; John 20:31; 1 John 5:13). I feel the need to make this point because, in the present epoch of doubt, some Christians have a bad conscience about believing! But no, *plērophoria*, meaning 'full assurance' and even 'certainty', is meant to characterize both our approach to God in prayer and our proclamation of Christ to the world. (Heb. 10:22; 1 Thess. 1:5) A Christian mind asks questions, probes problems, confesses ignorance, feels perplexity, but does these things within the context of a profound and growing confidence of the reality of God and of his Christ. We should not acquiesce in a condition of basic and chronic doubt, as if it were characteristic of Christian normality. It is not. It is rather a symptom of spiritual sickness in our spiritually sick age.

Secondly, we need to recognize that real and important questions are being asked by theologians today, which cannot be shirked. How far does the cultural conditioning of Scripture affect the normative nature of its teaching? Do we have liberty to reclothe this teaching in modern cultural dress without being guilty of manipulation? Does the language in which doctrines have been formulated – both in Scripture and in tradition – bind the Church for ever, or may we engage in a work of reformulation? What are the relations between history and faith, Jesus and Christ, Scripture and Church traditions? How can we present the good news of Jesus Christ intelligibly to the secular West without distorting it? These are some of the urgent questions which are facing all of us today. If we cannot agree with all the answers which are being offered, we have no quarrel with the questions.

Thirdly, we need to encourage Christian scholars to go to the frontiers and engage in the debate, while at the same time retaining their active participation in the community of faith. I know this is a delicate issue, and it is not easy to define the right relations between free enquiry and settled faith. Yet I have often been disturbed by the loneliness of some Christian scholars. Whether it is they who have drifted away from the fellowship, or the fellowship which has allowed them to drift, in either case their isolation is an unhealthy and dangerous condition. As part of their own integrity Christian scholars need both to preserve the tension between openness and commitment, and to accept some measure of accountability to one another and responsibility for one another in the Body of Christ. In such a caring fellowship I think we might witness fewer casualties on the one hand and more theological creativity on the other.

87

Fourthly, we need to pray more persistently and expectantly for grace from the Holy Spirit of truth. Christian understanding is not possible without his enlightenment, nor is Christian assurance possible without his witness. Vital as are both honest historical enquiry and membership of the believing community for growth in Christian understanding and certainty, yet ultimately only God can convince us about God. Our greatest need, as the Reformers kept insisting, is the *testimonium internum Spiritus sancti*. The witness of Christian experience down the ages is important, but we have to assign it a tertiary place. The testimony of the apostolic eye-witnesses is indispensable, but even this is only secondary. The primary witness is that of God the Father to God the Son through God the Holy Spirit (cf. John 15:26, 27). Yet we have to put ourselves in the way of receiving it, his objective witness as we study the Scriptures and his subjective witness as, in our biblical studies, we humble ourselves before him and cry to him for mercy.

Christians believe that the living God is the Lord of history. Some of us also believe that it is time for him to push back the forces of unbelief and to set the pendulum swinging in the direction of faith again. Indeed, there are signs that he is already doing so. In support of this statement, I appeal to Peter Berger, the American sociologist and author, and in particular to his 'Call for Authority in the Christian Community', in his book *Facing up to Modernity* (1977). He contrasts the contemporary crisis in American society and American churches with the situation in 1961 when his earlier book *The Noise of Solemn Assemblies* was published. What has happened in the intervening sixteen years? 'Then,' he writes, 'the critic appeared to be banging against the locked gates of majestically self-confident institutional edifices. Today he is more like a man storming through doors torn wide open by an earthquake. The ground on which we are standing has been profoundly shaken, and most of us feel it in our bones.'[66] Peter Berger goes on to argue that the Church's loss of nerve, with its 'orgies of self-doubt and self-denigration', is due to its capitulation to the prevailing secular culture. It is now necessary, however, 'to affirm the transcendence and the authority of Christianity over and beyond any cultural constellation in history, present or future, "established" or still striving for "establishment".'[67] Christian leaders should stop their 'dance round the golden calves of modernity'. Instead of asking 'what does modern man have to say to the Church?', they should start asking 'what does the Church have to say to modern man?'[68] For there is now 'a widespread and apparently deepening hunger for religious answers among people of many different sorts', which may herald 'a possibly powerful reversal of the secularization process'.[69] So, in preparation for the dawning of another age of faith, let the Church adopt a new 'stance of authority', in contrast to her present demoralization, and resume the bold proclamation of her unchanging message.[70] It is a stirring summons.

*   *   *

We have tried to face the three chief obstacles to preaching today. The anti-authority mood makes people unwilling to listen, addiction of television makes them unable to do so, and the contemporary atmosphere of doubt makes many preachers both unwilling and unable to speak. Thus there is paralysis at both ends, in the speaking and in the hearing. A dumb preacher with a deaf congregation presents a fearsome barrier to communication. So completely have these problems undermined the morale of some preachers that they have given up altogether. Others struggle on, but have lost heart. Indeed, all of us have been affected by the negative arguments, even if there are counter-arguments which we have begun to deploy. The best form of defence, however, is attack. So in the next chapter I propose to go over to the offensive and to argue theologically for the indispensable and permanent place of preaching in the purpose of God for his Church.

Notes

1 Welsh, p. 32.
2 H. Williams, *My Word*, pp. 1–17.
3 Coggan, *Stewards*, p. 13.
4 *Chambers' Dictionary*.
5 Trollope. p. 28.
6 ibid., p. 50.
7 ibid., pp. 46–7.
8 ibid., pp. 191–2.
9 The *Guardian Weekly*, 19 October 1967.
10 Forsyth, p. 81.
11 Ferris, pp. 22, 23.
12 ibid., p. 32.
13 Coggan, *Convictions*, p. 160.
14 Forsyth, p. 136.
15 Welsh, pp. 102–3.
16 ibid., p. 15.
17 ibid., pp. 109–10.
18 ibid., p. 104.
19 ibid., pp. 114–17.
20 White, R. E. O., *A Guide*, p. 5.
21 Mitchell, *Black Preaching*, pp. 26–43.
22 Mitchell, *The Recovery*, p. 116.
23 Mitchell, *Black Preaching*, p. 44.
24 Mitchell, *The Recovery*, p. 124.
25 Mitchell, *Black Preaching*, p. 106.
26 ibid., p. 98.
27 31 October 1970.
28 Stewart, *A Man in Christ*, pp. 57–8.
29 Warren, p. 143.
30 Miller, *McLuhan*, pp. 131–2.
31 McLuhan, *Understanding Media*, p. 93.
32 ibid., p. 25.
33 ibid., p. 263.
34 ibid., p. 264.
35 McLuhan, *Gutenberg*, p. 31.
36 ibid., p. 31.
37 ibid., p. 332; cf. *The Medium*, p. 125.
38 ibid., p. 87.
39 ibid., p. 90.
40 Evans, p. 142.
41 ibid., pp. 103–9.

42 *Broadcasting, Society and the Church*, p. 3.
43 Winn, p. 4.
44 McGinniss, p. 23.
45 ibid., p. 21.
46 ibid., p. 221.
47 ibid., p. 199.
48 McLuhan, *Understanding Media*, p. 303.
49 Muggeridge, *Christ and the Media*, p. 73.
50 ibid., p. 43.
51 *Screen Violence*, p. 126.
52 *The Future of Broadcasting*. See Chapter 16, 'Programme Standards'.
53 *Children and Television*, abbreviated report, p. 1.
54 Winn, p. 4.
55 The *New Internationalist*, No. 76, June 1979.
56 Winn, p. 80.
57 *Children and Television*, abbreviated report, p. 1.
58 From an article entitled 'Mass-Culture and Mimesis' in issue No. 22 of *Tract*.
59 McLuhan, *The Medium*, p. 117.
60 Reid, G., *The Gagging*, p. 108.
61 Berlo, p. 99.
62 Simpson, M., *Lectures*, p. 98.
63 Simpson, J. G., *Preachers*, pp. 222–3.
64 Green, p. 9.
65 Morgan, G. C., *Preaching*, p. 21.
66 Berger, p. 183.
67 ibid., p. 186.
68 ibid., p. 189.
69 ibid., pp. 190–1.
70 ibid., pp. 192–3.

CHAPTER THREE

Theological Foundations for Preaching[1]

In a world which seems either unwilling or unable to listen, how can we be persuaded to go on preaching, and learn to do so effectively? The essential secret is not mastering certain techniques but being mastered by certain convictions. In other words, theology is more important than methodology. By stating the matter thus bluntly, I am not despising homiletics as a topic for study in seminaries, but rather affirming that homiletics belongs properly to the department of practical theology and cannot be taught without a solid theological foundation. To be sure, there are principles of preaching to be learned, and a practice to be developed, but it is easy to put too much confidence in these. Technique can only make us orators; if we want to be preachers, theology is what we need. If our theology is right, then we have all the basic insights we need into what we ought to be doing, and all the incentives we need to induce us to do it faithfully.

. True Christian preaching (by which I mean 'biblical' or 'expository' preaching, as I shall argue later) is extremely rare in today's Church. Thoughtful young people in many countries are asking for it, but cannot find it. Why is this? The major reason must be a lack of conviction about its importance. For it is reasonable and charitable to suppose that if those of us who are called to preach (both pastors and lay preachers) were persuaded that this is what we ought to be doing, we should go away and do it. If then we are not doing it (which, in the main, we are not), the explanation must be that we lack the necessary conviction.

So my task in this chapter is to try to convince my readers of the indispensable necessity, for the glory of God and the good of the Church, of conscientious biblical preaching. I intend to marshal five theological arguments which underlie and undergird the practice of preaching. They concern the doctrines of God and Scripture, of the Church and the pastorate, and of the nature of preaching as exposition. Any one of these truths should be sufficient to convince us; the five together leave us without excuse.

A Conviction about God

Behind the concept and the act of preaching there lies a doctrine of God, a conviction about his being, his action and his purpose. The kind of God we believe in determines the kind of sermons we preach. A Christian must be at least an amateur theologian before he can aspire to be a preacher. Three affirmations about God are particularly relevant.

First, *God is light*. 'This is the message we have heard from him and proclaim to you, that God is light and in him is no darkness at all.' (1 John 1:5) Now the biblical symbolism of light is rich and diverse, and the assertion that God is light has been variously interpreted. It could mean that God is perfect in holiness, for often in Scripture light symbolizes purity, and darkness evil. But in the Johannine literature light more frequently stands for truth, as when Jesus claimed to be 'the light of the world' (John 8:12); he also told his followers to let their light shine into human society, instead of concealing it. (Matt. 5:14–16) In this case John's statement that God is light and contains no darkness means that he is open and not secretive, and that he delights to make himself known. We may say then that just as it is the nature of light to shine, so it is the nature of God to reveal himself. True, he hides himself from the wise and clever, but only because they are proud and do not want to know him; he reveals himself to 'babies', that is, to those humble enough to receive his self-disclosure. (Matt; 11:25, 26) The chief reason why people do not know God is not because he hides from them, but because they hide from him. People who are eager to share their thoughts with others we describe as 'communicative'. May we not accurately apply the same adjective to God? He does not play a game of 'hide and seek' with us, or lurk out of sight in the shadows. Darkness is the habitat of Satan; God is light.

Every preacher needs the strong encouragement which this assurance brings. Seated before us in church are people in a wide variety of states, some estranged from God, others perplexed, even bewildered, by the mysteries of human existence, yet others enveloped in the dark night of doubt and disbelief. We need to be sure as we speak to them that God is light and that he wants to shine his light into their darkness (cf. 2 Cor. 4:4–6).

Secondly, *God has acted*. That is, he has taken the initiative to reveal himself in deeds. To begin with, he has shown his power and deity in the created universe, so that both heaven and earth display his glory.[2] But God has revealed yet more of himself in redemption than in creation. For when man rebelled against his Creator, instead of destroying him God planned a rescue mission, whose outworking is central to human history. The Old Testament may be said to consist of three cycles of divine deliverance, as God called first Abraham from Ur, then the Israelite slaves from Egypt, and then the exiles from Babylon. Each was a liberation, and led to the making or renewing of the covenant by which Yahweh made them his people and pledged himself to be their God.

The New Testament focusses on another redemption and covenant, which it describes as both 'better' and 'eternal'.[3] For these were secured by God's most mighty acts, namely the birth, death and resurrection of his Son, Jesus Christ.

So the God of the Bible is a God of liberating activity, who came to the rescue of oppressed mankind, and who thus revealed himself as the God of grace or generosity.

Thirdly, *God has spoken*. He is not only communicative by nature, but has actually communicated with his people by speech. It is the constantly reiterated claim of the Old

Testament prophets that 'the Word of the Lord' came to them. In consequence, they used to poke fun at heathen idols because being dead, they were dumb: 'They have mouths, but do not speak' (e.g. Ps. 115:5). With these they contrasted the living God. Being spirit he had no mouth, yet they dared to say, 'The mouth of the Lord has spoken,' (cf. Isaiah 40:5; 55:11).

It is important to add that the speech of God was related to his activity: he took the trouble to explain what he was doing. Did he call Abraham from Ur? Then he spoke to him about his purpose and gave him the covenant of promise. Did he call the people of Israel out of their Egyptian slavery? Then he also commissioned Moses to teach them why he was doing it, namely to fulfil his promise to Abraham, Isaac and Jacob, to confirm his covenant with them, to give them his laws, and to instruct them in his worship. Did he call the people out of the humiliation of their Babylonian exile? Then he also raised up prophets to explain the reasons why his judgment had fallen upon them, the conditions on which he would restore them, and the kind of people he wanted them to be. Did he send his Son to become man, to live and serve on earth, to die, to rise, to reign and to pour out his Spirit? Then he also chose and equipped the apostles to see his works, hear his words, and bear witness to what they had seen and heard.

The modern theological tendency is to lay much emphasis on the historical activity of God and to deny that he has spoken; to say that God's self-revelation has been in deeds not words, personal not propositional; and in fact to insist that the redemption is itself the revelation. But this is a false distinction, which Scripture itself does not envisage. Instead, Scripture affirms that God has spoken both through historical deeds and through explanatory words, and that the two belong indissolubly together. Even the Word made flesh, the climax of God's progressive self-revelation, would have remained enigmatic if it were not that he also spoke and that his apostles both described and interpreted him.

Here then is a fundamental conviction about the living, redeeming and self-revealing God. It is the foundation on which all Christian preaching rests. We should never presume to occupy a pulpit unless we believe in this God. How dare we speak, if God has not spoken? By ourselves we have nothing to say. To address a congregation without any assurance that we are bearers of a divine message would be the height of arrogance and folly. It is when we are convinced that God is light (and so wanting to be known), that God has acted (and thus made himself known), and that God has spoken (and thus explained his actions), that we must speak and cannot remain silent. As Amos expressed it: 'The lion has roared; who will not fear? The Lord God has spoken; who can but prophesy?' (3:8) A similar logic lies behind Paul's statement, 'Since we have the same spirit of faith as he had who wrote "I believed, and so I spoke", we too believe, and so we speak.' (2 Cor. 4:13 quoting Ps. 116:10) The 'spirit of faith' to which he refers is the conviction that God has spoken. If we are not sure of this, it would be better to keep our mouth shut. Once we are persuaded that God has spoken, however, then we too must speak. A compulsion rests upon us. Nothing and nobody will be able to silence us.

A Conviction about Scripture

Our doctrine of God leads naturally and inevitably to our doctrine of Scripture. Although I have headed this section 'a conviction about Scripture', it is in fact a multiple conviction which may be analyzed into at least three distinct but related beliefs.

First, *Scripture is God's Word written*. This definition is taken from Article 20 of the Church of England's 39 Articles. Entitled 'The Authority of the Church', it declares that 'it is not lawful for the church to ordain anything that is contrary to God's Word written.' Moreover, although I shall qualify this in a later paragraph, 'God's Word written' is an excellent definition of Scripture.

For it is one thing to believe that 'God has acted', revealing himself in historical deeds of salvation, and supremely in the Word made flesh. It is another to believe that 'God has spoken', inspiring prophets and apostles to interpret his deeds. It is yet a third stage to believe that the divine speech, recording and explaining the divine activity, has been committed to writing. Yet only so could God's particular revelation become universal, and what he did and said in Israel and in Christ be made available to all people in all ages and places. Thus the action, the speech and the writing belong together in the purpose of God.

To define Scripture as 'God's Word written' says little if anything, however, about the human agents through whom God spoke and through whom his Word was written down. Hence the need for the qualification I said was necessary. When God spoke, his normal method was not to shout in an audible voice out of a clear blue sky. Inspiration is not dictation. Instead he put his Word into human minds and human mouths in such a way that the thoughts they conceived and the words they spoke were simultaneously and completely theirs as well as his. Inspiration was not in any way incompatible with either their historical researches or the free use of their minds. It is essential, therefore, if we are to be true to the Bible's own account of itself, to affirm its human as well as its divine authorship. Yet we must be careful to state the double authorship of the Bible (again, if we are to be true to the Bible's own self-understanding) in such a way as to maintain both the divine and the human factors, without allowing either to detract from the other. On the one hand, the divine inspiration did not override the human authorship; on the other, the human authorship did not override the divine inspiration. The Bible is equally the words of God and the words of men, as in a similar (though not identical) way Jesus Christ is both the Son of God and the son of man. The Bible is God's Word written, God's Word through men's words, spoken through human mouths and written through human hands.[4]

I come back now to the relevance of our doctrine of the

Bible to our ministry of preaching. All Christians believe that God did something and said something unique in Jesus Christ; we can scarcely call ourselves Christians if we do not believe this. But what would have been the point of this definitive deed and word of God through Jesus, if it had then been irrecoverably lost in the mists of antiquity? Since God's final deed and Word through Jesus were intended for all people of all ages, he inevitably made provision for a reliable record of them to be written and preserved. Without this he would have defeated his own purpose. As a result, today, although nearly 2000 years separate us from that deed and Word, Jesus Christ is accessible to us. We can reach him and know him. But he is accessible only through the Bible, as the Holy Spirit brings to life his own witness to him in its pages. True, Tacitus made a brief, passing reference to Jesus in his famous *Annals*, and – more questionably – there are allusions to Jesus in Suetonius and Josephus. True, also, the unbroken tradition of the Christian Church bears eloquent witness to the dynamic reality of its Founder. True again, contemporary Christians give their contemporary testimony to Jesus out of their own experience. Yet if we want to know the full facts of the birth and life, words and works, death and resurrection of Jesus, and God's own authoritative explanation of them, we can find them only in the Bible. That is, if we want to hear the Word which God himself has spoken, we must remember that he spoke it in Christ and in the biblical witness to Christ.

Our responsibility as preachers now begins to emerge. This is not primarily to give our twentieth-century testimony to Jesus (most Western preaching today tends to be too subjective), but rather to relay with faithfulness to the twentieth century (and endorse from our own experience) the only authoritative witness there is, namely God's own witness to Christ through the first-century apostolic eye-witnesses. In this respect the Bible is unique. It is 'God's Word written', since here and here only is God's own interpretation of his redeeming action to be found. To be sure, the New Testament documents came to be written within the milieu of the first-century Christian communities. These communities both preserved the tradition, and to some extent shaped it, in the sense that (humanly speaking) it was their needs of evangelism, instruction and worship which largely determined what was preserved. It is also increasingly recognized that the New Testament authors were writing as theologians, each of whom selected and presented his material according to his particular theological purpose. Yet neither the churches nor the writers invented or distorted their message. Nor does its authority derive from them or from their faith. For none of the apostles or evangelists wrote in the name of a church or churches. On the contrary, they confronted the churches in the name and with the authority of Jesus Christ. And when the time came to fix the New Testament canon, the Church was not conferring authority on the included books, but acknowledging the authority they already possessed because they contained the teaching of the apostles.

It is certain that we cannot handle Scripture adequately in the pulpit if our doctrine of Scripture is inadequate. Conversely, evangelical Christians, who have the highest doctrine of Scripture in the Church, should be conspicuously the most conscientious preachers. The fact that we are not should cause us to hang our heads in shame. If Scripture were largely a symposium of human ideas, though reflecting the faith of the earliest Christian communities, and lit up by an occasional flash of divine inspiration, then a fairly casual attitude to it would be pardonable. But if in Scripture we are handling the very words of the living God, 'words not taught by human wisdom but taught by the Spirit' (1 Cor. 2:13), God's words through men's, his own witness to his own Son, then no trouble should be too great in the study and exposition of them.

Further, we need to keep together in our preaching the saving acts and the written words of God. Some preachers love to speak about the 'mighty acts' of God, and really seem to believe in them, yet what they say tends to be their own interpretation of them, rather than what God has himself said about them in Scripture. Other preachers are entirely faithful in their exposition of God's Word, yet remain dull and academic because they have forgotten that the heart of the Bible is not what God has said, but what he has done for our salvation through Jesus Christ. The first group try to be 'heralds of God', proclaiming good news of salvation, but fail in their stewardship of his revelation. The second try to be 'stewards of God', dutifully guarding and dispensing his Word, but have lost the excitement of the herald's task. The true preacher is both a faithful steward of God's mysteries (1 Cor. 4:1, 2) and a fervent herald of God's good news.

We sometimes use the expression 'when all's said and done', referring to the conclusion of a matter. Well, Christians believe that all has been said and done. For God has said it and done it through Jesus Christ. Moreover, he has said and done it *hapax*, once and for all and for ever. In Christ his revelation and redemption are complete. Our task is to lift up our voices and make them known to others, and also ourselves to enter ever more deeply into an understanding and experience of them.

Our second conviction about Scripture is that *God still speaks through what he has spoken*. If we are content to make the statement 'Scripture is God's Word written' and to stop there, we would expose ourselves to the critical rejoinder that our God, if not dead, appears to be as good as dead. For we give the impression that he who spoke centuries ago is silent today; and that the only word we can hear from him comes out of a book, a faint echo from the distant past, smelling strongly of the mould of libraries. But no, this is not at all what we believe. Scripture is far more than a collection of ancient documents in which the words of God are preserved. It is not a kind of museum in which God's Word is exhibited behind glass like a relic or fossil. On the contrary, it is a living word to living people from the living God, a contemporary message for the contemporary world.

The apostles clearly understood and believed this about the Old Testament oracles. They introduced their biblical quotations with one or other of two formulae, either *gegraptai gar* ('for it stands written') or *legei gar* ('for it – or he – says'). The contrast between these formulae is not only between the perfect tense and the present continuous tense, and so between an event of the past and an activity of the present, but also between writing and speech. Both expressions assume that God has spoken, but in the one case what he has spoken has been written down and remains a permanent written record, while in the other case he is continuing to speak what he once spoke.

Take as an example Paul's statements in Galatians 4. Verse 22 begins, 'for it is written (*gegraptai gar*) that Abraham had two sons.' In the previous verse, however, Paul has asked 'do you not hear the law?' and in verse 30 he asks 'what does the Scripture say?' These are extraordinary expressions, for 'the law' and 'the Scripture' are ancient books. How can an old book be said to 'speak' in such a way that we can 'hear' it speaking? Only in one way, namely that God himself speaks through it, and that we must listen to his voice.

This concept of the contemporary voice of God is emphasized in Hebrews 3 and 4. the author quotes Psalm 95: 'Today, when you hear his voice, do not harden your hearts.' But he introduces the quotation with the words 'as the Holy Spirit says'. He thus implies that the Holy Spirit is 'today' making the same appeal to his people to listen to him as he made centuries previously when the psalm was written. Indeed, it is possible to detect here four successive stages in which God spoke and speaks. The first was the time of testing in the wilderness when God spoke but Israel hardened her heart. Next came the exhortation of Psalm 95 to the people of that day not to repeat Israel's earlier folly. Thirdly, there was the application of the same truth to the Hebrew Christians of the first century A.D., while, fourthly, the appeal comes to us as we read the Letter to the Hebrews today. It is in this way that God's Word is contemporary: it moves with the times and continues to address each fresh generation.

One further example may be given, in order to show that this principle applies as much to the New Testament Scriptures as to the Old. Each of the seven letters to the Asian churches recorded in Revelation 2 and 3 concludes with an identical entreaty from the ascended Lord Jesus, 'he who has an ear, let him hear what the Spirit says to the churches.' It is a remarkable sentence. Presumably each church will have heard its particular letter read out in the public assembly, and each knew that John had written it down on the island of Patmos some weeks, even months, previously. Yet each letter concluded with the same statement that the Spirit was speaking to the churches. This shows that what was addressed to each church in particular applied also to all 'the churches' in general; that what had come from John had originated with the Spirit; and that what John had written some time past the Holy Spirit was still speaking with a living voice, even to every individual church member who had an ear to listen to his message.

When once we have grasped the truth that 'God still speaks through what he has spoken', we shall be well protected against two opposite errors. The first is the belief that, though it was heard in ancient times, God's voice is silent today. The second is the claim that God is indeed speaking today, but that his Word has little or nothing to do with Scripture. The first leads to Christian antiquarianism, the second to Christian existentialism. Safety and truth are found in the related convictions that God has spoken, that God speaks, and that his two messages are closely connected to one another, because it is *through* what he spoke that he speaks. He makes his Word living, contemporary and relevant, until we find ourselves back on the Emmaus Road with Christ himself expounding the Scriptures to us, and with our hearts on fire. Another way of putting the same truth is to say that we must keep the Word of God and the Spirit of God together. For apart from the Spirit the Word is dead, while apart from the Word the Spirit is alien.

I cannot express this theme better than by borrowing an expression which I have heard Dr. James I. Packer use. 'Having studied the doctrine of Scripture for a generation', he has said, 'the most satisfactory model is to describe it thus: "The Bible is God preaching".'

The third conviction which preachers need about Scripture is that *God's Word is powerful*. For not only has God spoken; not only does God continue to speak through what he has spoken; but when God speaks he acts. His Word does more than explain his action; it is active in itself. God accomplishes his purpose by his Word; it 'prospers' in whatever he sends it forth to do. (Is. 55:11)

It is specially important for us to be assured of the power of God's Word, because there is in our day a widespread disenchantment with all words. Millions are spoken and written every day, apparently to very little effect. The Church is one of the worst offenders, and consequently some dismiss it as nothing but a useless talking shop. Moreover, the criticism proceeds, if the Church talks too much, it also does too little. It has a big mouth, but shrunken hands. Now the time has come to stop talking and start acting. In particular, let those garrulous clergy climb down from their pulpits, roll up their sleeves and do something productive for a change!

There is too much truth in this indictment for us to be able to shrug it off. The Church does indeed have a better record for talk than for action, and some of us have to confess that we have neglected to follow the Scriptures in defending the powerless and seeking social justice. But we should not set speech and action over against each other as if they were alternatives. It is written of Jesus both that 'he went about doing good' and that 'he went about . . . teaching . . . and preaching . . .' (Acts 10:38; Matt. 4:23, 9:35) He combined words and works in his ministry. He saw no need to choose. Neither should we. Moreover, whence this distrust of words? Words are far from being impotent. The devil uses them constantly in political propaganda and commercial exploitation. And if his lies are powerful, how much more powerful is God's truth? James Stalker put it like this:

> It seems the frailest of all weapons: for what is a word? It is only a puff of air, a vibration trembling in the atmosphere for a moment and then disappearing . . . (Yet) though it be only a weapon of air, the word is stronger than the sword of the warrior.[5]

Luther believed this. In his famous hymn *Ein' Feste Burg* (c. 1529), in which he alluded to the devil's might, he added *ein Wörtlein wird ihn fällen*, 'one little word will fell him'. Thomas Carlyle translated the hymn (1831), beginning *A safe stronghold our God is still*. Here is his rendering of the verse in question:

> And were this world all devils o'er
> And watching to devour us,
> We lay it not to heart so sore,
> Not they can overpower us.
> And let the prince of ill
> Look grim as e'er he will,
> He harms us not a whit;
> For why? His doom is writ;
> A word shall quickly slay him.

One of our contemporaries who has the same confidence in the power of words of truth is Alexander Solzhenitsyn. His 1970 Nobel Prize speech was entitled *One Word of Truth*. He asked:

> In this cruel, dynamic, explosive world, on the brink of a dozen destructions, what is the place and role of the writer? We writers have no rockets to blast off, we do not even trundle the most insignificant auxiliary vehicle, we are indeed altogether despised by those who respect only material power . . .[6]

So what can writers do 'in the face of the merciless on-slaught of open violence', especially when violence is 'bound up with the lie' and 'the lie can be maintained only by violence'?[7] Of course the courageous person will refuse to take part in the lie. But, Solzhenitsyn continued,

> writers and artists can do something more: they can vanquish the lie . . . We must not seek excuses on the grounds that we lack weapons . . . we must go out into battle . . . *One word of truth outweighs the whole world.* And on such a fantastic breach of the law of conservation of mass and energy are based my own activities and my appeal to the writers of the world.[8]

Not that our words are always heeded. Often they are ineffective. They fall on deaf ears and are disregarded. Yet the Word of God is different, for in his words speech and action are combined. He created the universe by his Word: 'he spoke, and it came to be; he commanded, and it stood forth.' (Ps. 33:9) And now through the same Word of authority he recreates and saves. The gospel of Christ is God's power for salvation to every believer, for it pleases God through the *kērygma*, the proclaimed message, to save those who believe. (Rom. 1:16; 1 Cor. 1:21 cf. 1 Thess. 2:13) Many similes are used in the Bible to illustrate the powerful influence which God's Word exerts. 'The word of God is living and active, sharper than any two-edged sword' (Heb. 4:12), for it pierces both mind and conscience. Like a hammer it can break stony hearts, and like fire it can burn up rubbish. It illumines our path, shining like a lamp on a dark night, and like a mirror it shows us both what we are and what we should be. It is also likened to seed causing birth, and milk causing growth, to wheat which strengthens and honey which sweetens, and to gold which immeasurably enriches its possessor.[9]

One preacher who knew from experience the power of the Word of God was John Wesley. His journal is full of references to it, especially to its power to subdue a hostile crowd and bring them under conviction of sin. On 10 September 1743, only five years after his conversion, Wesley preached in the open air to an exceptionally large congregation near St. Just in Cornwall, 'I cried out, with all the authority of love, "Why will ye die, O house of Israel?" The people trembled and were still. I had not known such an hour before in Cornwall.' On 18 October 1749 he met bitter opposition in Bolton, Lancashire. A mob surrounded the house, threw stones through the window, and then broke in through the door.

Believing the time was now come, I walked down into the thickest of them. They had now filled all the rooms below. I called for a chair. The winds were hushed, and all was calm and still. My heart was filled with love, my eyes with tears, and my mouth with arguments. They were amazed; they were ashamed; they were melted down; they devoured every word. What a turn was this!'

Twenty years later the same power was still attending Wesley's preaching. On 18 May 1770 he wrote, 'In the evening I trust God broke some of the stony hearts of Dunbar.' On 1 June 1777 he preached in a churchyard on the Isle of Man, and 'the Word of God was with power.' In St. Luke's Church, Old Street, London, on 28 November 1778, 'the fear of God seemed to possess the whole audience'. More than a decade later, when Wesley was eighty-five years old, 'God moved wonderfully on the hearts of the people' in Falmouth, Cornwall (17 August 1789), while in Redruth 'a huge multitude' gathered, and 'the Word seemed to sink deep into every heart.' (22 August 1789)

Let no one imagine that these experiences were peculiar to the eighteenth century or to John Wesley. Billy Graham, the world's best-known, most-travelled evangelist today, makes a similar claim. At the Pan African Christian Leadership Assembly at Nairobi in December 1976 I heard him say, 'I have had the privilege of preaching the gospel on every continent and in most countries of the world, and when I present the message of the simple gospel of Jesus Christ with authority, he takes the message and drives it supernaturally into human hearts.'

'It's all very well', someone may interject, 'for you to quote Luther and Wesley and Billy Graham. Without doubt their words have had power. But weren't they exceptional people, exceptionally gifted and endowed? What about me? I preach my heart out Sunday by Sunday, and the good seed falls by the wayside and is trodden under foot. Why isn't God's Word more powerful when it comes from *my* lips?' To these questions I reply that yes, of course, in every generation God raises us up special people, gives them special gifts and endows them with special power. It would be wrong for us to envy Luther or Wesley, and foolish to imagine that each of us has Billy Graham's evangelistic gift. Nevertheless, Scripture does justify the expectation that at least sometimes our preaching of the Word will be effective. Take the Parable of the Sower, to which an allusion was made above. On the one hand, Jesus taught us not to expect all our seed-sowing to bear fruit. We have to remember that some ground is hard and stony, and that the birds, the weeds and the scorching sun take their toll of the seed. So we should not grow too discouraged. On the other hand, Jesus did lead us to expect that some soil would prove good and productive, and that the seed falling into this would bear lasting fruit. There is life and power in the seed, and when the Spirit prepares the soil and waters the seed, the growth and fruitfulness will appear.

This is what P. T. Forsyth meant when he referred to the gospel as not just a statement or a doctrine or a promise. It is more. 'It is an act and a power: it is God's *act* of redemption . . . A true sermon is a real deed . . . The preacher's word, when he preaches the gospel and not only delivers a sermon, is an effective deed, charged with blessing or with judgment.'[10] This is because it brings dramatically into the here and now the historic redemptive work of Christ.

Perhaps no contemporary author has expressed this belief in the power of the Word more eloquently than Gustaf

Wingren, the Swedish Lutheran Professor of Theology in the University of Lund, in his book *The Living Word*. The theme of the whole Bible, he argues, is conflict, the duel between God and Satan, and it is the gospel which sets people free. Between Christ's victory and the consummation 'lies an empty space of waiting. It is in this gap, this empty space, that *preaching* sends forth its voice.'[11] Again, 'the time between Easter and the Parousia is the time for preaching.'[12] Preaching supplies the living Christ with both feet and a mouth: 'It is the Word that provides the feet on which Christ walks when he makes his approach to us and reaches us . . . Preaching has but one aim, that Christ may come to those who have assembled to listen.'[13] Again, 'preaching is not just talk about a Christ of the past, but is a mouth through which the Christ of the present offers us life today.'[14] Professor Wingren sees human beings as 'defeated', 'conquered', in bondage to sin, guilt and death, and he sees preaching as the means of their liberation. 'It belongs to the nature of the office of preaching that it has its place in the battle between God and the Devil.'[15] 'The word of the preacher is an attack on the prison in which man is held.'[16] It opens the prison, and sets him free.

These convictions about God and man, about man the prisoner and God the liberator by his Word, transform the work of preaching. We enter the pulpit with a Word in our hands, heart and mouth which has power. We expect results. We look for conversions. As Spurgeon put it in one of his addresses to pastors:

So pray and so preach that, if there are no conversions, you will be astonished, amazed, and broken-hearted. Look for the salvation of your hearers as much as the angel who will sound the last trump will look for the waking of the dead! Believe your own doctrine! Believe your own Saviour! Believe in the Holy Ghost who dwells in you! For thus shall you see your heart's desire, and God shall be glorified.[17]

A pleasant story is told about a travelling preacher who was passing through the security check at an airport. It was before the days of electronic scanning, and the security official was rummaging about in his brief-case. He came across the black cardboard box which contained the preacher's Bible, and was curious to discover its contents. 'What's in that box?' he asked suspiciously, and received the startling reply 'Dynamite!' Unfortunately, history does not relate what happened next. Yet to believe in the explosive power of God's Word – powerful not because it is like a magic spell but because the God who spoke it speaks it again – should be enough in itself to make an effective preacher out of every person who is called to this privileged ministry.

A Conviction about the Church

Doubtless we have numerous convictions about the Church. But for my purpose I have only this one in mind, that the Church is the creation of God by his Word. Moreover, God's new creation (the Church) is as dependent upon his Word as his old creation (the universe). Not only has he brought it into being by his Word, but he maintains and sustains it, directs and sanctifies it, reforms and renews it through the same Word. The Word of God is the sceptre by which Christ rules the Church and the food with which he nourishes it.

This dependence of the Church on the Word is not a doctrine readily acceptable to all. In former days of Roman Catholic polemic, for example, its champions would insist that 'the Church wrote the Bible' and therefore has authority over it. Still today one sometimes hears this rather simplistic argument. Now it is true, of course, that both Testaments were written within the context of the believing community, and that the substance of the New Testament in God's providence, as we have already noted, was to some extent determined by the needs of the local Christian congregations. In consequence, the Bible can neither be detached from the milieu in which it originated, nor be understood in isolation from it. Nevertheless, as Protestants have always emphasized, it is misleading to the point of inaccuracy to say that 'the Church wrote the Bible'; the truth is almost the opposite, namely that 'God's Word created the Church'. For the people of God may be said to have come into existence when his Word came to Abraham, calling him and making a covenant with him. Similarly, it was through the apostolic preaching of God's Word in the power of the Holy Spirit on the Day of Pentecost that the people of God became the Spirit-filled Body of Christ.

It is not difficult to demonstrate the dependence of the people of God on the Word of God. For throughout Scripture God is addressing his people, teaching them his way, and appealing to them both for his sake and for theirs to hear and heed his message. If it is true 'that man does not live by bread alone, but that man lives by everything that proceeds out of the mouth of the Lord' (Deut. 8:3, quoted by Jesus in Matt. 4:4), the same is true of the Church. God's people live and flourish only by believing and obeying his Word.

So the Old Testament is replete with God's exhortations to his people to listen to him. Adam's fall was due to his folly in listening to the serpent's voice instead of to his Creator's. When God established his covenant with Abraham, he justified him because he believed his promise, and he reiterated his blessing 'because you have obeyed my voice'. (Gen. 15:1-6; 22:15-18) When God confirmed his covenant with Israel, in fulfilment of his promises to Abraham, Isaac and Jacob, and pledged to make them his special possession among all peoples, the condition he made was 'if you will obey my voice' (Exod. 2:24; 19:3-6). So when the covenant was ratified by sacrifice, and 'all the words of the Lord and all the ordinances' were rehearsed in the hearing of the people, they responded in unison, 'all the words which the Lord has spoken we will do.' (Exod. 24:3) Because of the tragic history of disobedience during the forty years of wilderness wanderings ('they soon forgot' and 'did not obey the voice of the Lord', Ps. 106:13, 25), the covenant was renewed and the law repeated for the benefit of the new generation, before they entered the promised land. And one of the refrains of Deuteronomy is 'Hear, O Israel.' Its message is summed up in these words, 'And now, O Israel, give heed to the statutes and the ordinances which I teach you, and do them; that you may live and go in and take possession of the land . . .' and 'that it may go well with you'.[18]

Once the people had settled the land and the monarchy had begun, the same theme of divine blessing on the people's faith and obedience, and of divine judgment on their unbelief and disobedience, was continued in both the prophetic and wisdom literature. A small sample will be enough to show this.

Psalm 81:3, 13: 'Hear, O my people, while I admonish you! O Israel, if you would but listen to me! . . . But my people did not listen to my voice; Israel would have none of me.'

In the Book of Proverbs, Wisdom is personified and is represented as crying aloud in the street and in the market place:

> To you, O men, I call, and my cry is to the sons of men. O simple ones, learn prudence; O foolish men, pay attention . . . Take my instruction instead of silver, and knowledge rather than choice gold; for wisdom is better than jewels, and all that you may desire cannot compare with her . . . And now, my sons, listen to me: happy are those who keep my ways . . . Happy is the man who listens to me, watching daily at my gates, waiting beside my doors. For he who finds me finds life and obtains favour from the Lord; but he who misses me injures himself; all who hate me love death.[19]

In similar vein the prophets, to whom the Word of the Lord came, summoned Israel to listen to it. Take Isaiah as an example, who shocked people by likening the holy city of Jerusalem to Sodom and Gomorrah, 'Hear the Word of the Lord, you rulers of Sodom! Give ear to the teaching of our God, you people of Gomorrah . . . If you are willing and obedient, you shall eat the good of the land; but if you refuse and rebel, you shall be denounced by the sword; for the mouth of the Lord has spoken.' And again later, 'O that you had hearkened to my commandments! Then your peace would have been like a river, and your righteousness like the waves of the sea.' As it is, however, 'there is no peace . . . for the wicked.'[20]

Even more explicit is the prophet Jeremiah, close ally of good King Josiah, during whose reign the book of the law was rediscovered in the temple. Prophet and king together called for national repentance and rededication. But the people's response was superficial and short-lived. The divine complaint uttered through the lips of Jeremiah was straightforward:

This command I gave them, 'Obey my voice, and I will be your God, and you shall be my people; and walk in all the way that I command you, that it may be well with you.' But they did not obey or incline this ear, but walked in the stubbornness of their evil hearts, and went backward and not forward. From the day that your fathers came out of the land of Egypt to this day, I have persistently sent all my servants the prophets to them, day after day; yet they did not listen to me, or incline their ear, but stiffened their neck. They did worse than their fathers.[21]

So God's judgment fell upon them, Jerusalem was besieged and taken, the temple was razed to the ground, and the people were led away into Babylonian captivity. The national epitaph written by the Chronicler echoed the language of the prophets:

The Lord, the God of their fathers, sent persistently to them by his messengers, because he had compassion on

112

his people and on his dwelling place; but they kept mocking the messengers of God, despising his words, and scoffing at his prophets, till the wrath of the Lord rose against his people, till there was no remedy.[22]

It is clear from this brief rehearsal of the Old Testament story that God consistently hinged the welfare of his people on their listening to his voice, believing his promises and obeying his commands.

It is similar in the New Testament, although now God's spokesmen are apostles rather than prophets. They too claim to be bearers of God's Word (e.g. 1 Thess. 2:13). Appointed by Christ and invested with his authority, they speak boldly in his name, and they expect the churches to believe their instruction and obey their commands (e.g. 2 Thess. 3). So through their writings the exalted Jesus addresses his Church, just as much as through those letters of his to the seven churches. He instructs, admonishes, rebukes and encourages them, gives them promises and warnings, and appeals to them to listen, to believe, to obey and to hold fast until he comes. It is made plain throughout that the health of God's people depends on their attentiveness to his Word.

Today's preachers are neither prophets nor apostles, for we are not the recipients of any fresh, direct revelation. The Word of the Lord does not come to us at it came to them; rather we have to come to it. Nevertheless, if we faithfully expound the Scriptures, it is his Word which is in our hands and on our lips, and the Holy Spirit is able to make it a living and powerful word in the hearts of our hearers. Moreover, our responsibility will appear to us the more onerous when we remember the indissoluble link which we have traced between the Word of God and the people of God. A deaf church is a dead church: that is an unalterable principle. God quickens, feeds, inspires and guides his people by his Word. For whenever the Bible is truly and systematically expounded, God uses it to give his people the vision without which they perish. First, they begin to see what he wants them to be, his new society in the world. Then they go on to grasp the resources he has given them in Christ to fulfil his purpose. That is why it is only by humble and obedient listening to his voice that the Church can grow into maturity, serve the world and glorify its Lord.

In laying this emphasis on the Word of God as indispensable for the Church's welfare, I am not forgetting the gospel sacraments, and in particular the Lord's Supper. For Augustine's designation of the sacraments as 'visible words' (*verba visibilia*) supplies an essential clue to their function and value. They too speak. Both Word and sacrament bear witness to Christ. Both promise salvation in Christ. Both quicken our faith in Christ. Both enable us to feed on Christ in our hearts. The major difference between them is that the message of the one is directed to the eye, and of the other to the ear. So the sacraments need the Word to interpret them. The ministry of Word and sacrament is a single ministry, the Word proclaiming, and the sacrament dramatizing, God's promises. Yet the Word is primary, since without it the sign becomes dark in meaning, if not actually dumb.

History supplies ample evidence of the indivisible connection between Church and Word, between the state of the Christian community and the quality of Christian preaching. 'Is it not clear', asks Dr. D. M. Lloyd-Jones, 'as you take a bird's-eye view of Church history, that the decadent periods and eras in the history of the Church have always been those periods when preaching had declined?' 'What is it', he continues, 'that always heralds the dawn of a Reformation or of a Revival? It is renewed preaching.'[23]

Dr. E. C. Dargan's comprehensive two-volume *History of Preaching* from A.D. 70–1900 amply confirms this view. He writes:

Decline of spiritual life and activity in the churches is commonly accompanied by a lifeless, formal, unfruitful preaching, and this partly as cause, partly as effect. On the other hand, the great revivals of Christian history can

114

most usually be traced to the work of the pulpit, and in their progress they have developed and rendered possible a high order of preaching.[24]

It would be impossible to delineate the world-wide Church today by sweeping generalizations, for its condition varies greatly from country to country, and culture to culture. The secularization of Europe (together with those parts of the Western world which have retained close links with Europe) has been steadily progressing for about two centuries, although there are now some signs that the tide may be turning. In the United States there is an astonishing religious boom, which nevertheless perplexes friendly observers who cannot easily reconcile it with that nation's alarming statistics of crime, violence, abortion and divorce. In most Communist countries, and in some countries of predominantly Islamic culture, the Church is inhibited, if not actively opposed and persecuted. In some of the developing countries of Asia, Africa and Latin America, however, the rates of Church growth are so rapid that, if they continue, the international leadership of the Church will soon pass into Third World hands, if indeed this hand-over has not already taken place. Yet these very leaders themselves confess that, alongside the vigour and enthusiasm of their churches' life, there is much shallowness and instability.

In such a variegated situation, in which overall the Church is losing ground, is it possible to pinpoint a single cause of weakness? Many would say 'no'. And certainly the causes are many. Yet personally I do not hesitate to say that a (even the) major reason for the Church's decline in some areas and immaturity in others is what Amos called a 'famine of hearing the words of the Lord'. (8:11) The low level of Christian living is due, more than anything else, to the low level of Christian preaching. More often than we like to admit, the pew is a reflection of the pulpit. Seldom if ever can the pew rise higher than the pulpit.

On the last day of 1979 *Time* magazine carried an article

115

entitled *American Preaching*: *A Dying Art?* Its editor wrote, 'The chilling of the Word is a major contributor to the evident malaise in many a large Protestant denomination these days', while for Roman Catholics the sermon has never been very important but 'rather a kind of spiritual hors d'oeuvre before the Eucharist'. Two centuries previously, however, 'when Jonathan Edwards preached, all New England shook in its boots.'

So, if the Church is to flourish again, there is no greater need than a recovery of faithful, powerful, biblical preaching. God still says to his people, 'O that today you would listen to my Word' (cf. Ps. 95:7) and to preachers 'O that you would proclaim it.'

A Conviction about the Pastorate

There is much uncertainty in the modern Church about the nature and functions of the professional Christian ministry. To begin with, the social prestige which clergy once enjoyed in Western countries has now greatly diminished. Also, because the state has taken over much of the philanthropic work pioneered by the Church (e.g. in medicine, education and social welfare), some who would previously have offered themselves for ordination are finding that they can serve as well in the so-called 'secular city'. Then again, largely as a result of the charismatic movement, the New Testament doctrine of the Body of Christ has been recovered, with its corollary that every member has a gift and therefore a ministry. This being so, some are asking whether a professional ministry is necessary any longer? Have not the clergy been rendered redundant? These are some of the trends which have contributed to the contemporary loss of clerical morale.

In this situation, it is urgent to reassert the New Testament teaching that Jesus Christ still gives overseers to his Church and intends them to be a permanent feature of the Church's structure. 'It is a trustworthy statement: if any

116

man aspires to the office of overseer, it is a fine work he desires to do.' (1 Tim. 3:1 NASB)

Moreover, in seeking to reestablish this truth, it would be helpful simultaneously to recover for these overseers the New Testament designation 'pastor'. 'Minister' is a misleading term because it is generic rather than specific, and always therefore requires a qualifying adjective to indicate what kind of ministry is in mind. 'Priest' is unfortunately ambiguous. Those with knowledge of the etymology of English words are aware that 'priest' is simply a contraction of 'presbyter', meaning 'elder'. But it is also used to translate the Greek word *hiereus*, a sacrificing priest, which is never used of Christian ministers in the New Testament. To call clergy 'priests' (common as the practice is in Roman Catholic, Lutheran and Anglican circles) gives the false impression that their ministry is primarily directed towards God, whereas the New Testament portrays it as primarily directed towards the Church. So 'pastor' remains the most accurate term. The objection that it means 'shepherd', and that sheep and shepherds are irrelevant in the bustling cities of the twentieth century, can best be met by recalling that the Lord Jesus called himself 'the Good Shepherd', that even city-dwelling Christians will always think of him as such, and that his pastoral ministry (with its characteristics of intimate knowledge, sacrifice, leadership, protection and care) remains the permanent model for all pastors.

In England before the Reformation (as still in the Roman Catholic church), the sacerdotal concept of the ordained ministry was predominant. The ordaining bishop vested the candidate with a chasuble, saying 'Receive the sacerdotal vestment,' and gave him a paten and chalice, saying 'Receive power to offer sacrifice to God and to celebrate mass both for the living and for the dead.' This *porrectio instrumentorum*, or delivery of the symbols of office, was significantly altered by the English Reformers. Their first ordinal of 1550 directed that, in addition to the paten and chalice, a Bible be delivered to the ordinand, giving him authority 'to preach the Word of God and to minister the holy sacraments'. In 1552, only two years later, the delivery of paten and chalice was discontinued and the sole 'instrument' delivered to the candidate became the Bible. The Anglican ordinal has remained substantially unaltered until our own day.

This change in symbolism expressed the change in understanding of the ordained ministry. Its essence was now seen to be not priestly, but pastoral. It was and is a ministry of the Word. For the chief responsibility of the pastor who 'tends' his sheep is to 'feed' them. Whereas God rebuked the shepherds of Israel for feeding themselves instead of feeding their sheep, the Divine Shepherd causes his sheep to 'lie down in green pastures'. (Ezek. 34:1–3; Ps. 23:1, 2) Elaborating this Old Testament imagery, Jesus not only promised that his sheep, secure in his keeping, would 'go in and out and find pasture' but recommissioned Peter with the repeated instruction 'feed my lambs' and 'feed my sheep'. (John 10:9; 21:15, 17) This command the apostles never forgot. 'Tend the flock of God that is your charge' Peter himself wrote later, while Paul addressed the elders of the Ephesian church with the words, 'Take heed to yourselves and to all the flock, in which the Holy Spirit has made you guardians (or overseers), to feed the church of the Lord which he obtained with his own blood.' (1 Pet. 5:2; Acts 20:28) The elders would surely understand their privilege that the Chief Shepherd had delegated to them the pastoral care of his own sheep which he had purchased with his life-blood.

To feed God's flock is, of course, a metaphorical expression for teaching the Church. So the pastor is essentially the teacher. True, he is strictly forbidden by Christ to teach in the kind of authoritarian way which attempts to usurp the prerogative of the Spirit of truth and so to make the congregation docile in their dependence upon him. (Matt. 23:8) True also, in accordance with God's new covenant promise that 'they shall all know me', the Holy Spirit is now given to all believers, so that all 'have been anointed by the Holy One' and 'have been taught by God' and therefore in the

118

last resort do not need human teachers. (Jer. 31:34; 1 Thess. 4:9; 1 John 2:20–7) True again, all church members have a responsibility to let Christ's Word dwell richly within them so that they may 'teach and admonish one another in all wisdom' (Col. 3:16). Yet all these truths are not incompatible with the equipment, call and commissioning of specialists, that is, of pastors who devote themselves to a ministry of preaching and teaching. For among the many spiritual gifts which the ascended Lord bestows on his Church are those of 'pastors and teachers'. (Eph. 4:11) Commenting on this verse in its context, Calvin writes in the *Institutes*, 'We see how God, who could in a moment perfect his own, nevertheless desires them to grow up into manhood solely under the education of the Church. We see the way set for it: the preaching of the heavenly doctrine has been enjoined upon the pastors.' He goes on to warn his readers against the folly and arrogance of rejecting this divine provision. 'Many are led either by pride, dislike or rivalry to the conviction that they can profit enough from private reading and meditation; hence they despise public assemblies and deem preaching superfluous . . . This is like blotting out the face of God which shines upon us in teaching.'[25] 'For neither the light and heat of the sun, nor food and drink, are so necessary to nourish and sustain the present life, as the apostolic and pastoral office is necessary to preserve the Church on earth.'[26]

What Calvin was teaching in Geneva, the English Reformers were soon to grasp also. Nothing seemed more important to them than that the pastors should preach the pure Word of God and that the people should hear it. Here is John Jewel, Bishop of Salisbury:

Despise not, good brethren, despise not to hear God's Word declared. As you tender your own souls, be diligent to come to sermons; for that is the ordinary place where men's hearts be moved, and God's secrets be revealed. For, be the preacher never so weak, yet is the Word of God as mighty and as puissant as ever it was.[27]

In contrast, nothing could be more harmful to the Church than unfaithful preachers, as Thomas Becon outspokenly declared in the Preface to his book *The Demands of Holy Scripture*:

As there cannot be a greater jewel in a Christian commonwealth than an earnest, faithful and constant preacher of the Lord's Word, so can there not be a greater plague among any people than when they have reigning over them blind guides, dumb dogs, wicked wolves, hypocritical hirelings, popish prophets, which feed them not with the pure wheat of God's Word, but with the wormwood of men's trifling traditions. [28]

I know nobody in our own century who has expressed this fundamental understanding of the pastorate more forcefully than Samuel Volbeda, whose homiletical lectures at Calvin Theological Seminary, Grand Rapids, were edited and published after his death under the title *The Pastoral Genius of Preaching*. Having defined preaching as 'the proclamation by word of mouth of God's written instead of his spoken Word',[29] he goes on to affirm that 'that written Word of God is pastoral through and through in its message, spirit and purpose.' Therefore the true preacher will never be 'a mere speaking tube or trumpet . . . reproducing perfectly but mechanically the message of God's written Word'; he must rather be a pastor, 'who is himself in heart and mind in *perfect harmony* with the pastoral Scriptures which he must preach.'[30] Moreover, a good shepherd's care of his sheep is fourfold[31] – feeding, guiding (because sheep easily go astray), guarding (against predatory wolves) and healing (binding up the wounds of the injured). And all four of these activities are aspects of the ministry of the Word.

It must not be imagined, however, that this identification of pastors as being fundamentally teachers is an idiosyncracy of reformed or evangelical Christians. It is equally acknowledged by many with more catholic leanings. Let me quote, for instance, from an ordination charge given by Michael Ramsey while he was Archbishop of Canterbury. It is entitled 'Why the Priest?', and the first answer he gives to his own question is as follows:

> First, the priest is the teacher and preacher, and as such he is the *man of theology*. He is pledged to be a dedicated student of theology; and his study need not be vast in extent but it will be deep in its integrity, not in order that he may be erudite, but in order that he may be simple. It is those whose studies are shallow who are confused and confusing.[32]

In writing thus about a 'pastoral' ministry as a 'teaching' ministry, I do not think it is necessary for me to be drawn into the debate about 'ordination' and about what if anything distinguishes clergy and laity. Suffice it to say that God desires every local church to have the benefit of *episkopē* or pastoral oversight; that this oversight – at least over a congregation of any size – should be exercized by a team (the word 'elders' nearly always occurs in the plural in the New Testament, e.g. Acts 14:23, 20:17; 1 Tim. 4:14; Titus 1:5); and that such a team should include part-time and full-time, clerical and lay, stipendiary and voluntary ministers – and I believe women as well as men, although the New Testament indicates that their roles will not be identical. There is immense value in the team concept, as I know from experience as well as Scripture, because then we can capitalize one another's strengths and supplement one another's weaknesses. Moreover, gifted lay people should be encouraged to join the team, and exercize their ministry in a voluntary capacity according to their gifts. One of these is preaching, and the Church needs many more lay preachers. Nevertheless, the pastoral ministry of regular preaching and teaching is extremely exacting. It demands much time and energy in study. So a pastoral team in any sizeable church needs at least one full-time leader, who will give himself to the ministry of the Word. Without this the congregation is bound to be impoverished.

The task of feeding the flock or teaching the church can be accomplished by the pastoral team in a variety of contexts. The Good Shepherd himself preached to the crowds, spent time with individuals and trained the twelve. A pastoral ministry which is modelled on his will similarly include preaching to the congregation, counselling individuals, and training groups. Is there a difference, then, between preaching and teaching? Certainly the two words are not interchangeable, and C. H. Dodd popularized the thesis that in the New Testament the *kērygma* (preaching) was the proclamation of the death and resurrection of Jesus, according to the Scriptures and in an eschatological setting, with a summons to repent and believe, while the *didachē* (teaching) was instruction – mostly ethical – given to converts. This distinction is important, although probably it has been overpressed. For in the public ministry of Jesus 'teaching in their synagogues and preaching the gospel of the kingdom' (Matt. 4:23; 9:35) are not sharply distinguished, while the apostle Paul described himself as both a 'preacher' and a 'teacher' of the gospel (1 Tim. 2:7; 2 Tim. 1:11), and when Luke takes leave of him at the end of the Acts, he is 'preaching the kingdom of God and teaching about the Lord Jesus Christ'. (28:31) No doubt his preaching was more evangelistic in purpose and his teaching more systematic in character, but it is not clear that the one was entirely distinct from the other in content; probably they overlapped considerably.

It has sometimes been said that in the New Testament to preach (*kērusso*, 'herald') is entirely evangelistic, and that the modern brand of preaching (to a Christian congregation in church) neither occurs in the New Testament, nor is even contemplated. This is not so, however. The practice of assembling the people of God to hear his Word expounded goes back to the Old Testament, was continued in the synagogues, and was then taken over and christianized by the apostles. Thus Moses gave the law to the priests with

122

the instruction to gather the people and read it to them, presumably explaining and applying it as they went along. (Deut. 31:9–13; cf. Mal. 2:7–9) Ezra the priest and scribe 'brought the law before the assembly' and 'read from it'. The Levitical priests also shared in this ministry: 'they read from the book, from the law of God, clearly; and they gave the sense, so that the people understood the reading.' (Neh. 8:1–8) Later the synagogue services included readings from the law and the prophets, after which somebody preached. Thus Jesus in the Nazareth synagogue first read from Isaiah 61 and then in his subsequent message claimed that he was himself the fulfilment of this Scripture, and spoke other 'gracious words' which astonished his hearers. (Luke 4:16–22) Similarly, Paul in Pisidian Antioch, 'after the reading of the law and the prophets', was invited by the rulers of the synagogue to share with the people a 'word of exhortation', which he proceeded to do. (Acts 13:14–43)

It is not surprising, therefore, that when believers either left or were ejected from the synagogues, and began to arrange their own distinctively Christian assemblies, the same pattern of Bible reading followed by Bible exposition was preserved, except that there was now added to extracts from the law and prophets a reading from one of the apostles' letters (e.g. Col. 4:16; 1 Thess. 5:27; 2 Thess. 3:14). Luke gives us only one peep into such an assembly. It was the famous occasion at Troas when the Christians gathered 'on the first day of the week'. Their worship included both the breaking of bread and also a sermon from Paul which 'he prolonged . . . until midnight' with disastrous consequences. (Acts 20:7 ff.) Although this is the only Christian worship service in the New Testament which is specifically said to have included a sermon, there is no reason to suppose that it was exceptional. On the contrary, Paul gives Timothy specific instructions not only about the conduct of public prayer (1 Tim. 2:1 ff.) but also about preaching: 'Till I come, attend to the public reading of Scripture, to preaching, to teaching.' (1 Tim. 4:14) The clear implication is that after the reading from the Bible, and arising out of it, there should be both *paraklēsis* (exhortation) and *didaskalia* (instruction). This is not to say that there was no element of evangelistic proclamation as well, for there will have been fringe members in attendance like the 'godfearers' on the edge of the synagogue community, together with catechumens under instruction for baptism, and even sometimes heathen visitors. (1 Cor. 14:23) Yet the emphasis will have been on teaching the faithful. It is because the pastor had this responsibility to feed the flock that among the qualifications for the presbyterate are listed both loyalty to the apostolic faith (so that he could 'give instruction in sound doctrine and . . . confute those who contradict it') and a gift for teaching. (Titus 1:9; 1 Tim. 3:2)

If today's pastors were to take seriously the New Testament emphasis on the priority of preaching and teaching, not only would they find it extremely fulfilling themselves, but also it would undoubtedly have a very wholesome effect on the Church. Instead, tragic to relate, many are essentially administrators, whose symbols of ministry are the office rather than the study, and the telephone rather than the Bible. Preaching in August 1977 during the Centennial Thanksgiving Service of Wycliffe College, Toronto, Donald Coggan, at that time Archbishop of Canterbury, reminded the congregation that the Bishop gives each candidate a Bible at his ordination: 'he does not go forth . . . primarily as an organizer or a financier or an entertainer; he goes as a man authorized by the Lord of the Church, entrusted with the deposit of the Christian revelation, recorded in majestic outline in the Book in his hand, and incarnate in the Word made flesh.' Dr. Coggan went on to express the hope that during its second century Wycliffe College would send out a stream of men who would not only study the Bible themselves, feeding on it and digging into it, but also 'give all that they have to its exposition and application'.

If we were to establish 'the ministry of the Word and prayer' as our priority, as the apostles did (Acts 6:4), it would involve for most of us a radical restructuring of our programme and timetable, including a considerable delegation of other responsibilities to lay leaders, but it would express a truly New Testament conviction about the essential nature of the pastorate.

A Conviction about Preaching

Granted that pastors are preachers and teachers, what sort of sermons are they to preach? The textbooks on homiletics tend to give a long list of options. Perhaps the most thorough classification of sermon types is given by W. E. Sangster in his famous book *The Craft of the Sermon*. He distinguishes between three main kinds of sermon and assigns a chapter to each, although he adds that 'the range of combinations is almost infinite.'[33] The first is defined 'according to subject matter' (e.g. biblical, ethical, devotional, doctrinal, social or evangelistic), the second 'according to structural type' (e.g. direct exposition, progressive argument, or 'faceting') and the third 'according to psychological method' (i.e. according to whether the preacher sees himself as teacher, barrister, perplexed man or devil's advocate).

Other writers, less thorough than Sangster, have been content with simpler classifications. There are topical sermons and textual sermons, they say. Some are evangelistic or apologetic or prophetic, others doctrinal or devotional or ethical or hortatory, while somewhere down the line 'exegetical' or 'expository' sermons are included. I cannot myself acquiesce in this relegation (sometimes even grudging) of expository preaching to one alternative among many. It is my contention that all true Christian preaching is expository preaching. Of course if by an 'expository' sermon is meant a verse-by-verse explanation of a lengthy passage of Scripture, then indeed it is only one possible way of preaching, but this would be a misuse of the word. Properly speaking, 'exposition' has a much broader meaning. It refers to the content of the sermon (biblical truth) rather than its style (a running commentary). To expound

Scripture is to bring out of the text what is there and expose it to view. The expositor prizes open what appears to be closed, makes plain what is obscure, unravels what is knotted and unfolds what is tightly packed. The opposite of exposition is 'imposition', which is to impose on the text what is not there. But the 'text' in question could be a verse, or a sentence, or even a single word. It could equally be a paragraph, or a chapter, or a whole book. The size of the text is immaterial, so long as it is biblical. What matters is what we do with it. Whether it is long or short, our responsibility as expositors is to open it up in such a way that it speaks its message clearly, plainly, accurately, relevantly, without addition, subtraction or falsification. In expository preaching the biblical text is neither a conventional introduction to a sermon on a largely different theme, nor a convenient peg on which to hang a ragbag of miscellaneous thoughts, but a master which dictates and controls what is said.

Let me now draw attention to some of the principal benefits of this discipline.

First, *exposition sets us limits*. It restricts us to the scriptural text, since expository preaching is biblical preaching. We are not expounding a passage from either secular literature or a political speech or even a religious book, let alone our own opinions. No, our text is invariably taken from God's Word. The very first qualification of expositors is the recognition that we are guardians of a sacred 'deposit' of truth, 'trustees' of the gospel, 'stewards of the mysteries of God'.[34] As Donald Coggan expressed it in his first book on preaching:

The Christian preacher has a boundary set for him. When he enters the pulpit, he is not an entirely free man. There is a very real sense in which it may be said of him that the Almighty has set him his bounds that he shall not pass. He is not at liberty to invent or choose his message: it has been committed to him, and it is for him to declare, expound and commend it to his hearers . . . It is a great thing to come under the magnificent tyranny of the Gospel![35]

Secondly, *exposition demands integrity*. Not everybody is persuaded of this. It is commonly said that the Bible can be made to mean anything one wants – which is true only if one lacks integrity. Somerset Maugham in his novel *The Moon and Sixpence* describes how the Rev. Robert Strickland wrote a biography of his late father, which was more myth than history. In reality his father, driven by a strange demonic obsession to paint, had abandoned his wife, family and career. In the biography, however, he was portrayed as an excellent husband and father, and a man of kindness, industry and morality. This extraordinary distortion of the truth led Maugham to comment, 'The modern clergyman has acquired in his study of the science which I believe is called exegesis an astonishing facility for explaining things away.' He added with not a little sarcasm that the Rev. Robert Strickland's subtlety of interpretation 'must surely lead him in the fullness of time to the highest dignities of the Church. I see already his muscular calves encased in the gaiters episcopal.'[36]

The 'exegesis' which Somerset Maugham thus caricatures is in fact, or should be, a discipline of the utmost rigour. It is sometimes graced with the rather long-winded adjective 'grammatico-historical', because it signifies the interpretation of a text in accordance with both its historical origin and its grammatical construction. The sixteenth-century Reformers are rightly given the credit for having recovered this method by rescuing biblical interpretation from the fanciful allegorizations of medieval writers. When they spoke of the 'literal' meaning, they were contrasting it with the 'allegorical'; they were not denying that some passages of Scripture are deliberately poetical in style and figurative in meaning. They emphasized that what every Bible student must look for is the plain, natural, obvious meaning of each text, without subtleties. What did the original author intend his words to mean? That was the question. Moreover, it is a question which can with patience be answered, and answered confidently. We must not be infected by the modern cynical mood in literary criticism, which suspects every author of having secret purposes or occult meanings which need to be detected and unmasked. No, the biblical authors were honest men, not deceivers, and they intended their writings to be understood, not to be 'infinitely interpretable'.

The Reformers also spoke much of 'the analogy of faith', by which they meant their belief that Scripture possesses a unity given it by the mind of God, that it must therefore be allowed to interpret itself, one passage throwing light upon another, and that the Church has no liberty so to 'expound one place of Scripture that it be repugnant to another' (Article 20). They did not deny the diversity of formulation which Scripture contains, but they refused to emphasize it at the expense of Scripture's unity, as some modern scholars do. In contrast to these, they saw harmonization (which is not a synonym for manipulation) as a responsible Christian task.

At the end of April 1564, a month before he died, Calvin said goodbye to the pastors of Geneva. Would that every preacher were able to claim what he was able to say to them:

I have not corrupted one single passage of Scripture, nor twisted it as far as I know, and when I might well have brought in subtle meanings, if I had studied subtlety, I have trampled the whole lot underfoot, and I have always studied to be simple . . .[37]

Another expositor, some 250 years later, who made the same claim, was Charles Simeon of Cambridge. At one of his celebrated sermon parties, held every other Friday evening in term-time, he exhorted his student guests in these terms, 'Be most solicitous to ascertain from the original and from the context the true, faithful and primary meaning of every text.'[38] For this is what he took pains to do himself. 'The author has endeavoured,' he explained in his preface to the collection of his sermon outlines entitled *Horae Homileticae*, 'without prejudice or partiality, to give to every text its just meaning, its natural bearing and its legitimate use.'[39] And in a letter to his publisher he wrote, 'My endeavour is to bring out of Scripture what is there, and not to thrust in what I think might be there. I have a great jealousy on this head: never to speak more or less than I believe to be the mind of the Spirit in the passage I am expounding.'

It was this resolute determination to sit humbly under the authority of the Scriptures, instead of standing in judgment on them, which led Simeon to distrust all schemes and systems of divinity.

> The author . . . is no friend to systematizers in theology (he wrote). He has endeavoured to derive from the Scriptures alone *his* view of religion; and to them it is his wish to adhere, with scrupulous fidelity; never wresting any portion of the Word of God to favour a particular opinion, but giving to every part of it that sense which it seems to him to have been designed by its great Author to convey.[40]

The same, in his opinion, could not be claimed by the partisan Calvinists and Arminians of his day. On the contrary, as Simeon wrote with innocent humour, 'there is not a determined votary of either system who, if he had been in the company of St. Paul, whilst he was writing his different Epistles, would not have recommended him to alter one or other of his expressions.' As for Simeon himself, such an attitude of superiority towards the inspired text was out of the question. For he was entirely 'content to sit as a *learner* at the feet of the holy Apostles' and had 'no ambition to teach them how they ought to have spoken'.[41]

Thirdly, *exposition identifies the pitfalls* we must at all costs avoid. Since the resolve of the expositor is to be faithful to his text, the two main pitfalls may be termed forgetfulness and disloyalty. The forgetful expositior loses sight of his text by going off at a tangent and following his own fancy. The disloyal expositor appears to remain with his text, but strains and stretches it into something quite different from its original and natural meaning.

G. Campbell Morgan, one of the great expositors of this century, emphasized the necessity of having a text and elucidating it. By contrast, he wrote, Dr. Benjamin Jowett, Master of Balliol College Oxford, 'declared that it was his habit to write his sermons, and then choose a text as a peg on which to hang them. I am quite free to say', continued Campbell Morgan '. . . that the study of his sermons will reveal the accuracy of his statement, and show the peril of the method . . .' Yet more unscrupulous was another preacher who 'gave out his text and said "That is my text. I am now going to preach. Maybe we'll meet again, my text and I, and maybe not".'[42]

This kind of cavalier indifference to one's text at least has the merit of being candidly acknowledged. Much worse is the pretence of expounding a text when in reality one is exploiting it. The New Testament writers themselves warn us in vivid imagery against this wickedness. False teachers are condemned for 'swerving' from the truth, like an archer who misses the target, for 'peddling' God's Word, like a tradesman who sells by trickery, for 'perverting' the gospel by altering its content, and for 'twisting' the Scriptures into an unrecognizable shape. By contrast with all these crimes, Paul declares with great solemnity that he has 'renounced disgraceful, underhanded ways', that he utterly refuses 'to tamper with God's Word', and that instead he relies on 'the open statement of the truth'.[43]

Yet the wilful manipulation of Scripture by those who are determined to make it mean what they want it to mean has been a constant disgrace to the Church. As Professor A. Vinet of Lausanne put it in the middle of the last century, 'a passage of Scripture has a thousand times served for a passport to ideas which were not scriptural.'[44] Sometimes, it has been the comparatively harmless hunt for an appropriate text as when Dr. W. R. Matthews, Dean of St. Paul's Cathedral London on the cessation of hostilities at the end of World War II, wishing to preach on the need to go on from victory to reconstruction, preached on the text 'we are more than conquerors' (Rom. 8:37), or when an unidentified preacher, desiring to preach on the transitoriness of all human experience, hit on the common Old Testament expression 'It came to pass.'[45] Sometimes, however, a preacher misuses Scripture because he is riding a pet theological hobby-horse. Campbell Morgan told of a Baptist preacher who had such pronounced views about baptism that he simply could not leave the subject alone. One morning he announced his text, 'Adam, where art thou?' He then continued, 'There are three lines we shall follow. First, where Adam was; secondly, how he was to be got from where he was; and thirdly and lastly, a few words about baptism.'[46] More tendentious were the so-called 'Puseyites' of the Oxford Movement, who found Matthew 18:12 a convenient text to support their high view of the Church's authority. It reads, 'if he neglect to hear the church, let him be unto thee as a heathen man and a publican.' (AV) They 'preached so often on "Hear the church" as to provoke Archbishop Whately to reply with a homily upon "If any man refuse to hear the Church, let him . . ." '[47] This practice of wrenching a few words out of a text, let alone out of its context, reached its nadir when a preacher who thoroughly disliked the Old Testament is said to have based his diatribe on the words 'hang all the law and the prophets'.

Such unprincipled text-twisting on the part of preachers reminded R. W. Dale of conjurors, and prompted him in his 1878 Yale Lectures to say:

I always think of the tricks of those ingenious gentlemen who entertain the public by rubbing a sovereign between their hands till it becomes a canary, and drawing out of their coat sleeves half-a-dozen brilliant glass globes filled with water, and with four or five goldfish swimming in each of them. For myself, I like to listen to a good preacher, and I have no objection in the world to be amused by the tricks of a clever conjuror; but I prefer to keep the conjuring and the preaching separate: conjuring on Sunday morning, conjuring in church, conjuring with texts of Scripture, is not quite to my taste.[48]

Only the resolve to be a painstaking expositor will enable us to avoid these pitfalls.

Fourthly, *exposition gives us confidence to preach*. If we were expatiating upon our own views or those of some fallible fellow human being, we would be bound to do so diffidently. But if we are expounding God's Word with integrity and honesty, we can be very bold. Whoever speaks, wrote Peter, should do so 'as one who utters oracles of God'. (1 Pet. 4:11) This is not because we presume to regard our own words as an oracular utterance, but because like the ancient Jews we have been 'entrusted with the oracles of God' (Rom. 4:2), and because our overriding concern is to handle them with such scrupulous fidelity that they themselves are heard to speak, or rather that God speaks through them.

Professor Gustaf Wingren expresses this admirably when he writes:

The expositor is only to provide mouth and lips for the passage itself, so that the Word may advance . . . The really great preachers . . . are, in fact, only the servants of the Scriptures. When they have spoken for a time . . . the Word . . . gleams within the passage itself and is listened to: the voice makes itself heard . . . The passage itself is the voice, the speech of God; the preacher is the mouth and the lips, and the congregation . . . the ear in which the voice sounds . . . Only in order that the Word *may* advance – may go out into the world, and force its way through enemy walls to the prisoners within – is preaching necessary.[49]

*   *   *

Such is the theological foundation for the ministry of preaching. God is light; God has acted; God has spoken; and God has caused his action and speech to be preserved in writing. Through this written Word he continues to speak with a living voice powerfully. And the Church needs to listen attentively to his Word, since its health and maturity depend upon it. So pastors must expound it; it is to this they have been called. Whenever they do so with integrity, the voice of God is heard, and the Church is convicted and humbled, restored and reinvigorated, and transformed into an instrument for his use and glory.

These truths about God and Scripture, the Church, the pastorate and biblical exposition, need to reinforce our trembling convictions. Then the current objections to preaching will not deter us. On the contrary, we will give ourselves to this ministry with fresh zeal and determination. Nothing will be able to deflect us from our priority task.

Notes

1 Some of the material of this chapter has already appeared in the tribute to the late Dr. Wilbur Smith, entitled *Evangelical Roots*, ed. Kenneth S. Kantzer (Nelson, 1978).
2 cf. Ps. 19:1; Isa. 6:3; Rom. 1:19, 20.
3 cf. the use of these adjectives 'better' and 'eternal' in Heb. 7:19, 22; 8:6; 9:12; 14, 15, 23; 13:20 and the expression 'more glorious' in 2 Cor. 3:4–11 AV.
4 I have elaborated the implications of the double authorship of Scripture, especially in relation to human cultures, in my 1979 Olivier Beguin lecture, published by the Bible Society in Australia and U.K., and by Inter-Varsity Press in the United States.
5 Stalker, p. 93.
6 Solzhenitsyn, p. 22.
7 ibid., p. 26.
8 ibid., p. 27.
9 Jer. 23:29; Ps. 119:105; Jas. 1:18, 22–5; 1 Pet. 1:23–2:2; Ps. 19:10.

10 Forsyth, pp. 3, 15, 56.
11 Wingren, p. 45.
12 ibid., p. 146.
13 ibid., pp. 207–8.
14 ibid., p. 108.
15 ibid., p. 95.
16 ibid., p. 124.
17 Spurgeon, *All-Round Ministry*, p. 187.
18 e.g. Deut. 4:1, 30; 5:1; 6:1–3; 11:26–8; 12:28; 15:5; 28:1.
19 Prov. 8:1–36, cf. 1:20–33.
20 See Isa. 1:2, 10, 19, 20; 42:18–25; 43:8; 48:17–19, 22.
21 Jer. 7:23–6, cf. 25:3–7; 32:33; 35:12–16; 44:1–6.
22 2 Chr. 36:15, 16.
23 Lloyd-Jones, *Preaching*, p. 24.
24 Dargan, Vol. 1, p. 13.
25 Calvin IV.1.5.
26 ibid., IV.III.2.
27 *Works* Vol. II, p. 1034.
28 *Works* Vol. III, p. 598
29 Volbeda, p. 24.
30 ibid., p. 26.
31 ibid., pp. 79–85.
32 Ramsey, M., *The Christian Priest*, p. 7.
33 Sangster, *The Craft*, p. 92.
34 1 Tim. 6:20; 2 Tim. 1:12–14; 1 Thess. 2:4; 1 Cor. 4:1, 2.
35 Coggan, *Stewards*, pp. 46, 48.
36 Maugham, p. 8.
37 Cadier, pp. 173–5.
38 Smyth, *The Art*, p. 176.
39 Simeon, *Horae*, p. 12.
40 ibid., pp. 4–5 Preface to Vol. 1.
41 ibid., p. 6.
42 Morgan, G. C., *Preaching*, pp. 40, 42.
43 2 Tim, 2:18; 2 Cor. 2:17; Gal. 1:7; 2 Pet. 3:16; 1 Cor. 4:2.
44 Vinet, p. 76.
45 McWilliam, p. 39.
46 Jones, p. 288.
47 Quoted at the 1935 Islington Clerical Conference by the Rev.
    G. T. Manley. See *Authority and the Christian Faith*, Thynne
    1935, p. 50.
48 Dale, p. 127.
49 Wingren, pp. 201–3.

CHAPTER FOUR

Preaching as Bridge-building

Exactly what is preaching? I have tried so far both to face some current objections to it and to develop a theological defence of it. But I have not yet attempted to define it, except to insist that if it is to be authentically Christian it must be expository. Yet to assert that 'preaching is exposition' would not be a wholly satisfactory equation, for then preaching would be no more than the interpretation of the biblical documents and would have no necessary concern for any contemporary application.

The Bible itself uses a variety of images to illustrate what a Christian preacher is. The commonest is that of the herald or town crier (*kēryx*), who has been given a message of good news and been told to proclaim it. So in the market square or some other public place, without fear or favour, he lifts up his voice and makes it known. 'We herald Christ crucified' and 'we herald . . . Jesus Christ as Lord' are two of Paul's most direct descriptions of his evangelistic preaching.[1]

Next, the preacher is a sower (*speirōn*). As in Jesus' parable of the sower, he goes out into the world, like a farmer into his fields. There he broadcasts the precious seed of God's Word, hoping and praying that some of it will fall into well-prepared soil and in due course bear good fruit (cf. Luke 8:4ff.).

Thirdly, the preacher is an ambassador (*presbus*). He has been commissioned to serve as an envoy in a foreign – even hostile – land. In it he has the responsibility of representing his sovereign or government, whose cause he is proud to plead.[2]

The preacher is also a steward or housekeeper

(*oikonomos*). It is his privilege to have been put in charge of God's household and entrusted with the provisions they need. These are 'the mysteries of God', meaning God's revealed secrets. He is expected above all to be faithful in dispensing them to God's family.[3]

The preacher as pastor or shepherd (*poimēn*) we have already considered. The Chief Shepherd has delegated the care of his flock to under-shepherds, who are charged to protect them from wolves (false teachers) and lead them to pasture (sound teaching).[4]

The sixth metaphor of the preacher represents him as 'one approved, a workman who has no need to be ashamed' (2 Tim. 2:15). But what kind of a workman must he be if he is to be 'approved' in God's sight and 'not ashamed'? He must be skilful in his treatment of 'the word of truth'. The familiar AV translation of the verb *orthotomeō* has him 'rightly dividing' it, but this is mistaken. Modern versions prefer something like 'rightly handling' the Word (RSV), or handling it 'correctly' (NIV), but these are too vague. For the word has a more precise meaning, namely to 'cut straight', and the image conveyed is either that of the ploughman or of the road-maker. NEB opts for the former, and depicts the preacher as 'driving a straight furrow' in his proclamation. The other rendering seems the more likely, however, because in its only other two biblical occurrences (Prov. 3:6 and 11:5 LXX) it 'plainly means "cut a path in a straight direction" or "cut a road across country (that is forested or otherwise difficult to pass through) in a straight direction", so that the traveller may go directly to his destination.' (AG) This 'straight' teaching of the truth is in evident contrast to the false teachers who were 'swerving' from it (v. 18), and emphasizes the need for such loyalty and simplicity in our exposition that our hearers understand and follow it with ease.

What is immediately notable about these six pictures is their emphasis on the 'givenness' of the message. Preachers are not to invent it; it has been entrusted to them. Thus, good news has been given to the herald to proclaim, good seed to the farmer to sow and good food to the steward to dispense, while good pasture is available for the shepherd to lead his flock there. Similarly, the ambassador does not pursue his own policy but his country's, and the workman cuts a way for 'the word of truth', not for his own word. It is impressive that in all these New Testament metaphors the preacher is a servant under someone else's authority, and the communicator of somebody else's word.

What these models of the preacher's task make less clear is the need for him to relate the given message to the existential situation, or, to use the modern jargon, to 'contextualize' the Word of God. Not that this factor is altogether absent. The herald cannot be indifferent to those who listen to what he says, nor the ambassador to the people with whom he pleads, nor the steward to the household for whom he is responsible. So too the shepherd seeks pasture which will suit his sheep, and the road-maker is concerned about the travellers who will walk the way which he is cutting through the jungle. Perhaps the sower metaphor is the most suggestive of all in this respect, in spite of the fact that the actual picture is the least personal. Yet the different soils into which the seed falls represent different kinds of people who hear the Word, and a conscientious farmer is obviously concerned not only to sow the right seed but to sow it in the right soil.

Crossing the Cultural Gulf

It is because preaching is not exposition only but communication, not just the exegesis of a text but the conveying of a God-given message to living people who need to hear it, that I am going to develop a different metaphor to illustrate the essential nature of preaching. It is non-biblical in the sense that it is not explicitly used in Scripture, but I hope to show that what it lays upon us is a fundamentally biblical task. The metaphor is that of bridge-building.

Now a bridge is a means of communication between two places which would otherwise be cut off from one another by a river or a ravine. It makes possible a flow of traffic which without it would be impossible. What, then, does the gorge or chasm represent? And what is the bridge which spans it? The chasm is the deep rift between the biblical world and the modern world. In a famous essay published in 1955 Lord Snow spoke of 'The Two Cultures' – science and the arts – and bemoaned the increasing alienation of literary and scientific intellectuals from each other. He spoke of the 'gulf of mutual incomprehension' between them. But if the gulf between two contemporary cultures is so wide, the gulf between both of them and the ancient world is wider still. It is across this broad and deep divide of two thousand years of changing culture (more still in the case of the Old Testament) that Christian communicators have to throw bridges. Our task is to enable God's revealed truth to flow out of the Scriptures into the lives of the men and women of today.

A few years ago I was talking with two students who were brothers, one at Oxford University and the other at Edinburgh. They had been brought up in a traditional Christian home, both their parents being practising Christians. But now they had renounced their parents' faith and their Christian upbringing. One was a complete atheist, he told me; the other preferred to call himself an agnostic. What had happened? I asked. Was it that they no longer believed Christianity to be true? 'No', they replied, 'that's not our problem. We're not really interested to know whether Christianity is true. And if you were able to convince us that it is, we're not at all sure we would embrace it.' 'What *is* your problem, then?' I asked with some astonishment. 'What we want to know,' they went on, 'is not whether Christianity is *true*, but whether it's *relevant*. And frankly we don't see how it can be. Christianity was born two millenia ago in a first-century Palestinian culture. What can an ancient religion of the Middle East say to us who live in the exciting, kaleidoscopic world of the end of the twentieth century? We have men on the moon in the seventies, and shall have men on Mars in the eighties, transplant surgery today and genetic engineering tomorrow. What possible relevance can a primitive Palestinian religion have for us?' I have often thanked God for that conversation. Nothing has brought home to me more forcefully the gulf which people perceive between the Bible and themselves, and so the challenge which confronts Christian preachers today.

Before developing the concept of preaching as bridge-building, however, I think I need to qualify it in two ways, in order to avoid misunderstanding. First, although I have spoken of an unbridged chasm between the biblical and the modern worlds, I recognize that in fact there has been a long succession of bridge-builders; that throughout the history of the Church Christians have tried to relate the biblical message to their particular culture; and that each new Christian generation has entered into its predecessor's labours. So there has been more historical continuity in bridge-building than my analogy may seem to allow. Sometimes, instead of building a new bridge, the new generation is actually adapting and refurbishing an old one, adding a span here, replacing a girder there. Nevertheless, the world is now changing so rapidly that each rising generation feels challenged by the width of the gulf and by the need to construct a new bridge. There was no doubt in the minds of my two student friends of the yawning chasm which separated them from the message of the Bible.

Secondly, I recognize that there are perils in the clamant demand for relevance. If we become exclusively preoccupied with answering the questions people are asking, we may overlook the fact that they often ask the wrong questions and need to be helped to ask the right ones. If we acquiesce uncritically in the world's own self-understanding, we may find ourselves the servants rather of fashion than of God. So, in order to avoid the snare of being a 'populist' or a modern false prophet, the type of bridge to be built must be determined more by the biblical revelation than by the *zeitgeist* or spirit of the age. The Church's calling is to challenge secularism, not to surrender to it. Nevertheless, there is a great need for more understanding of, and sensitivity to, the modern world around us.

Faced with this problem (the communication gulf between two worlds), preachers tend to make one of two mistakes.

If we are conservatives (I am referring to our theology, not our temperament or our politics), and stand in the tradition of historic Christian orthodoxy, we live on the Bible side of the gulf. That is where we feel comfortable and safe. We believe the Bible, love the Bible, read the Bible, study the Bible and expound the Bible. But we are not at home in the modern world on the other side, especially if we have reached – or passed – middle age. It bewilders and threatens us. So we tend to insulate ourselves from it. If we read Alvin Toffler's *Future Shock*, which documents the rapidity with which Western culture is changing and the disturbance this causes people (a form of 'culture shock' though caused by our passage through time instead of space), we go into a state of profound shock from which, it seems, some of us never emerge. You can tell it from our preaching. We preach biblically. Why, of course; how else could we preach? Charles Simeon and Charles Spurgeon are our heroes. We are determined like them to expound the Scriptures, and to derive all our teaching from God's Word. But if I were to draw a diagram of the gulf between the two worlds, and then plot our sermons on the diagram, I would have to draw a straight line which begins in the biblical world, and then goes up in the air on a straight trajectory, but never lands on the other side. For our preaching is seldom if ever earthed. It fails to build a bridge into the modern world. It is biblical, but not contemporary. And if we are called to account for our practice of exposition without application, we piously reply that our trust is in the Holy Spirit to apply his Word to the realities of human life.

I hope my readers will forgive me if my diagram of conservative preaching is a hurtful caricature. In self-

140

defence I can only plead that it is my former self that I have been portraying. For, although I hope that in recent years I have begun to mend my ways, yet previously both my theory and my practice were to expoud the biblical text and leave the application largely to the Holy Spirit. Moreover, this method is by no means as ineffective as it may sound, for two reasons. First, the biblical text is itself amazingly contemporary, and secondly, the Holy Spirit does use it to bring the hearers to conviction of sin, faith in Christ and growth in holiness. No one has expressed this better than P. T. Forsyth:

> It is into the Bible world of the eternal redemption that the preacher must bring his people . . . To every age it is equally near, and it is equally authoritative for every age, however modern. The only preaching which is up to date for every time is the preaching of this eternity, which is opened up to us in the Bible alone – the eternal of holy love, grace and redemption, the eternal and immutable morality of saving grace for our indelible sin.[5]

At the same time, it would be quite inadmissible to use the perpetual relevance of the gospel and the up-to-date ministry of the Holy Spirit as an excuse for avoiding the communication problem. We should not follow the example of the Reverend Maynard Gilfil, the Ango-Catholic curate of Shepperton, whom George Eliot introduces to us as 'an excellent old gentleman, who smoked very long pipes and preached very short sermons'. In fact, 'he had a large heap of short sermons, rather yellow and worn at the edges, from which he took two every Sunday, securing perfect impartiality in the selection by taking them as they came, without reference to topics.'[6] A number of horror stories are current about inappropriate sermons. There was, for example, the chaplain who visited the construction works on the Great Dam being built on the Upper Nile. His congregation consisted of men who had to endure great heat, extreme isolation and the strong temptations which assault people who have too much time for recreation and too few facilities for it. So what do you think he preached about? 'The duty of observing all the saints' days in the church calendar – as if they had been a group of the devout widows and spinsters in the home congregation.' He was 'a first prize idiot', comments W. M. McGregor, who tells the story.[7] Then there was the 'Cambridge don of whom E. L. Mascall tells in one of his books' who 'began his sermon to a group of Cambridge bedmakers (college servants): "The ontological argument for the existence of God has in recent years, largely under Teutonic influence, been relegated to a position of comparative inferiority in the armoury of Christian apologetics".'[8] Yet even this crass stupidity was exceeded by Bishop John Wordsworth of Salisbury (1885–1911) who, in his sermon at a Confirmation service at Sherborne School, 'vehemently implored the boys, whatever else they might do, on no account to marry their Deceased Wives' Sisters.'[9]

Let C. H. Spurgeon expose the tragic folly of such irrelevancies, and of a preoccupation with the minutiae of doctrine:

For instance, the great problems of sublapsarianism and supralapsarianism, the trenchant debates concerning eternal filiation, the earnest dispute concerning the double procession, and the pre- and post-millenarian schemes, however important some may deem them, are practically of very little concern to that godly widow woman, with seven children to support by her needle, who wants far more to hear of the loving-kindness of the God of providence than of these mysteries profound. I know a minister who is great upon the ten toes of the beast, the four faces of the cherubim, the mystical meaning of badgers' skins, and the typical bearings of the staves of the ark, and the windows of Solomon's temple: but the sins of business men, the temptations of the

142

times, and the needs of the age, he scarcely ever touches upon.[10]

In other words, he is totally irrelevant.

I turn now to the characteristic fault in the preaching of those whose theology is 'liberal' or, more extreme, 'radical' rather than conservative.[11] They find it congenial to live on the contemporary side of the great divide. They are modern people who belong to the modern world. They are sensitive to the current mood and understand what is going on around them. They read modern poetry and philosophy. They are familiar with the writings of living novelists and the discoveries of modern scientists. They go to the theatre and the cinema, and they watch television. Toffler's *Future Shock* fails to shock them, for they have their built-in shock absorbers. They are moving with the moving times. So when they preach, I would have to draw another straight line on my diagram, although this time in the opposite direction. All their sermons are earthed in the real world, but where they come from (one is tempted to add) heaven alone knows. They certainly do not appear to come out of the Bible. On the contrary, these preachers have allowed the biblical revelation to slip through their fingers.

Those of us who criticize and condemn liberal theologians for their abandonment of historic Christianity, do not always honour their motivation or give them credit for what they are trying to do. The heart of their concern is not destruction but reconstruction. They know that large numbers of their contemporaries are contemptuously dismissive of Christianity, because they find its beliefs untenable, its formulations archaic and its vocabulary meaningless. This fact causes the best liberals profound pain, and it is this which lies behind their theologizing. They are anxious to restate the Christian faith in terms which are intelligible, meaningful and credible to their secular colleagues and friends. All honour to them in so far as they are genuinely wrestling with the need to discover the modern gospel for the modern world. I wish we conservatives shared this incentive, and were ourselves neither so entrenched in antique clichés, nor so offensively complacent about our failure to communicate. What is sad and reprehensible about liberals is that in discarding the ancient formulations they tend also to discard the truth formulated, and so to throw out the baby with the bathwater.

The contrast I have been drawing between the two main theological groupings in today's churches seems to me to be one of the greatest tragedies of our time. On the one hand, conservatives are biblical but not contemporary, while on the other liberals and radicals are contemporary but not biblical. Why must we polarize in this naive way, however? Each side has a legitimate concern, the one to conserve God's revelation, the other to relate meaningfully to real people in the real world. Why can we not combine each other's concerns? Is it not possible for liberals to learn from conservatives the necessity of conserving the fundamentals of historic, biblical Christianity, and for conservatives to learn from liberals the necessity of relating these radically and relevantly to the real world?

Meanwhile, each group stays on its favourite side of the cultural chasm, and almost nobody seems to be building bridges. Yet we preachers are supposed to be in the business of communication. A lecture has been wittily defined as the transfer of information from the lecturer's notes to the student's, without it passing through the mind of either; but sermons should not be equally dismal examples of non-communication. We should be praying that God will raise up a new generation of Christian communicators who are determined to bridge the chasm; who struggle to relate God's unchanging Word to our ever-changing world; who refuse to sacrifice truth to relevance or relevance to truth; but who resolve instead in equal measure to be faithful to Scripture and pertinent to today.

Biblical and Historical Precedents

This earthing of the Word in the world is not something optional; it is an indispensable characteristic of true Christian preaching. Indeed, it is an obligation laid upon us by the kind of God we believe in and by the way in which he has himself communicated with us, namely in Christ and in Scripture, through his living and his written Word. In Scripture he spoke his Word through human words to human beings in precise historical and cultural contexts; he did not speak in culture-free generalities. Similarly, his eternal Word became flesh, in all the particularity of a first-century Palestinian Jew. In both cases he reached down to where the people were to whom he desired to communicate. He spoke in human language; he appeared in human flesh. Thus the great doctrines of inspiration and incarnation have established a divine precedent for communication. God condescended to our humanity, though without surrendering his deity. Our bridges too must be firmly anchored on both sides of the chasm, by refusing either to compromise the divine content of the message or to ignore the human context in which it has to be spoken. We have to plunge fearlessly into both worlds, ancient and modern, biblical and contemporary, and to listen attentively to both. For only then shall we understand what each is saying, and so discern the Spirit's message to the present generation. We have to ask, in the controversial language of Dietrich Bonhoeffer, 'Who is Christ for us today?' Already in 1932 he had said, 'The point is not how are we to model the message, but what really *is* the message and its content' for the present age?[12]

All this will mean a greater thoughtfulness in our preaching. On the whole, if I may generalize, we do not make sufficient demands on the congregation. When they come to church, they have heard it all before. They have known it since they were in junior Sunday School. It is stale, boring and irrelevant. It fails to 'grab' or excite them. They can scarcely stifle their yawns. They come with their problems, and they leave with their problems. The sermon has not spoken to their need.

I am not of course advocating that we treat our congregation as if it were a university audience, or that we turn our sermon into an academic lecture. Nor do I forget Marshall McLuhan's dislike of literary man, who reads books in antisocial isolation, extinguishes his imagination and becomes a slave to linear logic. It is perfectly true that the conclusions which some reach through logic others reach through intuition; that it is possible to learn by images as well as by words; and that the human beings God has created are not only 'cerebral' (with brain power) but also 'visceral' (capable of what is vulgarly termed a 'gut reaction'). Therefore, there is a legitimate, even an essential, place in preaching for the intuitive, the imaginative and the emotional. I shall have more to say about these later. Nevertheless, it is also true that all human beings, including entirely illiterate people, are rational by creation; that God has addressed to them a rational revelation, speaking his message to their minds and expecting them to understand it; and that, even if we were to give up reading, we would still remain to some degree linear thinkers, since 'speech is just as linear as script – more so in fact.'[13] I have myself been struck how many modern films and plays (e.g. of Bergman, Woody Allen, Tom Stoppard and Brian Clark) contain very little action, but rely instead on rapid dialogue which demands of the audience a high degree of concentration.

Yet obviously we must preach in such a way that people can understand. Henry Paget, Bishop of Chester from 1919 to 1932, who described himself as 'far better at making friends than at making speeches', would have preferred to remain in East Suffolk where he had earlier served. For there in the farming villages it was possible gradually to get to know everybody and understand them. 'I am no preacher', a village clergyman had said to him one day, 'but my reach is a little longer than theirs, and I can pull down the fodder low enough for them to get it.'[14] To preach instead over people's heads, is to forget who they are. As Spurgeon once commented, 'Christ said, "Feed my sheep . . . Feed my lambs." Some preachers, however, put the food so high that neither lambs nor sheep can reach it. They seem to have read the text, "Feed my giraffes." '[15]

Although we must not overestimate our congregation's intellectual capacity, we must not underestimate it either. My plea is that we treat them as real people with real questions; that we grapple in our sermons with real issues; and that we build bridges into the real world in which they live and love, work and play, laugh and weep, struggle and suffer, grow old and die. We have to provoke them to think about their life in all its moods, to challenge them to make Jesus Christ the Lord of every area of it, and to demonstrate his contemporary relevance.

In developing the picture of preaching as a bridge-building operation, I am not proposing anything new. Christian preachers in every age have seen the need to relate God's revelation to the times in which they lived, and have responded to the challenge. Let me give you a few examples. Chrysostom (who died in A.D. 407), perhaps the most eloquent and forthright preacher of the first three Christian centuries, was summed up by C. S. Horne in these words, 'We have two qualities in Chrysostom, which in their combination make him unique – he is *a man of the Word and a man of the world.*' Again, 'As with all effective preachers, his message had both a *timeless* and a *timely* element in it.'[16] Somewhat similarly, S. E. Dwight wrote of Jonathan Edwards, who was at the heart of the Great Awakening in the eighteenth century, 'His knowledge of the Bible, evinced in his sermons . . . is probably unrivalled. His knowledge of the human heart, and its operations, has scarcely been equalled by that of any uninspired preacher.'[17]

A nineteenth century British example is F. W. Robertson (1816–1853). In stature he was tall and thin, and in personality sensitive, proud, nervous and lonely. After only six years as incumbent of Trinity Chapel, Brighton, his health broke down, and he died at the age of thirty-seven. Yet 'this relatively obscure Brighton preacher', said Hensley Henson in a lecture celebrating the centenary of his birth, left a mark on the spiritual life of his countrymen which was 'deep and permanent'.[18] Why so? Because 'whatever was agitating society he took up . . . in the pulpit.'[19] Bishop Henson explained his influence in three ways: (1) 'the deliberate reference of his preaching to modern conditions of thought and life', (2) 'the intensely personal note which runs through his preaching' and (3) 'the passionate devotion to the Person of the Lord Jesus Christ which inspires his words.'[20] Of these three the first was paramount. He can be criticized for his somewhat arbitrary use of Scripture, but he had great courage in fighting the reigning prejudices, and he maintained throughout 'his habit of "preaching to the times", by linking his argument to the subjects which at the moment were engaging the public mind.'[21] As Bishop Phillips Brooks put it, 'truth and timeliness together make the full preacher.'[22]

In the twentieth century it is perhaps Karl Barth who has spoken most persuasively about the need for relevant biblical preaching. At a ministers' meeting in 1922 he gave an address entitled 'The Need and Promise of Christian Preaching'. He spoke personally of his twelve years in the pastorate. During this period, he said,

> I sought to find my way between the problem of human life on the one hand and the content of the Bible on the other. As a minister I wanted to speak to the *people* in the infinite contradiction of their life, but to speak the no less infinite message of the *Bible*, which was as much of a riddle as life. Often enough these two magnitudes, life and the Bible, have risen before me (and still rise!) like Scylla and Charybdis: if *these* are the whence and whither of Christian preaching, who shall, who can, be a minister and preach?

It was this dilemma, he went on to explain, which finally led him to write his epoch-making commentary on the Letter to the Romans, and readers will understand it best if throughout they hear the minister's question 'what is preaching?' The standpoint of the 'man in the pulpit' is this: 'Before him lies the Bible, full of mystery; and before him are seated his . . . hearers, also full of mystery . . . *What now*? asks the minister.' When the church bells ring, 'there is in the air an *expectancy* that something great, crucial and even momentous is to *happen*.' What is this? It is the people's expectation that they will hear God's Word, that is, answers to their ultimate questions.[23] Years later 'someone . . . asked Karl Barth "What do you do to prepare your Sunday sermon?" Barth answered, "I take the Bible in one hand and the daily newspaper in the other." '[24] It is intriguing that some fifty years previously C. H. Spurgeon had written what he entitled 'My little shilling book *The Bible and the Newspaper*'.[25]

The same emphasis has been made by Professor Jean-Jacques von Allmen of Neuchatel, Switzerland, who wrote in his book *Preaching and Congregation* of 'the two poles of preaching', namely God's Word and our hearers. Neither is of much use without the other. 'To repeat from the pulpit "Jesus Christ our Lord", "Jesus Christ our Lord", rather as the Ephesians proclaimed the greatness of their Diana, is no guarantee that one has truly preached the lordship of Christ'; for this to happen, there must be listeners who hear, understand, relate and respond. But the contrary mistake is also possible: the listeners may assemble and no Word of God be proclaimed. Both errors, he suggests, correspond to Christological heresies. The first is Docetic preaching (denying the humanity of Christ) and the second Arian (denying his divinity). The preacher's task is faithfully to translate the Word of God into modern language and thought-categories, and to make it present in our day. Thus 'to translate the Word we must know two languages; to make it present we must know two epochs.'[26] As Bishop Yngve Brilioth of Sweden put it, two major elements in preaching are 'the expository or exegetical (it starts from and expounds a text of Scripture) and the prophetic (it is a message for the present time, making the Scriptural text a living word in the actual situation).'[27]

To sum up this necessity of holding together the biblical and the contemporary, I call four final witnesses. James Stalker quoted the German theologian Tholuck as saying 'a sermon ought to have heaven for its father and the earth for its mother.'[28] Dr. Martyn Lloyd-Jones has written that 'the business of preaching is to relate the teaching of the Scriptures to what is happening in our own day.'[29] And Professor Ian Pitt-Watson writes, 'Every sermon is stretched like a bowstring between the text of the Bible on the one hand and the problems of contemporary human life on the other. If the string is insecurely tethered to either end, the bow is useless.'[30] Fourthly, Bishop Stephen Neill develops yet another metaphor. 'Preaching is like weaving,' he writes. 'There are the two factors of the warp and the woof. There is the fixed, unalterable element, which for us is the Word of God, and there is the variable element, which enables the weaver to change and vary the pattern at his will. For us that variable element is the constantly changing pattern of people and of situations.'[31]

It is time now to turn from theory to practice. Supposing it is conceded that genuine Christian preaching is a bridge-building exercise, legitimized by ample biblical and historical precedents, what will be required of us? Not just renouncing theological jargon in favour of modern slang, though in some situations this will be necessary, but actually entering other people's worlds of thought and feeling. Incarnation (exchanging one world for another), not just translation (exchanging one language for another) is the Christian model of communication. I will try to develop two examples, the first personal and individual, the second ethical and social.

Christ our Contemporary

First, we must boldly handle the major themes of human life, the incessant questions which men and women have always asked, and which the great novelists and dramatists have treated in every age: What is the purpose of our existence? Has life any significance? Where did I come from, and where am I going to? What does it mean to be a human being, and how do humans differ from animals? Whence this thirst for transcendence, this universal quest for a Reality above and beyond us, this need to fall down and worship the Infinitely Great? What is freedom, and how can I experience personal liberation? Why the painful tension between what I am and what I long to be? Is there a way to be rid of guilt and of a guilty conscience? What about the hunger for love, sexual fulfilment, marriage, family life and community on the one hand, and on the other the pervasive sense of alienation, and the base, destructive passions of jealousy, malice, hate, lust and revenge? Is it possible truly to master oneself and love one's neighbour? Is there any light on the dark mysteries of evil and suffering? How can we find courage to face first life, then death, then what may lie beyond death? What hope can sustain us in the midst of our despair?

In every generation and every culture men and women have asked these questions and debated these issues. This is the stuff from which the world's great literature is formed. Have we Christians nothing to say about these things? Of course we have! We are convinced that the questions themselves reflect and bear witness to the paradoxical nature of human beings which the Bible teaches, namely their dignity as Godlike creatures and their depravity as fallen and guilty sinners. We are also convinced that Jesus Christ either has the answers to these questions or – in the case of intractable mysteries like pain and evil – that he throws more light on them than can be gathered from any other source. Jesus Christ, we believe, is the fulfilment of every truly human aspiration. To find him is to find ourselves.

Therefore, above all else, we must preach Christ. 'Enthusiasm for Christ is the soul of preaching,' wrote James Stalker in his Yale lectures of 1891.[32] 'If we can but teach Christ to our people,' Richard Baxter had written more than two centuries earlier, 'we teach them all.'[33] Not only so, but Jesus Christ exerts on people an almost irresistible attraction. Uplift him, and he draws people to himself, as he said he would. (John 12:32) Was this not the major secret of the power which attended the preaching of Whitefield and Wesley in the eighteenth century? In January 1739 in Bermondsey, South London, George Whitefield found the church packed to capacity, while outside perhaps another thousand people could not get in. 'I offered Jesus Christ freely to sinners,' he wrote of his sermon in the church, 'to all who would lay hold of him by faith.' And even while he was preaching, he dreamed of the possibility of going out into the churchyard, and of climbing on to a tombstone in order to preach Christ again.

John Wesley's favourite text, particularly during the first year of his itinerant ministry, seems to have been 1 Corinthians 1:30, which announces Jesus Christ as 'our wisdom, our righteousness and sanctification and redemption'. It thus declares the comprehensive adequacy of Jesus Christ for all our needs. If we want to find true wisdom, to enter into a right relationship with God, to grow in Christlikeness of character or to be one day fully and finally redeemed, it is to Jesus Christ alone that we must turn. For Christ crucified and risen has been designated by God to be all these things to his people. Wesley revelled in proclaiming this. Take these quotations from his journal, which all belong to 1739, the year following his conversion. On 14 June he preached in Blackheath to between twelve and fourteen thousand people 'on my favourite subject "Jesus Christ who of God is made unto us wisdom, righteousness, sanctification and redemption"'. On 17 July, on the top of a hill overlooking Bradford, five miles from Bath, 'I there offered Christ to about a thousand people for wisdom, righteousness, sanctification and redemption.' On 7 October, on the village green a few miles from Gloucester, 'I called on all who were

152

present (about 3,000 people) . . . to accept of Christ as their only wisdom, righteousness, sanctification and redemption. I was strengthened to speak as I never did before; and I continued speaking nearly two hours.' Then on 15 October, on a little green two or three miles beyond Chepstow in South Wales, he preached 'to 300 or 400 plain people on "Christ our wisdom, righteousness, sanctification and redemption" '. Although all these quotations come from the same year at the beginning of his ministry, Wesley never grew tired of preaching Christ. Twenty-two years later on 22 June 1761, his message was the same. He was in County Durham, in the north of England. The sun was hot and he was feeling physically weak. The place was unsuitable too, 'for there was so vehement a stench of stinking fish as was ready to suffocate me, and the people roared like the waves of the sea. But the voice of the Lord was mightier.' Neither weakness, nor heat, nor stench, nor hostility could silence him. 'In a few minutes the whole multitude was still and seriously attended while I proclaimed "Jesus Christ made of God unto us wisdom, righteousness, sanctification and redemption".'

In his lectures to his students, and in his addresses to pastors, Spurgeon continually reverted to the same glorious theme. 'What shall we preach?' he asks himself, and replies:

> Of all I would wish to say this is the sum; my brethren, preach Christ, always and evermore. He is the whole gospel. His person, offices and work must be our one great, all-comprehending theme. The world needs still to be told of its Saviour, and of the way to reach him . . . Salvation is a theme for which I would fain enlist every holy tongue. I am greedy after witnesses for the glorious gospel of the blessed God. O that Christ crucified were the universal burden of men of God.[34]

Later, at one of his annual conferences for pastors, in an address entitled 'How to Meet the Evils of the Age', Spurgeon said: 'Keep to the gospel, then, more and more. Give the people Christ and nothing but Christ.' Then, after expatiating on some current evils he concluded: 'We have only one remedy for them; preach Jesus Christ, and let us do it more and more. By the roadside, in the little room, in the theatre, anywhere, everywhere, let us preach Christ. Write books if you like and do anything else within your power; but whatever else you cannot do, preach Christ.'[35]

It should be plain from these quotations that the One we preach is not Christ-in-a-vacuum, nor a mystical Christ unrelated to the real world, nor even only the Jesus of ancient history, but rather the contemporary Christ who once lived and died, and now lives to meet human need in all its variety today. To encounter Christ is to touch reality and experience transcendence. He gives us a sense of self-worth or personal significance, because he assures us of God's love for us. He sets us free from guilt because he died for us, from the prison of our own self-centredness by the power of his resurrection, and from paralyzing fear because he reigns, all the principalities and powers of evil having been put under his feet. He gives meaning to marriage and home, work and leisure, personhood and citizenship. He introduces us into his new community, the new humanity he is creating. He challenges us to go out into some segment of the world which does not acknowledge him, there to give ourselves in witness and service for him. He promises us that history is neither meaningless nor endless, for one day he will return to terminate it, to destroy death and to usher in the new universe of righteousness and peace. 'In him (Christ) the whole fullness of deity dwells bodily, and you have come to fullness of life in him.' (Col. 2:9, 10) One of the most fascinating of all the preacher's tasks is to explore both the emptiness of fallen man and the fullness of Jesus Christ, in order then to demonstrate how he can fill our emptiness, lighten our darkness, enrich our poverty, and bring our human aspirations to fulfilment. The riches of Christ are unfathomable. (Eph. 3:8, NEB)

Ethics for Christians

From this personal example of bridge-building, of relating the Word to the world, or Christ to the individual, I turn to the sphere of ethical duty. All Christians of every conceivable tradition are agreed that the gospel has ethical implications. Justification leads inevitably to sanctification. Doctrine without duty is sterile; faith without works is dead. But what are the 'works' which are the fruit of faith? It is here that disagreement begins. It may be helpful to consider the matter as a series of concentric circles, beginning with personal ethics, and then moving on through the churchly, the domestic and the social to issues which have a political dimension.

Even *individual* Christian ethics, in at least some Christian circles, have been pitifully trivialized. There is, for example, an evangelical subculture which is obsessed with the questions of smoking and drinking, with what used to be called 'questionable amusements' (dancing, card-playing, theatre-going and visiting the cinema), together with styles of clothing (how short a woman may wear her skirt), coiffure (how long a man may grow his hair) and cosmetics (how much cream, powder, lipstick and mascara are permitted, if any). Now I am not saying that these issues have no importance. For example, alcohol dependence has become a serious problem in many countries, so that every Christian must come to a responsible decision whether to be a total abstainer or to drink occasionally and in moderation. Now that a link between heavy smoking and some forms of cancer has been scientifically established, the Christian's duty to his body as the Holy Spirit's temple is involved in his decision whether to smoke. Since Jesus taught that the discipline of the eyes is a major means to sexual self-control, Christians are forced to make a conscientious choice between what films and plays they will see, and what novels and magazines they will read, and those they will not. Further, in questions of clothing, cosmetics, coiffure and jewellery, further choices have to be made between modesty and vanity, simplicity and extravagance, as the apostles themselves taught. So these issues are not unimportant. In all of them we need to develop a Christian perspective and make a Christian decision. Nevertheless, some Christians lose their sense of proportion over these matters which, in comparison with the big moral and social issues of the day, can only be described as minuscule. They are 'micro-ethics' in distinction from 'macro-ethics'. To become preoccupied with them is to be guilty of an evangelical pharisaism ('straining out a gnat and swallowing a camel') which majors on minors and neglects what Jesus called 'the weightier matters of the law, justice and mercy and faith'. (Matt. 23:23, 24)

Individual or personal morality was taught in the Old Testament by prophets, priests, scribes and wise men, who sought to draw out the implications of the Ten Commandments. John the Baptist was the last representative of this honourable tradition, before Christ came. He not only exhorted the people to 'bear fruits that befit repentenance', but spelled out what this would mean to different people, instructing the tax-gatherers to collect no more than was appointed them, and the soldiers to rob nobody, accuse nobody falsely, and be content with their wages. (Luke 3:8–14) Similar teaching in personal ethics is given in the New Testament letters, sometimes in the general commendation of Christian virtues ('the fruit of the Spirit is love, joy, peace, patience, kindness, goodness, faithfulness, gentleness and self-control' Gal. 5:22, 23), and sometimes in a particular requirement like the control of that unruly organ and 'restless evil', the tongue. (Jas 3:1–12)

To me the most striking example, however, is to be found in the second chapter of the Letter to Titus. Here Titus is told to give detailed ethical instruction to different groups in the congregation: the older men are to be temperate, serious and mature; the older women are to be self-controlled and to teach the young wives their responsibilities to husband and children; the younger men are to learn self-mastery; Titus himself is to set a blameless example; and slaves are to be submissive, hard-working and honest. More impressive even than these particularities is their grounding in Christian doctrine. For the paragraph begins with the command to 'teach what befits sound doctrine' and ends with the statement that good behaviour will 'adorn the doctrine of God our Saviour'. There were, then, two parts to Titus' pedagogical responsibilities. On the one hand, he was to teach 'the sound doctrine' (the apostolic faith which, like the human body, is an integrated whole). On the other, he was to teach 'the things which befit it' (the ethical conduct which is appropriate to it and will 'adorn' it or display its beauty). It is of the utmost importance that we follow the apostles by keeping these two together in our preaching ministry and by refusing to divorce them. When we proclaim the gospel, we must go on to unfold its ethical implications, and when we teach Christian behaviour we must lay its gospel founda-tions. Christians need to grasp both that their faith in Christ has practical consequences and that the main incentive to good works is to be found in the gospel. God's saving grace in Christ is actually personified as our moral teacher, 'training us to renounce irreligion and worldly passions, and to live sober, upright and godly lives in this world'. (Titus 2:11, 12)

By our '*churchly*' duty ('ecclesiastical' sounds too pomp-ous and institutional), as distinct from our 'individual' duty, I am referring to our responsibilities to each other within the new community which Jesus founded. Much of the ethical teaching of the apostles refers to 'how one ought to behave in the household of God' (1 Tim. 3:15), and so to the new style and standards of conduct which are expected in God's new society. It is here that all the many 'one another' exhortations in the New Testament find their place. We are to love one another, to forgive and forbear one another, to encourage and admonish one another, to 'practice hospitality ungrudgingly to one another' (1 Pet. 4:9) and to 'bear one another's burdens'. (Gal. 6:2) This is

157

the context of Paul's catalogue of duties in Ephesians 4 and 5. We are to put away falsehood, anger, dishonesty, evil talk, bitterness, slander and impurity, as incompatible with the new fellowship (God's family, Christ's body and the Holy Spirit's temple) which has come into being through the cross. For 'we are members one of another' (4:25), and all our behaviour must be consistent with this fact of our belonging to one another in Christ. Such practices as litigation, or enjoying our liberty in a way that offends another's weak conscience, are absolutely at variance with the notion of being brothers and sisters through Christ. 'Brother goes to law against brother.' 'By your knowledge this weak man is destroyed, the brother for whom Christ died'. (1 Cor. 6:6; 8:11) One can hear the outrage in the apostle's voice as he dictated these sentences about violations of the brotherhood.

It is already quite evident that, although good behaviour is an inevitable consequence of the good news, it is not 'automatic' in the sense that it does not need to be taught. The apostles who proclaimed the gospel gave clear and concrete ethical instruction as well. The law and the gospel were thus related in their teaching. If the law is a 'schoolmaster' to bring us to Christ, placing us under such discipline and condemnation as to make Christ our only hope of salvation, Christ now sends us back to the law to tell us how to live. Even the purpose of his death for our sins was not only that we might be forgiven but that, having been forgiven, 'the just requirement of the law might be fulfilled in us, who walk not according to the flesh, but according to the Spirit'. (Rom. 8:3, 4) There are many pastors today who, for fear of being branded 'legalists', give their congregation no ethical teaching. How far we have strayed from the apostles! 'Legalism' is the misguided attempt to earn our salvation by obedience to the law. 'Pharisaism' is a preoccupation with the externals and the minutiae of religious duty. To teach the standards of moral conduct which adorn the gospel is neither legalism nor pharisaism but plain apostolic Christianity.

The third circle of ethical responsibility, to which we now turn our attention, is the *domestic*. The apostles Paul and Peter both include a section in their letters which specifies the reciprocal duties of husbands and wives, parents and children, masters and slaves.[36] They evidently set great store by the Christian home and the harmonious relationships which should characterize it. So they give straightforward instruction on this subject. Home, marriage, the upbringing of children and working for our living remain a major part of human life, and are daily concerns of nearly everybody in each Christian congregation. Moreover, Christian standards in each sphere differ markedly from those of the non-Christian world. So thorough teaching on the Christian doctrines and duties of marriage, parenthood and work is urgently needed today, and too few pulpits attempt to give it.

Social and Political Issues

Wider than our individual, ecclesiastical and domestic duties are the *social* questions which affect our behaviour in the community at large. Let me begin with our Lord's own teaching in the Sermon on the Mount about non-retaliation on the one hand and loving our enemies on the other. (Matt. 5:38–48 and Luke 6:27–36) Here is teaching which takes us out of our home and our church into the world where violence reigns and where there is hostility to the person and standards of Jesus. The question of the Christian attitude to the evil-doer and the enemy cannot be confined to the realm of personal ethics either. It immediately raises questions about the state and its officers (legislators, policemen, judges). This Paul makes clear by placing in deliberate juxtaposition the duty of the individual Christian to 'repay no one evil for evil' and the duty of the state to punish the evil-doer. (Rom. 12:14–13:5) Indeed, he makes the contrast the more stark by his teaching on both wrath and revenge. 'Never avenge yourselves,' he writes. Why not? Not because retribution is wrong in itself but because it is God's prerogative rather than ours: 'Vengeance is mine, I will repay, says the Lord.' Similarly, we are not to curse those who persecute us but to bless them, and never to retaliate but to live peaceably with everybody. Why so? Are anger against evil and judgment upon evil always incompatible with righteousness? No, but they belong to God. 'Leave it to the wrath of God,' Paul writes. (12:19) For God expresses his wrath partly through the state, which is 'the servant of God to execute his wrath on the wrongdoer'. (13:14)

The reason why I have tried briefly to elaborate this Pauline teaching is to show that the Sermon on the Mount cannot be simplistically confined to the realm of individual ethics; it raises questions about violence and non-violence in the community which cannot either be dodged in our own thinking or be eliminated from the pulpit.

Several other examples could be given. One is sexual ethics. Certain standards of sexual morality are clearly taught in the Bible, for instance that lifelong heterosexual marriage is the only context, and 'honour' as opposed to 'lust' the only style, in which sexual intercourse is to be enjoyed.[37] Moreover, since marriage is an ordinance of creation rather than of redemption, these divine standards apply to the whole human community, and not merely to a diminishing religious remnant. It is impossible, therefore, to rest content with the faithful teaching of biblical sex ethics to the congregation (though, to be sure, this is so rare that in itself it would be a welcome advance); we have to be concerned also with the public debate about marriage (is it not now dispensable?), about divorce and the remarriage of divorced persons (why make a fuss about these things?), and about homosexual partnerships (if characterized not by promiscuity but by fidelity, are they not an acceptable variation on heterosexual marriage?). Christians should enter vigorously into these debates, and fearlessly use the pulpit to do so. We have a responsibility not only to expound God's standards with clarity and courage, and without compromise, and to exhort our own congregations to maintain and exhibit these standards with joyful faithfulness, but to go on to commend them to the secular community. Just as we must not only preach the gospel but argue it, as the apostles did, so we must not only teach biblical ethics (including sex ethics), but go on to argue that they are as conducive to society's well-being as a departure from them is destructive of it.

From sex I move on to money. Jesus spoke much of the dangers of wealth, the sin of covetousness, the folly of materialistic ambition and the duty of generosity. James his brother includes in his letter a fierce denunciation (reminiscent of the Old Testament prophets) of those rich people who hoard their wealth like misers, oppress their workers by withholding their wages, and live in selfish luxury. (5:1-6) He and John and Paul all also emphasize the obligation of well-to-do Christians (people who possess 'the world's goods') so to share with the poor as to ensure that they have the necessities of life.[38] Yet how much do we hear of this biblical teaching today, even from those pulpits and in those churches which claim to adhere most strictly to biblical authority? Are we afraid of offending an affluent congregation by preaching on the perils of affluence and the joys of sacrifice and simplicity? Or do we try to evade the challenge of such biblical themes by restricting the scope of our concern to our impoverished fellow Christians? To be sure, even this would be a revolutionary step, for there are millions of deprived and even destitute Christians in the world, whose plight puts our Western Christian affluence to shame. Yet this restriction is inadmissible. For though the Bible does teach that our priority responsibility is to our brothers and sisters in the Christian fellowship, it commands us also to 'do good to all men'. (Gal. 6:10) And of course Jesus told us to love even our enemies and to express our love in action, for only then shall we prove to be genuine children of our heavenly Father who loves the evil and the good indiscriminately, and expresses his love in his gifts of rain and sunshine to all. (Matt. 5:43-8) So the gross economic inequality between the nations of the North and

161

the South is not just a legitimate concern of Christians, but a mandatory one. It is an unavoidable extension of the biblical doctrines of the unity of the human race, the stewardship of the earth's resources and the injustice which is inherent in inequalities of privilege.

I have now slipped into the fifth and widest of the concentric circles of Christian ethics, the *political*, that is, into situations of social injustice which may be ameliorated but cannot be remedied without political action. What attitude are preachers to take up towards the issues of 'macro-ethics'? They press upon us from every side – human oppression and the cry for liberation; poverty, hunger, illiteracy and disease; the pollution of the environment and the conservation of its natural resources; abortion, euthanasia, capital punishment and other life and death issues; work, leisure and unemployment; civil rights and civil liberties; dehumanization by the technocracy and the bureaucracy; the increase of crime, and society's responsibility for the criminal; racism, nationalism, tribalism and human community; violence and revolution; the armaments race, the nuclear horror and the threat of world war. The list seems almost endless. These are the questions which fill our newspapers and which thoughtful university students debate all day and all night. How then can we ban them from the pulpit? If we do so, in order to concentrate exclusively on 'spiritual' topics, we perpetuate the disastrous separation of the sacred from the secular (implying that these are distinct spheres and that God is concerned only for the one and not for the other); we divorce Christian faith from Christian life; we encourage a pietistic Christian withdrawal from the real world; we justify Marx's well-known criticism that religion is an opiate which drugs people into acquiescing in the status quo; and we confirm non-Christians in their sneaking suspicion that Christianity is irrelevant. All this is much too high a price to pay for our irresponsibility.

But I can hear my objectors rallying for their counter-attack. 'You are presuming to advocate in Christian preachers today', they will say, 'something which neither the biblical writers, nor Jesus, nor his apostles ever did. They never meddled in politics. They preached salvation. The ethical instruction they gave was limited to the individual, the home and the church. They did not concern themselves with social or socio-political questions in the outside world.' Are you so sure, my friend and critic? I reply. Think again, I beg you, and consider these arguments. The living God of the Bible is the God of creation as well as of the covenant, and his concern extends beyond his own covenant community to the whole human community. And since he is a God of justice and of compassion, he desires to see these flourish in every society. Look at the first two chapters of Amos, in which it is written that his judgment will fall not only on his own people, the kingdoms of Judah and Israel, for disregarding his law and oppressing the powerless, but on the surrounding heathen nations too, on Syria and Philistia, on Tyre, Edom, Ammon and Moab. And why? Because of their barbaric atrocities in warfare, their depopulation of conquered countries and enslavement of their peoples, and their desecration of the bones of an enemy king. This passage (with similar prophetic oracles against the nations) shows that God is concerned for justice and humane behaviour in every community.

Allied with this is the biblical doctrine of man, male and female, the crown of God's creation, bearing his likeness, possessing a unique worth and dignity, and on that account to be honoured, respected and served. To oppress the poor is to insult their Maker, the Scripture says, and to curse human beings is to dishonour people 'who are made in the likeness of God'. (Prov. 14:31; Jas. 3:9) This respect for human beings as Godlike beings is fundamental according to the Bible to our attitude to them. It moves us to oppose everything which dehumanizes human beings, and to support everything which makes them more human. Nothing, it is true, is more humanizing than the gospel. So we must proclaim it throughout the world with all possible energy, thoroughness, urgency and zeal. But once the good news of

Christ's salvation has brought people into right relationship with God, and caused them to stand upright and lift up their heads with a new self-respect as his adopted and beloved children, we cannot then leave them alone in the inhuman conditions of poverty, disease and illiteracy in which so many millions of them are condemned to live. Nor indeed can we consider the same inhuman conditions which oppress non-Christian people, and react to them with composure and idleness on the ground that their victims do not know Christ. What callous discrimination is this? Do they not bear the divine image too? Is not all oppression offensive to God? Then what displeases him must displease us. We cannot stand by, and do nothing.

As for our Lord Jesus Christ, his message had more far-reaching political implications than is commonly recognized. His contemporaries certainly thought so, for they had him arrested, tried and condemned on a charge of sedition. 'We found this man perverting our nation,' the Jewish leaders said to Pilate, 'and forbidding us to give tribute to Caesar, saying that he himself is Christ a king,' (Luke 23:1, 2) while the inscription over the cross, identifying the crime for which he was executed, read 'This is the king of the Jews.' (Luke 23:38) Of course the Jewish accusation was partly a lie. Jesus neither perverted the nation nor prohibited tribute to Caesar. Yet he did claim to be a king, indeed the King, God's King. And the Jewish leaders perceived something of the implications of his claim to kingship. Indeed, the Jews later continued the same campaign against his apostles. 'These men . . . have turned the world upside down,' they complained in Thessalonica. That is, they are political subversives, for 'they are all acting against the decrees of Caesar, saying that there is another king, Jesus.' (Acts 17:6, 7) Was it a slander? Or was the accusation true? It was both. Of course the apostles were not inciting the people to revolt. But they were proclaiming the supreme kingship of Jesus, and this necessarily meant denying to Caesar that which he coveted most, namely the absolute homage of his subjects, even their

164

worship. It meant, further, that King Jesus had a community of subjects who looked to him for directions about their values, standards and lifestyle; who knew they had a responsibility to be the world's salt and light; and who were prepared, whenever there was a collision between the two communities and their two value-systems, to defy Caesar and follow Christ, even at the cost of their lives. It was all very alarming to the political establishment whose chief concern was to maintain undisturbed the social status quo.

Yet these arguments will not convince my objectors. Even granted the rival kings and the alternative communities, they will say, Jesus and the apostles still did not instruct Caesar how to conduct his business, nor suggest how the law-code of the Roman Empire should be improved, nor even demand the abolition of slavery. No, it is quite true, they did not. But surely we are not going to argue from this that they condoned slavery (to continue with this example), and that those Christian politicians who finally succeeded in securing its abolition, first in Britain and then in the United States, were mistaken in their understanding of their duty and had no mandate from Christ for what they did? My objectors will certainly not pursue this line of argument. No, we surely all agree that William Wilberforce and his friends had discerned God's mind and were doing God's will in their courageous activity; that they correctly deduced from Scripture that slavery (the ownership of one human being by another) is incompatible both with the Christian doctrine of man and with the 'justice' which Paul himself required slave owners to give their slaves (Col. 4:1); and that they were rightly encouraged from Christian pulpits to translate these biblical principles into practice. So they campaigned, with indomitable perseverence, not only for the abolition of the slave-trade ('this most detestable and wicked practice' Wilberforce called it[39]) but also for the emancipation of the slaves.

Why then did Christians not make this deduction from Scripture and get rid of this evil centuries earlier? Leaving aside the tragedy of blind spots, the principal difference between New Testament times and the nineteenth century lies in the social status and political power of Christians. In the early centuries Christians were a tiny, persecuted, powerless minority. Direct political activity was out of the question for them. It is the same with Christians in many countries today, whose prevailing culture is Marxist, Moslem, Hindu, Buddhist or secular. In many such situations either there is no democratic government, or if there is, there are no (or extremely few) Christians in parliament. In such a state of political powerlessness, Christians can preach and teach, argue and persuade (though with differing degrees of liberty), and seek to exhibit their beliefs and standards in consistent Christian lives and homes. But they can take no direct political action.

What are we to say about the West, however, and about some countries of the Third World, where professing Christians are actually in a majority and the culture has been substantially Christian for centuries? Surely in this situation our Christian responsibilities are quite different. Although it is hardly the responsibility of a church or denomination as such to engage in direct political action, yet Christian individuals and Christian groups should be doing so, and should be encouraged from the pulpit to do so. For Christians should avoid the two opposite mistakes of *laissez faire* (making no Christian contribution to the nation's political well-being) and imposition (trying to force a minority view on an unwilling majority, as with the American liquor laws during the period of Prohibition). Instead, we remember that democracy means government with the consent of the governed, that 'consent' means majority public opinion, and that public opinion is a volatile thing, which is open to Christian influence. Pessimists will respond that human nature is depraved (which it is), that Utopia is unattainable (which it is), and that socio-political activity is therefore a waste of time (which it is not). It is really absurd to say that social amelioration by Christian influence is impossible. For the historical record demonstrates the contrary. Wherever the Christian gospel has gone and triumphed, it has brought in its wake a new concern for education, a new willingness to listen to dissidents, new standards of impartiality in the administration of justice, a new stewardship of the natural environment, new attitudes to marriage and sex, a new respect for women and children, and a new compassionate resolve to relieve the poor, heal the sick, rehabilitate prisoners, and care for the aged and dying. Moreover, these new values become expressed, as Christian influence grows, not only in philanthropic enterprise but also in humane legislation. This is still far from being Utopia. Nor is it the 'social gospel' of old-fashioned liberalism which made the mistake of equating the Kingdom of God with Christianized society. No, the Kingdom of God is his rule over his redeemed people through Christ. But this new people with their new life, new vision and new power are meant to be the salt and light of the world. They can hinder social decay and spread the light of Christ's love, peace and righteousness, and so help to shape a society which is more pleasing to the God of compassion and justice than the society which it replaced.

I am not suggesting that the pulpit is the place in which precise political programmes are framed or from which they are commended. Rather that it is the preacher's responsibility to open up the biblical principles which relate to the problems of contemporary society, in such a way as to help everybody to develop a Christian judgment about them, and to inspire and encourage the opinion-formers and policy-makers in the congregation, who occupy influential positions in public life, to apply these biblical principles to their professional life. There may be politicians in the congregation, or lawyers, teachers, doctors, industrialists, business people, novelists, journalists, actors, radio and television producers and scriptwriters. The pulpit should help them to develop their Christian thinking and so to penetrate their segment of the human community more deeply for Christ.

What is certain is that the pulpit has political influence, even if nothing remotely connected with politics is ever uttered from it. For then the preacher's silence endorses the contemporary socio-political conditions, and instead of helping to change society and make it more pleasing to God, the pulpit becomes a mirror which reflects contemporary society, and the Church conforms to the world. The neutrality of the pulpit is impossible. We can find ample evidence to substantiate this fact in Paul Welsby's anthology of forty-five Anglican sermons preached during the 400 years ending in 1947, published under the title *Sermons and Society*. He begins his preface with these words:

> The object of this anthology is to illustrate the attitude of Anglican preachers, from the Reformation onwards, towards social conditions in this country. In the process of reading their sermons we can also see, through the eyes of the preacher, what life in England was like at the time the sermon was preached.[40]

Some preachers acquiesced in the status quo, while others denounced it. Some disapproved of reform, while others actively promoted it. Their sermons tell us something, therefore, about both society and the Church, and about the impact of each on the other. For most of this long period, sad to relate, 'the social teaching of the Church had ceased to count, because the Church itself had ceased to think.' That was the judgment of R. H. Tawney which Paul Welsby quotes.[41] Only from the end of the nineteenth century, he argues, did the Church of England become more influential for social change.

Handling Controversial Questions

If, then, we are to include in our preaching themes which have social, moral and political implications, how shall we

168

handle the controversial ones? It is indubitable that even equally biblical Christians, with an equal desire to discover the mind of God in the Word of God and to submit to it when discovered, come to different conclusions and find themselves in painful disagreement with each other. How, then, should we tackle such topics? We can go any one of three ways.

First, we can avoid these topics altogether. 'Controversy has no place in the pulpit,' we may say. 'I want to be able to preach with authority, to echo the prophetic formula "Thus says the Lord" or to declare with dogmatism "The Bible says". But I cannot preach on these subjects with authority, partly because they are acknowledged to be controversial even among Christians, and partly because I do not possess the necessary knowledge or expertise to do so. I have no alternative, therefore: I will avoid them.'

This attitude is understandable, but irresponsible. Christian people are crying out for guidance in these areas. They want to be helped to think about them as Christians. Shall we abandon them to swim in these deep waters alone? This is the way of the coward.

Secondly, we can adopt a partisan position. In this case, if preaching about war, we will become an uncompromising pacifist (dove) or militarist (hawk); if preaching about economic realities, we will either defend capitalism or advocate socialism; or if preaching about the relations between man and woman, husband and wife, we will embrace either a total feminism or a total male chauvinism. This way we can preach with dogmatism and passion. Since we have a clear-cut position to commend, we can do so with all the eloquence and argument we can muster, meanwhile ignoring alternative viewpoints.

But this is to misuse the pulpit, which is for the exposition and application of God's Word, and neither for the ventilation of private opinions, nor for the pretension that we have the infallibility of a biblical prophet and apostle. It is also deceitful, because it gives the impression that there is only one position for biblical Christians to hold, and it conceals the fact that other biblical Christians think differently. This is the way of the dogmatist, and even, I think, of the fool.

Can we find a third way? Is there a way to handle controversial topics in the pulpit which is brave not cowardly, humble not dogmatic, and prudent not foolish? I think there is. It is to help Christians to develop a Christian mind. The Christian mind (an expression popularized by Harry Blamires in his book of that title) is not a mind which is thinking about specifically Christian or even religious topics, but a mind which is thinking about everything, however apparently 'secular', and doing so 'Christianly' or within a Christian frame of reference. It is not a mind stuffed full with pat answers to every question, all neatly filed as in the memory bank of a computer; it is rather a mind which has absorbed biblical truths and Christian presuppositions so thoroughly that it is able to view every issue from a Christian perspective and so reach a Christian judgment about it. Mr. Blamires bemoans the almost total loss of a Christian mind among Church leaders today: 'The Christian mind has succumbed to the secular drift with a degree of weakness and nervelessness unmatched in Christian history . . . As a *thinking* being the modern Christian has succumbed to secularization.'[42]

Preachers should facilitate the recovery of the lost Christian mind. For by our systematic exposition of the Bible over the years we should be giving our congregation a framework of truth. This will include such basic convictions as the reality and loving personality of the living God, the dignity of human beings by creation and their depravity by the fall, the pervasiveness of evil and the primacy of love, the victory and reign of Jesus Christ, the centrality of the new community in God's historical purpose, the transcience of time and the certainty of the *eschaton* of judgment and salvation. More simply, a mind may be said to be Christian when it has firmly grasped the fourfold biblical scheme of creation, fall, redemption and consummation, and is able to evaluate the phenomena of life in the light of it. So all our preaching, week in and week out, should gradually unfold 'the whole counsel of God' and so contribute to the development of Christian minds in the congregation.

How, then, does this task relate to controversial preaching? How can we help church members to think Christianly about a particular topic of debate? It seems that we have a fourfold duty. First, we must expound with courage, clarity and conviction the biblical principle or principles which are involved, and those aspects of the subject on which God has plainly revealed his will. Secondly, we should seek to summarize fairly the alternative applications which biblical Christians have made, and the arguments they have used to buttress their conclusions. Thirdly, we should feel free, if we judge it wise, to indicate which position we hold and why. And fourthly, we should leave the congregation free, after grasping the principles we have taught and weighing the issues we have sketched, to make up their own minds.

My first illustration comes from the Middle East. On two or three occasions I have had the opportunity to travel through several Arab countries, and so to experience at first hand the Arab–Israeli tension, and feel something of the Arab sense of injustice over the Palestinian question. How should Arab Christians react to this situation? I was asked. And what should their pastors say about it? It seems to me that it would not be possible either to banish from the pulpit what is the main topic of conversation outside it, or to adopt an extreme partisan position as if justice were entirely and exclusively on one side, although I believe there are pastors following both these courses. It is perhaps presumptuous for an outsider like myself to express an opinion on such a delicate situation, but after discussion with some local Christian leaders I feel able to say something like this. On the one hand, there are certain plain truths of Scripture which pastors should be preaching with confidence, e.g. that the God of the Bible is the God of justice and does not condone injustice in any individuals or nations; that personal hatred and revenge are completely forbidden to Christians, that Jesus commanded his followers to love their enemies, and to express their love constructively in deeds and prayers; that therefore every Christian Arab church which meets for worship should spend time specifically praying for Israel, and every Christian group in Israel should pray for their Arab neighbours; that Jesus expects his disciples to bear unjust suffering patiently and without retaliation; that he calls them to be peacemakers; and that Christians who obey all this teaching of Jesus (whether Jews or Arabs) would have to disassociate themselves from the blind, vindictive fanaticism of many of their compatriots, and might therefore be misunderstood, accused of being unpatriotic, and vilified. None of this teaching could be called controversial.

On the other hand, perplexing areas of controversy remain, on which the Christian pastor would need to be much more tentative. What does the Bible teach about nations, about national sovereignty over territory in general, and in particular about the right to occupy the promised land? Is it ever right to seek to secure justice by violent means? Should Christians in the militia ever shoot to kill? What constructive Christian peacemaking is possible? In these areas the pastor would have to open up the debate. On the issue of violence and pacifism, for example, he would have to concede that throughout Church history Christians have ranged themselves on opposite sides; that although all Christians condemn war as evil and agree that it is wrong to kill innocent civilians, some have gone further and urged that the way of the cross demands the unconditional renunciation of violence, while others have developed the theory of the 'just war', namely that war may be in certain specific situations (relating especially to its object, the means employed, the suffering involved and the outcome anticipated) the lesser of two evils. Church members would have to be encouraged to face the issue, consider the arguments and reach their own conclusion.

Perhaps, as a second example, I could take the Western debate over abortion. If one were preaching about this, the plain biblical principle to teach with authority would be the sanctity of human life. That is, the reason why murder is regarded in Scripture as such a heinous crime is not so much because of the sanctity of all life (which, carried to its extreme, is more a Buddhist than a Christian concept) as because of the sanctity of *human* life, 'for God made man in his own image'. (Gen. 9:6) The area of debate concerns the point at which the foetus should be regarded as a human being. The Roman Catholic position is that from the moment of fusion a full human being exists, with both body and soul. The Protestant view is that certainly God knew us before we were born; that it is he who formed us in our mother's womb (Psalm 139:13–16); and that the foetus from the moment of fusion is at the very least a 'human being in the making'. Protestant theologians have therefore emphasized that the unborn child (and not the mother only) has 'rights' which must be protected. On these grounds they have not only regarded 'abortion on demand' with horror, but have also opposed all abortions except in the rare cases when a choice has to be made between the mother's life and that of the unborn child. Whether there are other extreme cases in which a medical termination of pregnancy may be morally justified (e.g. when a young, unmarried girl is pregnant after being raped) is a matter of anxious, conscientious debate. But Christians will find it easier to reach a decision in such cases when their Christian mind has strongly grasped the sanctity of the life of Godlike human beings both when they are 'in the making' and when they are fully developed.

Our task as preachers, then, is neither to avoid all areas of controversy, nor to supply slick answers to complex questions in order to save people the bother of thinking. Either way is to treat them like children who are unable to think for themselves, and to condemn them to perpetual immaturity. Instead, it is our responsibility to teach them with clarity and conviction the plain truths of Scripture, in order to help them develop a Christian mind, and to encourage them to think with it about the great problems of the day, and so to grow into maturity in Christ.

Conscientious thought and decision-making are an indispensable aspect of human maturity, which is the reason for the so-called 'non-directive' element in modern counselling procedures. To make choices for other people is to treat them as children and keep them as such; to help them make their own choices is to treat them as adults and help them to become such. Christian teachers and preachers need to do their utmost to safeguard this human freedom, and defend it against the inhuman manipulations of the secular world, such as we see in some forms of advertizing and of education.

In his famous book *The Hidden Persuaders*, subtitled 'an introduction into the techniques of mass-persuasion through the unconscious', the author and journalist Vance Packard described Americans as 'the most manipulated people outside the Iron Curtain'[43] because of their constant exposure to 'mental-depth advertizers' or 'depth persuaders'. Using the findings of 'motivational research' (experiments relating to our subconscious reasons for making choices), he argues, merchandizers, public relations experts, fund raisers, politicians, industrialists and others are systematically exploiting our hidden frailties (e.g. our vanity, ambition, fears and sexual desires). The book is amusing. But it is also disturbing, because it uncovers the possibilities of persuading people beneath the surface of their conscious mind. 'Large-scale efforts are being made,' Vance Packard writes, 'often with impressive success, to channel our unthinking habits, our purchasing decisions, and our thought processes by the use of insights gleaned from psychiatry and the social sciences.'[44] Whether we are thought of as 'consumers'[45] or as 'citizens',[46] the hidden persuaders are at work, trying 'to invade the privacy of our minds'.[47]

The other sphere of manipulation is education. Many have written about it. But the author I have chosen to illustrate this danger is Paulo Freire, who was born in Recife, North-East Brazil, in 1921. Experiencing himself the pangs of hunger when he was a boy of only eleven, he vowed to fight against hunger in the world. He became Education Secretary and General Coordinator of Brazil's 'National Plan of Adult Literacy', but after the military coup of 1964 he was first jailed and then exiled. Since then he has worked in Chile, at Harvard and in Geneva. His main concern is what he calls 'the culture of silence', that is, the condition of ignorance and passivity in which the Latin American masses are submerged. So in his book *Pedagogy of the Oppressed* he advocates their 'conscientization', an educational process in which they first perceive their social reality with accuracy and then take action to transform it. Now Paulo Freire is evidently a Marxist, and there are therefore some features of his book which I find distasteful and unacceptable. Yet I do not think his Marxist commitment gives us any reason to reject his main educational thesis. He contrasts two concepts of education. The first is 'narrative education', so called because it involves 'a narrating subject (the teacher) and patient, listening objects (the students)'. It turns students into 'containers' or 'receptacles' which the teachers proceed to fill. 'Education thus becomes an act of depositing, in which the students are the depositories and the teacher is the depositor. Instead of communicating, the teacher issues communiqués. This is the "banking" concept of education.'[48]

The alternative concept, which Paulo Freire himself advocates, he calls 'problem-posing' as opposed to 'deposit-making'.[49] It presupposes a dialogical situation in which teachers and students together confront reality and help each other to reflect on it critically. He sums up the difference between the two concepts in this way:

Whereas banking education anaesthetizes and inhibits creative power, problem-posing education involves a constant unveiling of reality. The former attempts to maintain the *submersion* of consciousness; the latter strives for the *emergence* of consciousness and *critical intervention* in reality.[50]

Further, it is here that man is most clearly to be distinguished from the animals. Animals, he argues, are 'a-historical' because they can neither reflect on their situation, nor 'set objectives', nor 'commit themselves' purposefully to the transformation of reality. By contrast, human beings are aware of themselves and of the world, and can set objectives for change.[51] Again, 'animals do not consider the world; they are immersed in it. In contrast, men emerge from the world, objectify it, and in so doing can understand and transform it with their labour.'[52] Without this reflection and action they would not be fully human. For it is by thinking and acting that they cease to be mere objects of the domination and manipulation of others, and themselves become subjects, taking history into their own hands.[53]

In both advertizing and educating, then, it is possible either to manipulate people or to serve them, either to dehumanize them or to help them to grow into human maturity. The same alternative confronts the preacher. It is true that preaching is a different process, and indeed unique because it involves handling the inspired and authoritative Word of God. And yet we must never wield the authority of God's Word in such a way as to destroy people's humanness. For God himself, out of love for the people he has made in his own image, addresses us as human beings. He respects the mind and will he has given us; he refuses to coerce us, and instead asks for our thoughtful, loving and free response. Is this not the reason why the biblical writers encourage their readers to develop critical listening? Elihu was right to say that 'the ear tests words as the palate tastes food', namely with a view either to savouring it or to spitting it out. As with food, so with ideas, Elihu continues, 'let us choose what is right; let us determine among ourselves what is good.' (Job 34:1–4) Similarly in the New Testament, Christians were told to 'test the spirits to see whether they are of God', indeed to 'test everything', for only then could they 'hold fast what is good' and 'abstain from every form of evil'. (1 John 4:1; 1 Thess. 5:19–22) That is, even messages claiming to be inspired had to be evaluated in the light of apostolic teaching. In this way Christian knowledge and discernment would gradually grow, and Christians would become 'mature', having 'their faculties trained by practice to distinguish good from evil'. (Phil. 1:9, 10; Heb. 5:14)

We who are called to be Christian preachers today should do all we can to help the congregation to grow out of dependence on borrowed slogans and ill-considered clichés, and instead to develop their powers of intellectual and moral criticism, that is, their ability to distinguish between truth and error, good and evil. Of course we should encourage an attitude of humble submission to Scripture, but at the same time make it clear that we claim no infallibility for our interpretations of Scripture. We should urge our hearers to 'test' and 'evaluate' our teaching. We should welcome questions, not resent them. We should not want people to be moonstruck by our preaching, to hang spellbound on our words, and to soak them up like sponges. To desire such an uncritical dependence on us is to deserve the fierce denunciation of Jesus for wanting to be called 'rabbi' by men. (Matt. 23:7, 8) By contrast, the people of Beroea are commended as 'noble', more noble in fact than the Thessalonians, because they combined enthusiastic receptivity with critical listening: 'they received the word with all eagerness, examining the Scriptures daily to see if these things were so.' (Acts 17:11)

This kind of open but questioning mind is implicit even in the 'pastoral' metaphor. Sheep, it is true, are often described as 'docile' creatures, which may be so, but they are fairly discriminating in what they eat, and are certainly not uncritically omnivorous like goats. Moreover, the way in which the shepherd feeds them is significant. In reality, he does not feed them at all (except perhaps in the case of a sick lamb which he may take up in his arms and bottle-feed); instead he leads them to good grazing pasture where they feed themselves.

*   *   *

In conclusion, let me summarize the principal features of a preaching ministry which is conceived as an activity of bridge-building between the revealed Word and the contemporary world. Such preaching will be authoritative in expounding biblical principles, but tentative in applying them to the complex issues of the day. This combination of the authoritative and the tentative, the dogmatic and the agnostic, conviction and open-mindedness, teaching the people and leaving them free to make up their own minds, is exceedingly difficult to maintain. But it seems to me to be the only way on the one hand to handle the Word of God with integrity (declaring what is plain, but not pretending that everything is plain when it is not) and on the other to lead the people of God into maturity (by encouraging them to develop a Christian mind, and use it).

Notes

1 1 Cor. 1:23; 2 Cor. 4:5 cf. Isa. 40:9; 52:7.
2 cf. 2 Cor. 5:20; Eph. 6:20.
3 1 Cor. 4:1, 2; cf. 1 Tim. 3:4, 5; Titus 1:7.
4 cf. Ezekiel 34; John 21:15 ff.; Acts 20:28–31.
5 Forsyth, p. 22.
6 Eliot, pp. 43, 121.
7 McGregor, pp. 45, 46.
8 Coggan, *Stewards*, p. 70.
9 Quoted from Bishop W. S. Swayne's *Parson's Pleasure*, 1934, p. 79 in Smyth, *Garbett*, p. 470.
10 Spurgeon, *Lectures*, First Series, pp. 78, 79.
11 I do not like the stereotypes that labels perpetuate, but I do not know how to avoid them.
12 Fant, *Bonhoeffer*, p. 107.
13 Miller, J., *McLuhan*, p. 113.
14 Paget, pp. vii, 145.
15 Williams, W., *Reminiscences*, p. 145.
16 Horne, pp. 135, 144–5.
17 Dwight, Vol. 1, p. 606.
18 Henson, *Robertson*, p. 19.
19 ibid., p. 66.
20 ibid., p. 92.

21 Henson, *Church and Parson*, pp. 60, 61.
22 Brooks, *Lectures*, pp. 220–1.
23 Barth, pp. 100–4.
24 Ramsey and Suenens, *The Future*, pp. 13, 14.
25 Spurgeon, *Lectures*, Third Series, p. 54.
26 Von Allmen, pp. 20–9.
27 Brilioth, p. 3.
28 Stalker, p. 107.
29 Lloyd-Jones, *Warfare*, p. 109.
30 Pitt-Watson, p. 57.
31 Neill, p. 74.
32 Stalker, p. 199.
33 Baxter, *Reformed Pastor*, p. 136.
34 Spurgeon, *Lectures*, First Series, pp. 82, 83.
35 Spurgeon, *All-Round Ministry*, pp. 117, 127.
36 Eph. 5:21–6:9; Col. 3:18–4:1; 1 Pet. 2:18–3:7.
37 Gen. 2:24; Mark 10:5–9; 1 Thess. 4:3–5.
38 Jas. 2:14–18; 1 John 3:17, 18; 2 Cor. 8:1–15.
39 Pollock, *Wilberforce*, p. 53.
40 Welsby, p. 9.
41 *Religion and the Rise of Capitalism* by R. H. Tawney (Pelican 1938), p. 171, in Welsby, p. 16.
42 Blamires, p. 3.
43 Packard, p. 9.
44 ibid., p. 11.
45 ibid., Part 1.
46 ibid., Part 2.
47 ibid., p. 216.
48 Freire, pp. 45–6.
49 ibid., p. 52.
50 ibid., p. 54.
51 ibid., pp. 70–3.
52 ibid., p. 96.
53 ibid. *See* pp. 97, 101, 135.

CHAPTER FIVE

The Call to Study

If we are to build bridges into the real world, and seek to relate the Word of God to the major themes of life and the major issues of the day, then we have to take seriously both the biblical text and the contemproary scene. We cannot afford to remain on either side of the cultural divide. To withdraw from the world into the Bible (which is escapism), or from the Bible into the world (which is conformity), will be fatal to our preaching ministry. Either mistake makes bridge-building impossible and non-communication inevitable. Instead, it is our responsibility to explore the territories on both sides of the ravine until we become thoroughly familiar with them. Only then shall we discern the connections between them and be able to speak the divine Word to the human situation with any degree of sensitivity and accuracy.

Such exploration means study. There is no doubt that the best teachers in any field of knowledge are those who remain students all their lives. It is particularly true of the ministry of the Word. 'None will ever be a good minister of the Word of God unless he is first of all a scholar.' (Calvin)[1] Spurgeon had the same conviction. 'He who has ceased to learn has ceased to teach. He who no longer sows in the study will no more reap in the pulpit.'[2]

There is a freshness and a vitality about every sermon which is born of study; without study, however, our eyes become glazed, our breath stale and our touch clumsy. 'The preacher's life must be a life of large accumulation,' said Bishop Phillips Brooks in his 1877 Yale Lectures. He went on:

He must not be always trying to make sermons, but always seeking truth, and out of the truth which he has won the sermons will make themselves . . . Here is the need of broad and generous culture. Learn to study for the sake of truth, learn to think for the profit and the joy of thinking. Then your sermons shall be like the leaping of a fountain, and not like the pumping of a pump.[3]

The best-known living evangelist addresses the same exhortation to preachers today. Speaking to about 600 clergy in London in November 1979, Billy Graham said that, if he had his ministry all over again, he would make two changes. People looked startled. What could he possibly mean? First, he continued, he would study three times as much as he had done. He would take on fewer engagements. 'I've preached too much,' he said, 'and studied too little.' The second change was that he would give more time to prayer. Moreover, in making these emphases, he must have been deliberately echoing the apostolic resolve: 'we will devote ourselves to prayer and to the ministry of the Word.' (Acts 6:4) Because afterwards I commented appreciatively on what he had said, Dr. Graham wrote to me the following day and added: 'I remember that Dr. Donald Grey Barnhouse (of Tenth Presbyterian Church, Philadelphia) once said: "If I had only three years to serve the Lord, I would spend two of them studying and preparing."'

Bible Study

Since the Christian pastor is primarily called to the ministry of the Word, the study of Scripture is one of his foremost responsibilities, to which he commits himself at his ordination. This is very plain in the Church of England Ordinal of 1662. In his exhortation to the candidates the Bishop says:

Seeing that you cannot by any other means compass the doing of so weighty a work, pertaining to the salvation of man, but with doctrine and exhortation taken out of the holy Scriptures, and with a life agreeable to the same, consider how studious ye ought to be in reading and learning the Scriptures . . . We have good hope that you have well weighed and pondered these things with yourselves long before this time; and that you have clearly determined, by God's grace, to give yourselves wholly to this Office, whereunto it hath pleased God to call you: so that, as much as lieth in you, you will apply yourselves wholly to this one thing, and draw all your cares and studies this way; and that you will continually pray to God the Father, by the mediation of our only Saviour Jesus Christ, for the heavenly assistance of the Holy Ghost; that, by daily reading and weighing of the Scriptures, ye may wax riper and stronger in your ministry . . .

The higher our view of the Bible, the more painstaking and conscientious our study of it should be. If this book is indeed the Word of God, then away with slovenly, slipshod exegesis! We have to make time to penetrate the text until it yields up its treasures. Only when we have ourselves absorbed its message, can we confidently share it with others. God spoke to Samuel when he listened to God; then, when Samuel spoke to Israel, they listened to him. (1 Sam. 3:9–4:1) Similarly, before Ezekiel was in a position to speak God's Word to the people, he had himself to devour and digest it. God said to him: 'Son of man, . . . eat this scroll, and go, speak to the house of Israel.' (Ezek. 3:1)

Our Bible study should have at least three characteristics.

First, it must be *comprehensive*. A man 'does not qualify to be a preacher of the Word', John Huxtable has written, 'by making weekly sallies into the good book to discover some peg on which to hang some scattered observations about men and affairs.'[4] Sporadic and haphazard dipping into the Scriptures is not enough. Nor must we limit ourselves to our favourite passages, or concentrate on the microscopic examination of a few key texts. Such selective knowledge and use of Scripture plays into the devil's hands. Every heresy is due to an overemphasis upon some truth, without allowing other truths to qualify and balance it. Biblical induction is the only safe way to begin theology, moving, that is, from a wide variety of particular texts to general conclusions. But it presupposes a thorough knowledge of the diverse particularities of Scripture. It is in this way that the grand themes of Scripture emerge. Only then are we ready for a more deductive approach, as we view each part in the light of the whole.

I am personally grateful to Dr. Martyn Lloyd-Jones, formerly minister of Westminster Chapel, for introducing me perhaps twenty years ago to Robert Murray McCheyne's 'Bible Reading Calendar'. McCheyne produced it in 1842 for the members of St. Peter's Church in Dundee, Scotland, which he was serving at that time.[5] It enables one to read the whole Bible through every year, the Old Testament once and the New Testament twice. As Dr. Lloyd-Jones has subsequently written in *Preaching and Preachers*, 'I would say that all preachers should read through the whole Bible in its entirety at least once every year . . . That should be the very minimum of the preacher's Bible reading.'[6] McCheyne's lectionary sets four chapters to be read daily. His intention in those tranquil Victorian days was for two to be read in private devotions (morning and evening) and the other two in family prayers (also morning and evening) every day. My own practice has been rather to take three chapters each morning, if possible reading two and studying the third, and to keep the fourth chapter for the evening. What is particularly helpful about McCheyne's scheme is the way in which he allocates the chapters. We do not begin on 1 January with Genesis 1–4, continuing with Genesis 5–8 on 2 January and Genesis 9–12 on 3 January. Instead, we start on New Year's Day with the four great beginnings of Scripture, namely Genesis 1 (the birth of creation), Ezra 1 (the re-birth of the nation), Matthew 1 (the birth of the Christ) and Acts 1 (the birth of the Christian Church). In this way we follow the parallel lines of God's unfolding purpose. One day we may be reading about the patriarchs, Esther, the ministry of Jesus and the Pauline journeys; on another day we may be following the fortunes of the monarchy, listening to the message of a prophet, studying John's portrait of Jesus, and peering into the future disclosed by the Revelation. Nothing has helped me more than this to survey the rolling landscape of Scripture, and to grasp its underlying and recurring themes.

If we hope to help our congregation to develop a Christian mind, we have to develop one ourselves. And the only way to do this is to soak our mind in the Scriptures. 'Be masters of your Bibles, brethren,' said Spurgeon to his students; 'whatever other works you have not searched, be at home with the writings of the prophets and apostles. "Let the Word of God dwell in you richly." '[7] 'To understand the Bible should be our ambition; we should be familiar with it, as familiar as the housewife with her needle, the merchant with his ledger, the mariner with his ship.'[8] Again, 'it is blessed to eat into the very soul of the Bible until, at last . . . your blood is *Bibline* and the very essence of the Bible flows from you.'[9] This steeping of the mind in Scripture was a major secret of the powerful preachers of the past. 'Origen, the greatest scholar of the early Church . . . seems to have held the whole of Scripture in solution in his mind,' Bishop Stephen Neill has written, while Chrysostom's sermons contain 7,000 quotations from the Old Testament, and 11,000 from the New.[10]

If our study of the Bible must be comprehensive, it must also be *open-minded*. That is, we must genuinely desire through our Bible reading to hear and heed God's Word, without distorting its meaning or avoiding its challenge. How is this possible? So far, in thinking of preaching as a bridge-building exercise between the biblical and modern worlds or cultures, we have concentrated on the need to relate the one to the other. But we have said little about the third factor in the operation, namely the bridge-builder himself who may belong to yet another culture. In fact, the exciting though demanding discipline of Christian communication is concerned with the interplay between these three cultures. The preacher or evangelist says to himself: 'How can I, who have been brought up in one culture, take a particular biblical text which was given in a second culture, and expound it to people who belong to a third culture, without either falsifying the message or rendering it unintelligible?' At this moment our concern is not so much with the exposition of Scripture, as with our personal reading and understanding of it. For this we have to take the two cultures involved with the utmost seriousness, namely, that of the biblical text on the one hand and our own who are seeking to interpret it on the other. It is the great merit of what is now referred to as the 'new hermeneutic' that it emphasizes this necessity.

To begin with, we have to transport ourselves back, by the use of both our knowledge and our imagination, into the biblical writer's context, until we begin to think what he thought and feel what he felt. Our responsibility is not to assimilate his views to ours, by reading our opinions back into what he wrote, but to assimilate our views to his, by struggling to penetrate into his heart and mind. In order to do this, we need more than imaginative insight into his situation; we need also to be self-critical with regard to ours. It is essential to give up the illusion that we come to the biblical text as innocent, objective, impartial, culture-free investigators, for we are nothing of the kind. No, the spectacles through which we look at the Bible have cultural lenses. And the mind with which we think about the Bible, however open we keep it, is not empty. On the contrary, it is filled with cultural prejudices. So, though we cannot altogether rid ourselves of our cultural inheritance, we should be aware of our cultural bias. We should also seek increasingly to ensure that the presuppositions with which we approach the Bible are not drawn from outside it (e.g. those of the humanist, the capitalist, the Marxist or the scientific secularist) but are Christian presuppositions supplied by the Bible itself.

Here, then, are two cultural horizons, that of the biblical author and that of the Bible reader. As Dr. Tony Thiselton sums up in his thoroughly researched and closely argued book *Two Horizons* (1980), 'understanding takes place when two sets of horizons are brought into relation to each other, namely those of the text and those of the interpreter.'[11] How, then, are they to relate? The expression 'the hermeneutical circle' has been used in a variety of ways, some of which are unacceptable because they give the impression that the interpreter controls the meaning of the text. But, on the contrary, it is the text which challenges the interpreter. The true 'hermeneutical circle' is a kind of dialogue between Scripture and us, in which Scripture is the senior partner, or a 'dynamic interplay between text and interpreters'. It is not difficult to grasp why this is necessary. When we approach the Bible, the questions we have in our minds, and the answers which we expect to get, are both determined by our cultural background. 'What is received back, however, will not be answers only, but more questions. As we address Scripture, Scripture addresses us. We find that our culturally conditioned presuppositions are being challenged and our questions corrected. In fact, we are compelled to re-formulate our previous questions and to ask fresh ones. So the living interaction proceeds.' As it does so, our understanding of God and of his will, our faith and obedience, continuously grow and deepen. It is 'a kind of upward spiral, in which Scripture remains always central and normative'.[12]

These are some of the implications of an 'open-minded' approach to Scripture. We have to open our minds wide enough to risk hearing what we do not want to hear. For we have been taught to come to the Bible for solace. Does not Paul himself write of 'the encouragement of the Scriptures' (Rom. 15:4)? So naturally we cherish the hope that through our Bible reading we shall be comforted; we have no wish to be disturbed. Hence we tend to come to it with our minds made up, anxious to hear only the reassuring echoes of our own prejudice. Moreover, it is not difficult to insulate ourselves against the challenges of God's Word, or to barricade ourselves against his unwelcome incursions. The very two cultures we have been thinking about – of Bible authors and Bible readers – can act like two layers of thick cushioning to protect us against the impact, sometimes the shock, of the Word he wants to speak to us. The first step towards opening ourselves up to his Word, is to be aware of the protective padding which has to be removed. We have to be willing for God himself to lay down the ground rules, and to decide what he wants to say to us, however uncongenial we may find it. We have no liberty to circumscribe him, or to suggest lines of demarcation within which we are prepared to negotiate. No, we have to break down the cultural barriers, and struggle to open our hearts and minds to listen to whatever he has to say.

Thirdly, our Bible study needs to be *expectant*. At least two conditions are hostile to the joyful expectancy with which we should come to the Scriptures. The first is pessimism, aroused in some by the current hermeneutical debate itself. The interpretation of Scripture now appears to them so complicated that they become cynical, and despair of ever gaining a true and balanced understanding of God's Word. But if the new hermeneutic had really put biblical interpretation beyond the reach of all but the professionals, then we would have to condemn it as a dangerous abberation. For Scripture is intended for ordinary people like us. Even First Corinthians, with all its profound teaching on doctrine, ethics and church order, was addressed to a Christian community to which 'not many wise' belonged. The new hermeneutic has not reversed the blessing of the Reformation, however, and taken Scripture out of the hands of the lay people again. A little patience in learning to grasp and apply its unfamiliar principles should cure us of premature pessimism.

The second condition which militates against expectancy is spiritual staleness, and this can be a major problem for all pastors. If we read through the whole Bible annually, then after a few years we feel we know it fairly well. The temptation is to become blasé and to come to our daily reading with no very lively expectation that God is going to speak to us through it. Instead, we should be confident, in the famous words of John Robinson, pastor of the separatists' church in Holland from which the Pilgrim Fathers sailed in the *Mayflower* in 1620, that God has 'more truth and light yet to break forth out of his holy Word'. We need therefore to 'present ourselves before the Lord' each day like the angels (Job 1:6; 2:1), to ask for an 'awakened ear' like his servant (Isa. 50:4), and to request him as Samuel did to speak, because his servant is listening (1 Sam. 3:10). We need to 'cry out for insight and raise our voice for understanding', to 'seek it like silver and search for it as for hidden treasures', for then we shall understand and 'find the knowledge of God'. (Prov. 2:3–5) Such seeking perseveres even in the face of an apparent rebuff. It lays hold of God like Jacob and refuses to let him go until and unless he blesses us. (Gen. 32:26) It is this spirit of eager and determined expectation which God honours. He promises to fill the hungry with good things; it is only the complacent whom he sends away empty-handed. (Luke 1:53) So we must not give in to spiritual staleness as if it were normal or even tolerable, but must pray for the refreshment of the Holy Spirit so that, if our appetite is blunt he will sharpen it, and if our heart is cold he will rekindle within us the fires of expectancy.

In this comprehensive, open-minded and expectant study, although the Bible itself is always our text bok, we shall of course take advantage of the many aids to biblical understanding which are available to us today. Books are the preacher's stock-in-trade. How widely we spread our theological reading will depend on the time we have available, and where we concentrate our studies will depend on our individual interests. In any case, since such a cataract of theological books pours off the presses of Europe and North America, we all have to be severely selective, which means that we need to look at the book reviews and ask each other for suggestions of the most important books.

We shall be wise to read old books as well as new, especially the Christian classics which expound biblical passages and doctrines, and which, having stood the test of time, are often more valuable than transitory modern writing. At the same time, we shall need to keep abreast of the modern theological debates, at least in general if not in the particulars, and through summary articles in journals if not by reading the books themselves. For these debates do not stay in academic ivory towers for long; they are soon given publicity on radio and television, and it is not long before they filter down into school textbooks. So our congregation will expect us not only to be aware of current controversy but also to be able to help them respond to it thoughtfully. History is another vital dimension of theological study. Few truths or heresies are new; most are a rehash of ancient ideas. Some knowledge of historical theology gives us a well-adjusted perspective from which to view the latest doctrinal fashions. Biography, too, brings balance, wisdom and encouragement, as we learn how God has dealt with other Christians in other times and places. And in all this reading, our objective is not so much the accumulation of knowledge as the stimulation to think Christianly.

As books get ever more expensive, Western city-dwellers are increasingly grateful for access to good public libraries. In addition, every local church should be able to manage a small lending and reference library, and pastors can lend books both to one another and to their church members.

As for the 'well contrived library' which John Wilkins, seventeenth-century Bishop of Chester, recommended clergy to build,[13] we shall probably concentrate on essential reference books, especially dictionaries and commentaries, to which we shall need to turn again and again.

I often find myself wishing that local clergy gatherings, whether denominational or interdenominational, could be more effective in stimulating thought. When we meet, we are no doubt obliged to transact some business, but we could also encourage one another in study. The second half

of the eighteenth century was the great time for the founding of societies for English clergy, especially evangelicals.
The first was Samuel Walker's 'Clerical Club' in Truro (c.
1750), whose purpose was to 'strengthen each other's hands
in the work of the Lord'. During the following years about
ten others arose in different parts of the country. 'Why may
we not meet to pray, when others meet to play at bowls?'
asked Thomas Robinson of Leicester. 'Why may we not
have deliberative assemblies, when others of our brethren
have their dancing and drinking assemblies? Why may we
not seek to edify one another, whilst they care not if they
corrupt one another?' The most famous and influential of
these clubs was the Eclectic Society, founded in 1783 by
John Newton, ex-sea captain and slave trader, but at that
time Rector of St. Mary Woolnoth in the City of London,
and his friends. They met every other Monday. 'We begin
with tea,' wrote Newton (the teapot is preserved in Church
Missionary House in London); 'then a short prayer introduces a conversation for about three hours upon a proposed subject, and we seldom flag.' He added that the
group deserved to be called the Royal Society since 'I trust
the members are all of the royal family, and the King
Himself condescends to meet with us.'[14]

The Modern World

Biblical and theological studies do not by themselves make
for good preaching. They are indispensable. But unless
they are supplemented by contemporary studies, they can
keep us disastrously isolated on one side of the cultural
chasm. David Read addressed himself to this danger when,
as Chaplain to the University of Edinburgh, he gave the
1951 Warrack Lectures. '"O for the wings of a dove! Far,
far away would I rove" is all too often the appropriate
anthem before the sermon,' he said. For frequently our
preaching sounds remote, detached from society, 'un-
touched by its agonies, immaculate in its irrelevant
ideals'.[15] He went on to give a young minister's description

190

of what he regarded as 'the ideal building-plan for church and manse'. Here it is:

> The salient feature was a long straight corridor with a door at one end leading out of the manse study and a door at the other end opening into the pulpit of the church, . . . the highway for the Word of the Lord, the straight path from the mind of the preacher to the hearts of his hearers.

No interruptions, no distractions. But, David Read went on,

> that theologically-cushioned, isolated study is a lethal chamber, and it is a dead word that is carried out along the corridor . . . not the living Word, spoken as it must be, from heart to heart and from life to life.[16]

He then added his own understanding of how sermons are born:

> It remains an axiom of Christian preaching that the road from study to pulpit runs through a living, demanding interrupting manse; out into the noisy street; in and out of houses and hospitals, farms and factories, buses, trains, cinemas . . . up between rows of puzzled people to the place where you are called to preach . . . For the living Word there is no by-pass road from study to pulpit.[17]

We need, then, to study on both sides of the divide. As Austin Phelps put it at the end of the last century, a thoroughly trained preacher is first a human being, at home among human beings, and then a scholar, at home in libraries: 'No other profession equals that of the pulpit in its power to absorb and appropriate to its own uses the world of real life in the present and the world of the past as it lives in books.' Phelps' whole series of lectures, published under the title *Men and Books*, was devoted to this theme, and to the need for preachers to exploit these two resources.[18]

I am glad for this emphasis that our study of the modern world begins with people, not books. The best preachers are always diligent pastors, who know the people of their district and congregation, and understand the human scene in all its pain and pleasure, glory and tragedy. And the quickest way to gain such an understanding is to shut our mouth (a hard task for compulsive preachers) and open our eyes and ears. It has been well said that God has given us two ears and two eyes, but only one mouth, so that he obviously intends us to look and listen twice as much as we talk.

> A wise old owl lived in an oak.
> The more he saw, the less he spoke;
> The less he spoke, the more he heard;
> Why can't we all be like that bird?

We need, then, to ask people questions and get them talking. We ought to know more about the Bible than they do, but they are likely to know more about the real world than we do. So we should encourage them to tell us about their home and family life, their job, their expertise and their spare-time interests. We also need to penetrate beyond their doing to their thinking. What makes them tick? How does their Christian faith motivate them? What problems do they have which impede their believing or inhibit them from applying their faith to their life? The more diverse people's backgrounds, the more we have to learn. It is important for us to listen to representatives of different generations as well as of different cultures, especially of the younger generation. The married pastor who has teenage children has no excuse not to be earthed in reality. Humble listening is indispensable to relevant preaching. It also makes preaching a co-operative enterprise as our knowledge of the Bible and other people's knowledge of the world combine to construct bridges.

I take it for granted that, in addition to careful listening, we shall read a daily or weekly newspaper (for many years now I have found a thorough reading of a weekly much more profitable than the cursory scanning of a daily), watch some television, and peruse the secular book reviews in order to discover the most influential contemporary books to get and read. It seems clear that we shall also find it necessary to see some of the most notable films and plays, since nothing mirrors contemporary society more faithfully than the stage and the screen.

Because I guess that some of my readers will have received their spiritual nurture, as I did, in a Christian sub-culture which frowns on the cinema and the theatre, it may be right for me at this point to anticipate possible criticism. First, a reader may ask, are there not some plays, films and books which we would be wise to avoid, lest we expose ourselves to unnecessary temptation? Yes, indeed there are. Although we have no liberty to legislate for others, we should certainly keep away from anything likely to upset our own moral or spiritual equilibrium. The teaching of Jesus about the offending eye, foot or hand still applies. So it is sensible to make careful enquiries about recommended novels and plays, in order to be discriminating in what we see and read. In the case of borderline plays and films, and of those whose influence is particularly insidious because its spirit of antichrist is more subtle than overt, I have found it helpful to go not alone but with a group of friends, for it is then easier to retain one's critical detachment and refuse to be sucked into the atmosphere.

Secondly, what about the 'weaker brother' (or sister), of whom Paul wrote so much to the Romans and Corinthians? Even if we feel ourselves to be strong enough to risk con-tamination, might not our example lead weak Christians astray? Yes, this is another important question. Scripture has much to say about our responsibility for other people, and about the power for good or evil of our example. One of our Lord's fiercest denunciations and most solemn warn-ings was reserved for anybody who causes 'little ones' (i.e.

children, either literally or spiritually) to stumble. It would be better for him to be drowned, he said. Nevertheless, we have to recognize that the 'weakness' of weaker brothers and sisters refers not to their will, so much as to their conscience. A weak conscience is an over-scrupulous conscience. And although, even when mistaken, it is not to be violated, it does need to be educated. If, therefore, we have 'weaker brethren' in our congregation, who would be offended by our going to the theatre or cinema, we have no one to blame but ourselves: it is up to us to educate or 'strengthen' their conscience!

Thirdly, some disagree with the call to study the modern novel, stage and screen because they consider it a compromise with fashion. They regard the quest for 'relevance' in preaching as a surrender to worldiness. Those who give in to it are dismissed as men-pleasers, whose main objective is to be trendy rather than godly. Once again, we need to heed this criticism. The lust for popularity is indeed imperious, and many of us are twentieth-century Pharisees who love 'the praise of men more than the praise of God'. (John 10:43) One of the most trenchant critics of this tendency was W. R. Inge, Dean of St. Paul's Cathedral from 1911 to 1934. Invited to lecture in 1911 on 'The co-operation of the Church with the spirit of the age', he declared in his diary that this topic was 'a red rag for me'. He went on, 'there are many spirits of the age, most of them evil' and 'if you marry the spirit of your own generation, you will be a widow in the next.'[19] This is a wise warning. But it does not condemn a study of contemporary trends. For what I am proposing is not co-operation with the spirit of the age, still less marriage to it, but rather an understanding of it with a view to confronting it with a relevant word from God.

Reading and Resource Groups

What kind of study, then, will increase our understanding of the modern world? I want to bear witness to the immense stimulus which I have myself received from the reading group which I helped to bring into being in 1974. It consists of about a dozen young graduates and professional people, and includes doctors, lawyers, teachers, a housing officer, an architect, a personnel manager and some post-graduate students. We meet monthly when I am in London, and at the end of each meeting decide what we will read before next time. Then we spend a whole evening together, sharing our reactions to the book, discussing its message and implications, and trying to develop a Christian response to it. Some of the books selected are written from a Christian perspective, like Jacques Ellul's *Violence* and *The Meaning of the City*, E. F. Schumacher's *Small is Beautiful*, Donald McKay's *Clockwork Image*, John Howard Yoder's *The Politics of Jesus*, Colin Morris's *Unyoung, Uncoloured, Unpoor* and John V. Taylor's *Enough is Enough*. Other books we have studied present some rival ideology to the evangelical Christianity we represent. We have read the *Koran*, tried to understand the contemporary appeal of eastern mysticism, studied other 'isms' with the help of James Sire's *The Universe Next Door*, been fascinated by the Yaqui way of knowledge advocated by Carlos Castaneda, felt the pull of Marxism through *Christians and Marxists* (the mutual challenge to revolution) by José Miguez Bonino, and looked at Hans Küng's liberal Roman Catholicism outlined with such erudition in his *On Being a Christian* (1977).

But we have tried to concentrate on secular rather than religious books, because the main purpose of our group is to help us understand the secular mind of the post-Christian West, in order to combat it with a Christian mind. I have tried, therefore, to encourage the group to take responsibility for each month's choice, and they have certainly selected some titles which I would otherwise never have heard of, like R. M. Pirsig's *Zen and the Art of Motor-cycle Maintenance*. We have profited from several analyses of modern culture like Theodore Roszak's *The Making of a Counterculture*, Charles Reich's *The Greening of America* and Alvin Toffler's *Future Shock*. We have tried to grapple with popular modern philosophers like Herbert Marcuse (the students' cult hero in the 1960s) and Erich Fromm. We have struggled to understand the issues involved in the debates about feminism, abortion and euthanasia, and we spent one sensational evening examining the evidence for U.F.O.s. We have also attempted to come to grips with popular novelists (different group members reading different works) like Camus, Kafka, William Golding, Hermann Hesse and John Fowles.

On several occasions we have been to a film or play instead of reading a book. *Star Wars* and *Close Encounters of the Third Kind* introduced us to the whole realm of science fiction, and *Whose Life is it Anyway?* and *Sentenced to Life* to the campaign for voluntary euthanasia and its opponents. Bergman's *Autumn Sonata* made a profound impact on us. We sat silently glued to our seats when it was over, overwhelmed by the tragic effects which being deprived of love has on successive generations in the same family. We had to walk to church and pray together, in order to relieve our pent-up emotions. We were deeply moved in *Kramer v. Kramer* by the tug-of-war over the custody of the child which divorce brings. Then that tragicomedian Woody Allen in his recent films, combining humour and humanity, searching for love yet bouncing helplessly from one sexual liaison to the next without finding it, has enforced for us the Christian truth that there is no authentic love without responsible commitment.

The experience of the reading group – of the books we have read, the films and plays we have seen, and the discussion they have provoked – has not only increased our understanding of the modern world, but excited our compassion for human beings in their lostness and despair, confirmed our Christian faith, and rekindled our sense of Christian mission. I commend the value of such a group to all my fellow-clergy. There can hardly be a congregation in any culture, however small, which could not supply a few thoughtful people to meet with their pastor to discuss the engagement of the church with the world, the Christian mind with the secular mind, Jesus Christ with his rivals. The London group has given me the necessary stimulus to read at least some of the books I ought to be reading and has provided me with some sharp-witted, warm-hearted young people as a congenial context in which to discuss the issues raised. They have helped to drag me into the modern world and have planted my feet on the soil of contemporary reality; I am very grateful to them.

In addition to the reading group which meets regularly, I have derived great benefit from several ad hoc resource groups. The staff team of All Souls Church, chaired by Michael Baughen the Rector, decided about two years ago that we should have a series of quarterly sermons entitled 'Issues Facing Britain Today' and invited me to preach them. The topics chosen were 'The Multi-Racial Dream', 'Work and Unemployment', 'Industrial Relations', 'The Arms Race' and 'The New International Economic Order'. Although I accepted the invitation (or challenge), I knew at once that I was out of my depth. To be sure, I cherished certain biblical convictions relating to these issues, but I had little factual knowledge of race relations or armaments or economics, and no personal experience of industry or unemployment. How, then, could I presume to address myself to such questions with integrity? Here was a situation in which I plainly needed help.

First, I needed some well-informed, up-to-date literature which would supply me with facts and figures, and also stimulate my thinking. Let me at this point defend the inclusion of factual non-biblical information in our sermons. Without it the biblical message is proclaimed into a vacuum. Thus, we can expound the Christian doctrine of work from the Bible, but our exposition becomes much more significant if we can set it against the background of rising unemployment. We can preach on Christ's command to his disciples to be peace-makers, but his call sounds much more urgent when we know the appalling size of the super-powers' arsenals. Again, we can teach from Scripture that God cares for the poor, defends the powerless, demands justice, and calls his people to generous sharing, but this message becomes much more poignant if we add that 800 million people in the world are destitute and that 10,000 die of starvation or related diseases every day. Similarly, we can summarize the biblical basis for world mission, and preach our hearts out in calling a congregation to pray, to give and to serve, but our appeal becomes much more compelling when we add that approximately 3,000 million people, about three-quarters of the world population, have had no adequate opportunity to hear and respond to the gospel.

Secondly, I felt the need before each quarterly sermon of discussion with an ad hoc group of specialists, who would be willing to spend a couple of hours with me. Each group was representative of different, and sometimes conflicting, viewpoints. Before the sermon on industrial relations, for example, it included a full-time union official who had previously been a shop steward and branch secretary, and now looked after nearly 6,000 workers, a postal union worker who was a chairman of his local branch, a man who had worked in a brewery for fifteen years both as a manager and as marketing director, and was now studying for the ordained ministry, a health insurance consultant and broker who had served both management and union members, and an economics lecturer specializing in the impact of inflation on the bargaining process, together with a doctoral student who had 'never done a paid day's labour in his life'. Then before the even more controversial topic of the arms race, the group included a committed pacifist from the Anabaptist tradition, a civil servant with a Ph.D. in war studies, a naval commander taking a mid-career course at the National Defence College, and a Chief Education Officer for the Army in one of the regions of England. The third example I would like to mention relates to the group advising me on the sermon about work and unemployment. It comprised an employer, a personnel controller (who had the unpleasant task of breaking the news to staff who were being made redundant), a young lecturer and researcher in economics, the Chaplain to the Oxford Street stores, an insurance company employee, and two people with experience of unemployment. One was a man who had worked as a journalist, a press officer and in public relations, and who was made redundant at the age of thirty-five. The other was a lady hospital worker, a graduate in chemistry with a diploma in social administration, who had been passionately committed to the cancer and disabled patients she served, but, despite assurances to the contrary, was made redundant with only two weeks' notice. Since then she had applied for forty-three jobs, had been granted only six interviews and was still unemployed. These two friends enabled me to see unemployment in personal rather than statistical terms. They helped me to feel what they felt – the shock, the rejection, the hurt, the humiliation and the sense of helplessness, which are all caused by unemployment.

Before each group assembled, it was essential for me to do a bit of preparatory homework myself, so that I could identify some key issues and formulate the questions I wanted to put to them. The discussion was invariably lively, and on a number of occasions I found myself sitting back and listening to the debate as it developed between different opinions. Eavesdropping in this way proved extremely stimulating and enlightening. In fact, the whole experience was creative, as we struggled to relate biblical principles and contemporary contexts to one another.

Let me try now to face head on the critical reaction which my suggestion of resource groups is likely to provoke in some clergy. Here is an overworked pastor in an inner city or industrial area, who is already stretched to capacity. He could not possibly contemplate adding to his work load, he says. Besides, his congregation consists of only twenty-five people, none of whom is a specialist in any field. In a situation like this a resource group would be out of the question: he lacks the time and they the expertise for such a thing.

In response, I certainly recognize that large urban and

suburban congregations are in a much better position to recruit resource groups. Yet I am very reluctant to concede that even the small inner city church and its hard-pressed pastor can manage nothing. If a carefully considered sermon on a current issue is impossible quarterly, is it really impossible annually? And if a congregation cannot produce from its own membership mature Christians who are specialists in their field, there must surely be some within reach who belong to other churches, but who would be willing to contribute their expertise to an occasional discussion group, and would even be surprised and gratified to be asked to do so?

At all events, I am convinced that there ought to be more co-operation between clergy and laity in the process of sermon-making, and that this is required by the New Testament picture of the Church as the multi-gifted Body of Christ.

As Michael Ramsey, formerly Archbishop of Canterbury, put it in a lecture in New York:

> The priest (i.e. the presbyter or pastor) is one who learns theology and teaches it. His study is deep and constant . . . His teaching of theology is not done *de haut en bas* for, while he teaches the laity what they do not know without his help, he must all the while be learning from them about the questions to which theology is applied. In this partnership of priest and laity, the authority of the priest to teach in Christ's name is a real authority, but it will be exercized with the humility of Christ and in the spirit of one who learns.[20]

Personally, I would go further than Dr. Ramsey in seeking to develop 'this partnership of priest and laity' and to express 'the humility of Christ'. It is not just that the laity ask the questions and we answer them, since we too have to ask our questions for them to answer. It is rather that, by asking each other questions, we from the biblical perspective and they from the contemporary, we may together discern what answers should be given if the Word is to be contextualized in the world.

Habits of Study

I have enlarged on the need to focus our studies on the two sides of the deep divide. We have to study both the ancient text and the modern scene, both Scripture and culture, both the Word and the world. So, alongside our systematic, comprehensive, open and expectant reflection upon the Bible, we shall listen, look and read, watch plays, films and television, and summon groups to our aid, in our endeavour to understand the human society in which and to which we are called to expound God's Word. It is a mammoth task. It demands a lifetime of study. How can it be done?

Our forebears managed it mostly by the studied neglect of distracting duties. Take Joseph Parker, the first minister of the City Temple in London. He began his studies at seven-thirty every morning. Moreover, he refused to get involved in public life or business. 'I have lived for my work,' he explained. 'That is all. If I had talked all the week, I could not have preached on Sunday. That is all. If I had attended committee meetings, immersed myself in politics and undertaken the general care of the Empire, my strength would have been consumed. That is all. Mystery there is none.'[21] Campbell Morgan, who had received no seminary education and obtained no university degree, was in his study by six o'clock every morning.[22]

Alexander MacLaren, the eloquent Baptist preacher in Manchester, who died in 1903, also declined many social and speaking engagements in order to concentrate on his study and preparation. But he added another explanation of his massive learning. It was that he was content to spend the early years of his pastorate in an isolated countryside situation. 'I thank God,' he said, 'that I was stuck down in a quiet, little, obscure place to begin my ministry.'[23] In that relative seclusion he was able to store up material for his future years which were spent in the busy limelight of Manchester.

We seem to live in a very different world, however. True, students were still being taught in the theological college I attended that the diligent pastor spends his mornings with his books and his afternoons in visiting. Some, I know, still succeed. But for myself, I found from the beginning that this was an impossible ideal to attain. I made valiant efforts, but I failed. Mornings? Why, on Sunday morning I was at public worship in church; on Monday morning there was a staff meeting; Tuesday was my day off; by Wednesday there were urgent letters to write; on Thursday morning I taught in our Church Day School; on Friday morning there was sure to be a funeral; and Saturday morning I had to reserve for actual sermon preparation. Thus the week went by without a single morning being free for those books which I was supposed to be reading. So I found myself obliged to lower my expectations and set myself more realistic goals. I have come to believe in the cumulative value of shorter periods of study. Thus, I doubt if any pastor is so busy that he cannot manage one hour a day for reading, in addition to his personal Bible study and prayer-time. Most will also find it possible to keep one four-hour period a week – whether a morning, an afternoon or an evening – for more prolonged study. It only needs the discipline of blocking off such a weekly period in one's engagement book, and refusing to allow it to be invaded, except by an emergency.

Next, I have discovered the immense profit of a quiet day at least once a month. I learned this from the Rev. L. F. E. Wilkinson during an address he gave at the Islington Clerical Conference in about 1951. It is the only thing I remember from the whole conference. But it came to me as a message from God. I had been precipitated into being Rector of All Souls at the age of twenty-nine, when I was much too young and inexperienced for such a responsibility. I began living from hand to mouth. Everything piled up and got on top of me. I felt crushed by the heavy administrative load. I started having the typical clerical night-mare: I was half-way up the pulpit steps when I suddenly realized that I had forgotten to prepare a sermon. Then came L. F. E. Wilkinson's address. 'Take a quiet day once a month,' he said, or words to that effect. 'Go away into the country, if you can, where you can be sure of being undisturbed. Stand back, look ahead, and consider where you are going. Allow yourself to be drawn up into the mind and perspective of God. Try to see things as he sees them. Relax!' I did. I went home, and immediately marked one day a month in my engagement book with the letter 'Q' for Quiet. And as I began to enjoy these days, the intolerable burden lifted and has never returned. In fact, so valuable did these days prove to be, that for many years now I have tried to manage one a week instead of only one a month. I keep for them those items which need unhurried and uninterrupted time – some long-term planning, some problem to think and pray over, some difficult letters to draft, some preparation, reading and writing. I could not exaggerate the blessing which these quiet days have brought to my life and ministry.

Now let me come to the question of our annual holiday. The famous preachers of the nineteenth century, so far as I can tell, used to take two months for their summer vacation, and during this lengthy period would sketch out their whole year's preaching and do a great deal of the initial preparation. Alexander Whyte of Edinburgh, for example, took 'never less than two, and in later years three, summer months' away from the city, 'and shorter times at Christmas and Easter'. He was working, not relaxing, however. These periods were 'closely packed with reading, meditation, and sometimes writing'.[24] Nowadays, a clergyman's holiday is considerably shorter. Yet in the course of it he should be able to read several books. Even a married man with a quiverful of children should be able to find some time each day for quiet reading and study.

Dr. Lloyd-Jones tells us in *Preaching and Preachers* not only that he usually took the latest Bampton Lectures or

Hibbert Lectures with him on holiday, but also that he struck a kind of bargain with his wife and children. 'They gave me the mornings to myself that I might do this (sc. some serious reading); then, having done that, I was prepared to do anything they proposed.'[25] The Council of All Souls Church agreed many years ago that the pastoral staff should be encouraged to take off at least an annual week in addition to their vacation, either to attend an education course or conference of some kind or simply for a bona fide reading week. Ought not every church to make a similar provision for its pastors, and thus recognize their indispensable need for time to study?

What I have suggested in the previous paragraphs seems to me to be an absolute minimum of time for study, which even the busiest pastors should be able to manage. Many will achieve more. But the minimum would amount to this: every day at least one hour; every week one morning, afternoon or evening; every month a full day; every year a week. Set out like this, it sounds very little. Indeed, it is too little. Yet everybody who tries it is surprised to discover how much reading can be done within such a disciplined framework. It tots up to nearly 600 hours in the course of a year.

Whatever habits of study we develop, it is obviously important to garner its fruits. 'A preacher has to be like a squirrel and has to learn to collect and store matter for the future days of winter.'[26] Every reader of books develops his own practice of marking, underlining or note-taking. As one passes through middle age into old age, and one's powers of recall abate, some means of aiding and jogging the memory become essential. I have found it helpful, while the theme of an important book is fresh in my mind, to make a brief synopsis of its argument. After finishing each book I also try not to begin another until I have written out, or asked my secretary to type out, a few of its striking quotations. For many years now these summaries and quotations have been preserved on five- by three-inch cards, which can be both stored in a cabinet and (being punched with two holes) fitted into a loose-leaf book. We all know the American definition of a filing system as 'a device for losing things alphabetically'. So I keep two files, the one running from Genesis to Revelation, and the other from A to Z, and file each card where I think I am most likely to find it again, or at any rate least likely to lose it. This system has served me well. It is both simple and flexible. I find I can get the notes of an average sermon on to four cards, and can then add other cards containing appropriate quotations or illustrations. If I were to begin my ministry again, I would adopt the same system. The only change I would make would be to up-grade the cards from five- by three-inch to six- by four-inch, as a concession to my deteriorating eyesight.

Hindrances to Study

Some readers may find themselves in disagreement even with the minimum suggestions I have made as a framework for study. 'I am far too busy,' someone may say. 'Your programme is hopelessly unrealistic for my situation. You refer to a pastoral team, a secretary and resource groups. But you don't realize how favoured you are. I have none of these luxuries. I'm entirely on my own.' Well, I cannot deny that I have been and am extremely favoured. Indeed, I cannot speak too strongly of the benefits of working in a team. Nevertheless, I must deny that being overworked and understaffed can properly be made an excuse for having no time to study. Almost always what lies behind this contention is a false or 'clericalist' image of the Church. If the pastor holds all the ecclesiastical reins in his own hands, and has no concept of a shared responsibility which involves lay leaders, then of course he has no time to study. But if he has grasped the New Testament image of the church as the Body of Christ, every member of which has been gifted for some form of ministry, then he will be continuously on the look-out for the gifts which God has given, in order to encourage people to recognize, develop and exercize them. 'As each has received a gift, employ it for one another, as good stewards of God's varied grace.' (1 Pet. 4:10) Even 'delegation' is the wrong word for this, since it suggests that the work is rightfully the pastor's but that he rather condescendingly deigns to hand some of it over to others. 'Partnership' is the more biblical concept, so that clergy and laity rejoice in the variety of gifts which God has given, and help each other to use their gifts and fulfil their callings for the building up of Christ's Body.

The Church of every generation has to re-learn the lesson of Acts 6. There was nothing wrong with the apostles' zeal for God and his Church. They were busily engaged in a Christlike, compassionate ministry to needy widows. But it was not the ministry to which they, as apostles, had been called. Their vocation was 'the ministry of the Word and prayer'; the social care of the widows was the responsibility of others. So the necessary adjustments were made. Today, of course, pastors are not apostles. Yet part of the apostles' teaching ministry does belong to pastors, and it is tragic to see many making the very same mistake which the apostles made. They are extremely conscientious people. In fact, they respond to every conceivable need, and feel guilty if they are not readily available to anybody at any time. One cannot fault their dedication, their enthusiasm or their commitment. And indeed the pastor *is* called to serve people, as Christ himself did. But they have forgotten that there were times when Jesus himself sent the crowds away, in order to withdraw into the mountains to pray. They have also allowed themselves to be deflected from another priority task to which Christ has called them, namely the ministry of the Word. Their energies and zeal are being channelled in other directions. At the same time, usually without realizing it, they are inhibiting gifted lay leaders by denying them the opportunity to serve. Overworked clergy and frustrated laity form a dangerous combination; the Body of Christ does not grow into maturity that way.

Writing thus about lay leadership, I am not only referring to social and administrative responsibilities, which in any case lay men and women usually undertake more competently than clergy, but also to a share in the pastoral oversight of the congregation, whether as elders or deacons or readers or lay preachers or leaders of fellowship groups or house churches. Just as in the beginning Paul appointed 'elders' (in the plural) in every church (Acts 14:23 cf. 20:17; Phil. 1:1) and instructed Titus to do the same in every Cretan town (Titus 1:5), so today every church should be pastored not by a single shepherd but by a team. In many cases, especially where inflation is hitting the church, the team may consist largely of lay people, together perhaps with one or two non-stipendiary clergy who are exercizing a so-called 'tent-making ministry', that is, supporting themselves. But the team is there, seeking to care for the church together.

At the same time, a congregation of any size needs to have on its team at least one full-time stipendiary pastor. The New Testament seems clearly to envisage this situation. Paul not only urges that he 'who is taught the word shares all good things with him who teaches' (Gal. 6:6; cf. 1 Tim. 5:17, 18), but he insists on the right of evangelists and pastors to be supported, though he had waived this right in his own case. (1 Cor. 9:1–18) The reason for a full-time paid pastorate is that, freed from the need to earn his own living, he is able to devote himself exclusively to the pastoral care of the people, and particularly to 'the ministry of the Word and prayer'. Such a ministry, involving individual counselling and group work, intercession and study, preparing and preaching, is extremely exacting. It cannot be satisfactorily accomplished by part-time pastors alone, although such are essential to the team. This was apparent already in Old Testament times. Thus King Hezekiah 'commanded the people who lived in Jerusalem to give the portion due to the priests and the Levites, that they might give themselves to the law of the Lord.' (2 Chron. 31:4) The same principle was carried over into New Testament days: 'No soldier on service gets entangled in civilian pursuits, since his aim is to satisfy the one who enlisted him.' (2 Tim.

2:4) It is these 'entanglements' which prevent a pastor from giving adequate time to his studies. A church without a full-time pastor, even when there is a team of part-timers, is bound to be impoverished. We need more full-timers, who 'labour in preaching and teaching'. (1 Tim. 5:17)

Supposing then a pastor has this support, what else could keep him from study? Let me be frank. Only one thing: laziness. Was it not Ralph Waldo Emerson who said that 'man is as lazy as he dares to be'? It is true. And we pastors can be very daring in this area, because we have no employer to supervise our work or to reproach us for our neglect of it. Besides, we have neither set tasks to do, nor set times in which to do them. We are our own master and have to organize our own schedule. So it is possible for us to fritter our days away, until our time-wasting lapses degenerate into a life of gross indiscipline. Moreover, it becomes painfully evident in our ministry. As Cyril Garbett remarked privately to a friend, while he was Bishop of Southwark (1919–32): 'I can always tell when the clergy have given up any serious attempt to read or think: it becomes obvious at about the age of forty-five. If a man is an Anglo-Catholic, he becomes a bigot; if he is an Evangelical, he becomes a sentimentalist.'[27]

Alexander Whyte spoke some stern words on this subject. He ministered for forty-seven years (1860–1907) at Free St. George's Church in Edinburgh. In 1898 he was Moderator of the General Assembly of the Church of Scotland, and in 1909, at the age of seventy-three, he accepted the Principalship of New College Edinburgh, in addition to his other responsibilities. He disciplined himself rigorously and abominated laziness in others. 'I would have all lazy students drummed out of the college,' he said in 1904, 'and all lazy ministers out of the Assembly . . . I would have laziness held to be the one unpardonable sin in all our students and in all our ministers.'[28] Then in his closing address at the end of the 1898 General Assembly, of which he was Moderator, he said:

We have plenty of time for all our work, did we husband our time and hoard it up aright . . . Did we work as many hours every day, and as hard, as the people who support us work? As early in the morning, and as late at night, and as hard all the livelong day? Oh no! We cannot look seriously at one another's faces and say it is want of time. It is want of intention. It is want of determination. It is want of method. It is want of motive. It is want of conscience. It is want of heart. It is want of anything and everything but time.[29]

So we need, as I find myself, constantly to repent, and to renew our resolve to discipline our lives and our schedule. Only a constantly fresh vision of Christ and of his commission can rescue us from idleness, and keep our priorities correctly adjusted. Then we shall make time to read and think, and, as the fruit of our conscientious studies, our preaching will be fresh, faithful and relevant, yet also simple enough for people to understand.

Notes

1 From his commentary on Deut. 5:23 ff.
2 Spurgeon, *All-Round Ministry*, p. 236.
3 Brooks, *Lectures,* pp. 159–60.
4 Huxtable, p. 25.
5 It is still available from the Banner of Truth Trust, 3 Murrayfield Road, Edinburgh, Scotland.
6 Lloyd-Jones, *Preaching*, p. 172.
7 Spurgeon, *Lectures*, Second Series, p. 25.
8 Spurgeon, *Lectures*, First Series, p. 195.
9 Day, p. 131.
10 Neill, p. 67.
11 Thiselton, p. 103.
12 *Willowbank Report*, p. 11.
13 *Ecclesiastes*, p. 31.
14 Hennell, p. 84. Josiah Pratt's Notes of the discussions of the Eclectic Society between 1798 and 1814, edited by his son John H. Pratt, were first published in 1856 and reissued by the

Banner of Truth Trust in 1978. The original Eclectic Society lapsed at some time in the middle of the nineteenth century. In April 1955, having recognized the need in our generation (which Newton saw in his) for 'mutual religious intercourse . . . and the investigation of spiritual truth', an invitation went out from All Souls Church, Langham Place, to twenty-two younger evangelical clergy to spend a day off together and to re-found the Eclectic Society. From that modest beginning it grew spontaneously until by 1966 it had a membership of over 1,000 in seventeen regional groups. It is now limited to evangelical clergy and laity under forty years of age, and is therefore smaller, but still influential.

15 Read, p. 47.
16 ibid., pp. 62–3.
17 ibid., p. 63.
18 Phelps, Preface and p. 3.
19 Inge, p. 12.
20 Ramsey and Suenens, *The Future*, p. 35.
21 Wiersbe, p. 56.
22 ibid., p. 133.
23 ibid., p. 37.
24 Barbour, p. 286.
25 Lloyd-Jones, *Preaching*, pp. 182–3.
26 ibid., p. 173.
27 Smyth, p. 167.
28 Barbour, p. 282.
29 ibid., pp. 284–5.

Note: Because of the indispensability of books to preachers, one of the principal projects of the Evangelical Literature Trust is the promotion of Pastors' Book Clubs in countries of the Third World. These enable members to buy a number of books each year at greatly reduced prices. (The E.L.T. address is c/o 12 Weymouth Street, London, W1N 3FB. England.)

CHAPTER SIX

Preparing Sermons

Once upon a time there was an Anglican clergyman who was lazy. He had long ago given up the bother of preparing his sermons. He had considerable native intelligence and fluency of speech, and his congregation were simple people. So he got by pretty well with his unprepared sermons. Yet in order to live with his conscience, he took a vow that he would always preach extempore and put his trust in the Holy Spirit. Everything was fine until one day, a few minutes before the morning service began, who should walk into church and find a place in one of the pews but the bishop, enjoying a Sunday off. The parson was embarrassed. He had managed for years to bluff his uneducated congregation, but he was much less sure of his ability to hoodwink the bishop. So he went over to welcome his unexpected visitor and, in an endeavour to forestall his criticism, told him of the solemn vow he had taken always to preach extemporaneous sermons. The bishop seemed to understand, and the service began. Half-way through the sermon, however, to the preacher's great consternation, the bishop got up and walked out. And after the service a scribbled note from the bishop lay on the vestry table: 'I absolve you from your vow'!

Then there was the young American Presbyterian minister, whose besetting sin was not laziness, but conceit. He frequently boasted in public that all the time he needed to prepare his Sunday sermon was the few minutes it took him to walk to the church from his manse next door. Perhaps you can guess what his elders did: they bought him a new manse five miles away!

My little ecumenical parable is not yet finished. For there

was a Baptist preacher who had no besetting sins like his Episcopal and Presbyterian colleagues. His trouble – if one may call it a trouble – was super-spirituality. He did not prepare his sermons either, but this had nothing to do with laziness or pride. On the contrary, it was due to genuine piety. Like his Episcopal brother he placed his confidence in the Holy Spirit, but unlike him he appealed for support to Scripture itself, not to a vow of his own. 'Have you not read the words of Jesus in Matthew 10:19 and 20?' he asked his friends in unfeigned astonishment, when they ventured to take him to task: '"Do not be anxious how you are to speak or what you are to say," Jesus commanded, "for what you are to say will be given you in that hour, for it is not you who speak but the Spirit of your Father speaking through you."' What this ingenuous brother failed to do, however, was to read his Lord's words in their context. They actually began, 'When they deliver you up', and refer not to the church, but to the law court. 'You will be dragged before governors and kings for my sake,' Jesus said (v. 18). In such a situation, he implied, we may have no time to prepare our defence. It is then that the Holy Spirit will give us words to speak. Jesus' promise has brought great comfort to prisoners who lack a counsel for the defence; it offers no comfort to preachers who are either too lazy or too proud or too pious to prepare their sermons.

I think we must agree with Spurgeon that 'habitually to come into the pulpit unprepared is unpardonable presumption.'[1] What would we think of a lawyer who enters court to defend his client without having prepared his case? J. H. Jowett quotes the dictum of a distinguished English judge that 'cases are won in chambers.' That is, 'so far as the barrister is concerned, his critical arena is not the public court but his own private room.' The same principle applies to the preacher: 'if the study is a lounge, the pulpit will be an impertinence.'[2]

The great preachers who have influenced their generation have all borne witness to the need for conscientious preparation. You might not think so as you listen to them. For as the sermon proceeds, it all sounds deceptively simple. The opening up of the text, its illustration and application, the straightforward outline, the framing of sentences and choice of words – what could be easier? Yet behind it lies a lifetime's discipline and industry. Let me give one example only. After the death of Dr. Leslie Weatherhead in the New Year of 1976, Roy Trevivian wrote an obituary or personal appreciation which appeared in the *Church of England Newspaper* on 9 January 1977. It included these words:

> What was the secret of his extraordinary influence with people? Poor and rich, powerful and dispossessed, known and unknown, all came and all received his undivided attention. And what was the secret of the spell he could cast over a huge congregation who had withdrawal symptoms when he finished preaching? I must have asked him this twenty times, and always he replied 'Preparation'.

How, then, shall we prepare? This is a very subjective matter. There is no one way to prepare sermons. Every preacher has to work out his own method, which suits his temperament and situation; it is a mistake to copy others uncritically. Nevertheless, we can learn from one another. As Erasmus once rather playfully said, 'If elephants can be trained to dance, lions to play, and leopards to hunt, surely preachers can be taught to preach.'[3] There seem, in fact, to be six stages through which, in one way or another, most of us find it necessary to pass.

(1) Choose Your Text

I take it for granted that we shall have a text. For we are not speculators, but expositors. Yet how shall we choose our text for a particular sermon? Many a preacher has asked that question as he sat at his desk, sucked and even chewed his pencil, and stared vacantly at a blank sheet of paper before him. Yet the headache in selection is due not to the paucity of texts but to their abundance. If we are regular Bible students, and are keeping notes of our study, then our memory becomes like a well-stocked food cupboard, and biblical texts are lining up, asking to be preached on. How, then, shall we make our selection? There are, it seems, four main factors which will influence our choice.

The first is *liturgical*. Large sections of Christendom (in particular, Roman Catholic, Orthodox, Lutheran and Anglican) continue to observe the seasons of the Church's year, which are set out in a calendar and supplied, Sunday by Sunday, with appropriate lections. In 1967 the British interdenominational 'Joint Liturgical Group' produced an essay entitled *The Calendar and Lectionary: A Reconsideration*.[4] The following year the Church of England's Liturgical Commission followed it up with their report *The Calendar and Lessons for the Church's Year*.[5] This advocated 'a more rational presentation of the Church's year in the pastoral interest of worshippers'.[6] Let me simplify its recommendations in a way which may appeal also to members of non-liturgical churches. Most Christians observe at least three major Christian festivals every year – Christmas (celebrating the birth of Christ), Easter (his resurrection) and Pentecost (his gift of the Spirit). Taking these as pivotal points, each has a natural preparation leading up to it and a natural sequel following it. In this way the Church's year divides itself into three periods.

The first, running from October to December, is a lengthened Advent season. Because in Europe the harvest festival normally comes at the end of September or beginning of October, and in America in November, this is a convenient time to think about creation, to go on to the fall, and to take the Old Testament story and expectation up to the birth of Christ and his 'epiphany' or manifestation to the Gentiles.

The second period runs from Christmas to Pentecost, and thus covers the months from January to May. It is the natural season in which to rehearse the mighty acts of God in Christ, his birth and life, character and example, words and works, passion and death, resurrection and ascension, culminating in the outpouring of the Holy Spirit.

The third period should be thought of more as 'the Sundays after Pentecost' than as 'the Sundays after Trinity'. From May to September inclusive we have the opportunity to think about the Christian life as life in the Spirit and the Christian Church as the fellowship of the Spirit. It is a good time to give our minds to Christian ethical, social and missionary responsibilities, and to the Christian hope, our expectation of the triumphant return of Jesus Christ.

In this way, every year the Church calendar recapitulates the story of the biblical revelation, the Old Testament from creation to Christmas in the period from October to December, the Gospels as they portray the life of Christ from January to May, and the Acts, Epistles and Revelation in the post-Pentecost period from May to September. It is also inevitably a Trinitarian structure as we rehearse how God revealed himself progressively as Creator and Father, as Son of God made flesh, and in the person and work of the Holy Spirit.

Since the set lessons (the Old Testament reading, the Epistle, the Gospel and others) are appropriate to the season in the Church's calendar, the preacher may sometimes, even often, take his text from one of these readings. A slavish attachment to the prescribed lections can be an unnecessary bondage, however. It is better to regard them rather as suggestive pointers to the day's theme.

To be sure, one must not be in bondage to the church calendar either. For then one would feel inhibited, for example, from preaching on the Incarnation except at Christmas or on the Resurrection except at Easter. Colin Morris justly asks: 'Pentecost in autumn? Ascension in the bleak mid-winter? Why not? Are not these great verities universally relevant? Certainly they ought not to be subject to the tyranny of the calendar.'[7]

Nevertheless, the value of the calendar is obvious. James Stewart, Professor Emeritus of New Testament Language, Literature and Theology at New College, Edinburgh, who retired in 1966 but remains one of the most popular contemporary preachers, has commended 'a due observance of the Christian Year' in these words:

The great landmarks of the Christian Year – Advent, Christmas, Lent, Good Friday, Easter, Whit Sunday, Trinity – set us our course, and suggest our basic themes. They compel us to keep close to the fundamental doctrines of the faith. They summon us back from the by-paths where we might be prone to linger, to the great highway of redemption. They ensure that in our preaching we shall constantly be returning to those mighty acts of God which the Church exists to declare.[8]

The second factor which helps us to determine our text I will call *external*, by which I mean some event in the life of our nation (e.g. an election, the death of a public figure or a national scandal), some issue of public debate (e.g. the arms race, abortion, capital punishment, unemployment, homosexual practice, or divorce), a natural disaster (flood, famine or earthquake) or some other catastrophe (a plane or train crash). When Christian people come to church, they neither can nor should shut out of their minds such matters as these which are being given wide radio, television and newspaper coverage. On the contrary, they bring these anxieties with them to worship, and are asking 'is there any word from the Lord?' and 'how should Christian people react to such things?' Preachers need to be sensitive to the big public questions in people's minds.

Thirdly, there is the *pastoral* factor, that is, some discovered need in the congregation's spiritual pilgrimage. It is often and rightly said that the best preachers are always good pastors, for they know the needs and problems, doubts, fears and hopes of their people. A conscientious pastor can never preach 'regardless of his hearers' requirements'. 'As well might a physician prescribe ointment for eczema on the neck,' comments Douglas Cleverley Ford, 'when the patient has corns on his toes.'[9] The assessment of a congregation's current need, and the decision how to preach to it, are best made by the pastoral team together. Even if a local church has only one full-time, stipendiary pastor, one hopes that he is supported by both part-time and voluntary ministers or elders who share the pastoral oversight with him. They will doubtless spend regular times together for prayer, discussion and planning, and one of the items on their agenda should be their preaching ministry. At least three times a year Michael Baughen, Rector of All Souls since 1975, calls his team together specifically for this purpose. Sometimes he tells the congregation in advance, in order to solicit their prayers, and sometimes invites them, and Fellowship Group leaders in particular, to send in suggestions and requests for sermon topics or sermon series. At times, too, some lay leaders of the church family join us when we discuss our preaching syllabus for the next few months. This gives us the opportunity to plan courses to cover major Christian doctrines and duties, to expound whole books of the Bible, and to ask ourselves if there are areas which we have overlooked. Planned preaching of this kind helps church members to grasp the rich unity-in-diversity of the biblical revelation; one of the dangers of taking an isolated text each Sunday is that it gives the impression that the Bible is a mere anthology of unrelated fragments, with no common themes or overall message.

It may be helpful if I list the main series which we have taken at All Souls Church during the last six years. Doctrinal courses have included the character of God, the life of Christ, the Cross, the Resurrection appearances, God's family and the Bible. More practical series have related to both ethical questions (e.g. discipleship, the Ten Commandments, the Sermon on the Mount, the Imitation of Christ, and a series of fourteen on the implications of love) and topical issues (e.g. divine guidance, women's ministry, suffering, and spiritual gifts). There was also a series of fourteen on prayer.

During the same period we have sought to expound some lengthy biblical passages. In the Old Testament we have had series on the early chapters of Genesis, the lives of the patriarchs, selected Psalms, parts of Isaiah and the Book of Daniel. In the New Testament we have studied both shorter letters (Ephesians, Philippians, 1 Peter and 1 and 2 Thessalonians) and two longer letters, namely 2 Corinthians and Romans (the latter in forty-three sermons, requring two sessions from November to March and from May to July). Our longest series has also perhaps been the most appreciated. This has been to take the whole Gospel of Mark in sixty-two sermons, dividing the text into seven sections and running from September 1978 to April 1981.

In addition to these overviews, paragraph by paragraph, we have found it profitable sometimes to work much more slowly, verse by verse, through shorter passages. Using this method, we have taken Acts 20:19–38 (Paul's address to the Ephesian elders), Ephesians 1 ('A People for God's Glory'), Ephesians 4 and 5 (Christian moral standards), Hebrews 11 (the heroes of faith), and a less well-known chapter, Hebrew 13. This was divided up as follows:

1 Let brotherly love continue (v. 1)
2 Hospitality to strangers (v. 2)
3 Remember those in prison (v. 3)
4 Let marriage be held in honour (v. 4)
5 Contentment (vv. 5, 6)
6 Remember your leaders (vv. 7, 17–19)
8 Danger! (v. 9)
9 Suffering with Christ (vv. 10–17)
10 Temporary residents (v. 14)
11 Sacrifices that please God (vv. 15, 16)
12 Equipped for action (vv. 20, 21)

All these series were decided on in staff conferences, in response to perceived pastoral needs of the church family.

The fourth factor to guide us in our choice of text is *personal*. Without doubt the best sermons we ever preach to others are those we have first preached to ourselves. Or, to put the same truth somewhat differently, when God himself speaks to us through a text of Scripture, and it becomes luminous or phosphorescent to us, it is then that it continues to glow with divine glory when we seek to open it up to others. Campbell Morgan tells how he was in Dr. Joseph Parker's vestry at the City Temple one day when a man came in and said to him 'I want to thank you for that sermon. It did me good.' Dr. Parker looked at him and replied: 'Sir, I preached it because it had done me good.'[10] This does not mean that every sermon has to be born out of our personal experience. Some of us have to preach on marriage while remaining unmarried, or on divorce while remaining married, and all of us have to preach on death before we have died. Yet sermons which emerge from deep personal conviction have a rich self-authenticating quality. This is what James Stalker called 'the blood-streak of experience'. He added that 'truth is doubly and trebly true when it comes from a man who speaks as if he had learned it by his own work and suffering.'[11]

It is for this reason that most preachers find it necessary to have handy at all times a notebook or (as it was called from about the seventeenth century onwards) a 'commonplace book'. I wonder if your experience resembles mine. My mind is usually enveloped in a fairly thick fog, so that I do not see things at all plainly. Occasionally, however, the fog lifts, the light breaks through, and I see with limpid clarity. These fleeting moments of illumination need to be seized. We have to learn to surrender ourselves to them, before the fog descends again. Such times often come at awkward moments, in the middle of the night, when somebody else is preaching or lecturing, while we are reading a book, even during a conversation. However inconvenient the time, we cannot afford to lose it. In order to take fullest advantage of it, we may need to write fast and furiously.

Here, then, are four factors – liturgical, external,

pastoral and personal – which will help us to choose our sermon text. We are now ready for the second stage of preparation.

(2) Meditate on it

If our text is part of a consecutive exposition, or for some other reason has been determined weeks or months in advance, we have the great benefit of a long period of 'subconscious incubation',[12] or what Americans call 'maturation'. Certainly Sunday's text should, at the latest, be chosen by the preceding Monday, so that something of the incubation process can go on. The longer this period, the better. Robert Louis Stevenson once said of himself, 'I . . . sit a long while silent on my eggs.'[13] Dietrich Bonhoeffer made a practice of choosing his text in good time. He would then consider it every day and 'try to sink deeply into it, so as really to hear what it is saying'.[14]

Sooner or later the time for more concentrated preparation arrives. What should the preacher do now? Read the text, re-read it, re-read it, and read it again. Turn it over and over in your mind, like Mary the mother of Jesus who wondered at all the things the shepherds had told her, 'pondering them in her heart'. (Luke 2:18, 19) Probe your text, like a bee with a spring blossom, or like a humming-bird probing a hibiscus flower for its nectar. Worry at it like a dog with a bone. Suck it as a child sucks an orange. Chew it as a cow chews the cud. To these similes Spurgeon adds two more, the worm and the bath. 'It is a great thing to pray one's self into the spirit and marrow of a text; working into it by sacred feeding thereon, even as the worm bores its way into the kernel of the nut.'[15] Again, 'let us, dear brethren, try to *get saturated with the gospel*. I always find that I can preach best when I can manage to lie asoak in my text. I like to get a text, and find out its meaning and bearings, and so on; and then, after I have bathed in it, I delight to lie down in it, and let it soak into me.'[16]

These vivid metaphors may not, however, indicate

clearly enough what the preacher is actually doing while he meditates on his text. Let me put it in this way. He addresses questions to his text, especially two. First, *what does it mean*? Perhaps better, what *did* it mean when first spoken or written, for E. D. Hirsch is right to emphasize that 'a text means what its author meant.'[17] As we have seen, we cannot avoid the discipline of thinking ourselves back into the text's historical and geographical context, into its cultural milieu, into its words and images, and so into the mind and purpose of its author. What did he mean? What was he intending to affirm or condemn or promise or command?

The second question to ask is *what does it say*? That is, what is its contemporary message? How does it speak to us today? This is a different question. It involves the further 'bridge-building' discipline of relating the ancient Word to the modern world, and translating it into today's cultural terms.

It is essential to keep these two questions both distinct and together. To discover the text's *meaning* is of purely academic interest unless we go on to discern its *message* for today, or (as some theologians prefer to say) its 'significance'. But to search for its contemporary message without first wrestling with its original meaning is to attempt a forbidden short cut. It dishonours God (disregarding his chosen way of revealing himself in particular historical and cultural contexts), it misuses his Word (treating it like an almanac or book of magic spells) and it misleads his people (confusing them about how to interpret Scripture).

As we address our two questions to the text, respecting its meaning and its message, we may well need to turn to a lexicon, concordance or commentary for help. They can save us from misinterpreting the passage, illumine it and stimulate our thinking about it. But they can never be more than aids. They cannot replace our own direct and personal encounter with the text, as we cross-examine it for ourselves and allow it to cross-examine us. Besides, after a few years of Bible study we shall never come to a text as a complete stranger, but rather approach it in the light of our previous meditation.

All the time we shall be praying, crying humbly to God for illumination by the Spirit of truth. We shall repeat Moses' petition 'I pray you, show me your glory' (Exod. 33:18) and Samuel's 'Speak, Lord, for your servant is listening'. (1 Sam. 3:9, 10) Christian meditation differs from other kinds in being a combination of study and prayer. Some preachers are very diligent students. Their desk is piled high with theological works, and they give their mind to the elucidation of the text. But they hardly if ever pray for light. Others are very diligent in prayer, but hardly ever engage in any serious study. We must not separate what God has joined. Speaking personally, I have always found it helpful to do as much of my sermon preparation as possible on my knees, with the Bible open before me, in prayerful study. This is not because I am a bibliolater and worship the Bible; but because I worship the God of the Bible and desire to humble myself before him and his revelation, and, even while I am giving my mind to the study of the text, to pray earnestly that the eyes of my heart may be enlightened. (Eph. 1:18)

Of this combination of prayer and thought Daniel supplies an excellent Old Testament example. Having 'perceived in the books the number of years' that Jerusalem would lie derelict, he turned his face to the Lord God, 'seeking him by prayer and supplications with fasting and sackcloth and ashes'. Then, while he was still praying, Gabriel came to him and said, 'O Daniel, I have now come out to give you wisdom and understanding . . .' (9:1–3, 20–23) In a subsequent vision a human figure appeared to him, touched him and said to him: 'Fear not, Daniel, for from the first day that you set your mind to understand, and humbled yourself before your God, your words have been heard . . .' (10:1–14) The New Testament equivalent seems to be Paul's word to Timothy: 'Think over what I say, for the Lord will grant you understanding in everything.' (2 Tim. 2:7) In both cases there was on the one hand the reading of books, serious thought and the setting of the mind to understand, while on the other there was self-humbling in prayer and in confession. It was only in response to both study and petition that the desired insight was given. As R. W. Dale wrote, quoting an old English writer, 'work without prayer is atheism; and prayer without work is presumption.'[18]

It goes without saying that during this period of prayerful study called 'meditation', we are scribbling down, though haphazardly, the thoughts which clarify in our minds. 'How long does this stage last?' I have often been asked. 'As long as it has to' is the only answer I can give. There is no substitute for spending time with the text. Take as long as you need. Go on probing the flower until there is no nectar left. Go on sucking the orange until you have sucked it dry.

I have so far assumed that our study of the text will be private and individual. There is also a place for corporate sermon preparation, however, and Bishop Lesslie Newbigin has described to me his experiment in Madras Diocese (South India), when he was Bishop:[19]

'Once a month clergy from a group of pastorates gathered either for half a day or for a full day.' They began with 'thorough exegetical study of the passages prescribed for the Sunday in question'. This was done both in plenary session and in groups, four or five groups being asked to prepare a sermon outline each for the Sundays of the ensuing month. 'The outlines would then be submitted to the plenary for comment, criticism and discussion.' Usually, the sermon texts would be chosen from the lectionary published by the Church of South India. 'On some occasions, however, especially when something of over-riding importance was happening in the life of the Church or in the life of the nation . . . the groups would be asked to consider what the proper Christian response to the situation should be, and what passages of Scripture would be appropriate for the worship of the Sunday in question.' Bishop Newbigin's final comment was that, although 'in the end each one had to go home and prepare his own sermons', yet 'these exercises helped to ensure that there was more meat in them than would otherwise have been the case.'

(3) Isolate the Dominant Thought

As we continue to meditate by prayer and study, and jot down a miscellany of ideas, we should be looking for our text's dominant thought. Indeed, we should persevere in meditation until it emerges and clarifies. Why so?

First, because every text has a main theme. If, as we argued in Chapter Three, God speaks through what he has spoken, then it is essential to ask ourselves 'What is he saying? Where does his emphasis lie?' I am not denying that there may be several legitimate ways of handling a text, and several different lessons to learn from it; what I am asserting, however, is that every text has an overriding thrust. We need the integrity to discern this and to resist the temptation to give the text a twist or stress of our own.

For example, it would surely be permissible to teach from the Parable of the Good Samaritan that true love always expresses itself in sacrificial and constructive service. Yet the main thrust of Jesus' story is the shocking fact that a despised Samaritan outsider did what the two religious Jews were unwilling to do. It would therefore be impossible to expound the parable accurately without stressing this racial point and its implied criticism of all religion which, however orthodox, is yet bogus because loveless. Again, it would be possible to teach several truths from Romans 5:8, 'But God shows his love for us in that while we were yet sinners Christ died for us.' We could preach on the sin of man or the death of Christ or the love of God, for all three are mentioned in this verse. Yet the text's dominant thought is that Christ's death for sinners like us is 'God's own proof of his love towards us' (NEB). So a sermon on Roman 5:8 would have to be on 'how God proves his love', and would also have to relate the objective proof through Christ (his cross, v. 8) with the subjective experience through the Holy Spirit (in our hearts, v. 5).

Then there is a second reason why we should look for each text's dominant thought, namely that one of the chief ways in which a sermon differs from a lecture is that it aims to convey only one major message. Students are expected to take copious notes during lectures, and to revise them afterwards. On this assumption the lecturer feels free to be discursive, to cover a wide territory, and even to digress. Indeed, the eccentric digressions of an absent-minded professor constitute one of the chief delights of listening to him; otherwise one might just as well cull his material direct from books. A sermon is quite different, however. It is true that in some congregations note-taking goes on, while in others duplicated summaries and cassette recordings are made available. Each is valuable as an aide-mémoire. Yet this provision is exceptional. It can also prove harmful if people stop listening to the sermon because they intend on some later occasion to study the notes or play back the cassette. For the sermon, as a living word from God to his people, should make its impact on them then and there. They will not remember the details. We should not expect to do so. But they should remember the dominant thought, because all the sermon's details have been marshalled to help them grasp its message and feel its power.

The masters of sermon craft all seem to be agreed on this matter. In olden days the dominant thought was usually called 'the proposition', and preachers laboured to clarify it. 'I think that every sermon', said Charles Simeon, 'should have like a telescope but one object in the field.'[20] Here is his account of his own method in his Preface to *Horae Homileticae*:

It may perhaps be not unuseful to point out *the manner in which these discourses are formed*. As soon as the subject is chosen, the first enquiry is, *What is the principal scope and meaning of the text*? (I BEG EVERY YOUNG MINISTER ESPECIALLY TO REMEMBER THIS.)[21]

When a text's principal meaning has been discerned, Simeon continues, the next step is to express it in 'a categorical proposition'; to do this is *the great secret* of all composition for the pulpit'.[22] In an anonymous article in the *Christian Observer* in December 1821, Simeon emphasized the practical importance of this method for fixing a truth in people's memories:

> Reduce your text to a simple proposition, and lay that down as the warp; and then make use of the text itself as the woof; illustrating the main idea by the various terms in which it is contained. Screw the word into the minds of your hearers. A screw is the strongest of all mechanical powers . . . when it has turned a few times, scarcely any power can pull it out.[23]

Richard Baxter also wrote, 'screw the truth into their minds'.[24]

J. H. Jowett went further:

> I have a conviction that no sermon is ready for preaching . . . until we can express its theme in a short, pregnant sentence as clear as a crystal. I find the getting of that sentence is the hardest, the most exacting and the most fruitful labour in my study . . . I do not think any sermon ought to be preached, or even written, until that sentence has emerged, clear and lucid as a cloudless moon.[25]

Similarly, Professor Ian Pitt-Watson declares, 'Every sermon should be ruthlessly unitary in its theme. "This is the first and great commandment!"'[26]

Once the text has yielded its secret and the principal sermon theme has been clarified, ideally the whole service should be built round it. Although doubtless the opening worship can express penitence and praise in more general terms, and although the intercessions should embrace many concerns for the world, the Church and the needy, yet even in these sections of the service it is helpful to begin to draw the minds and hearts of the congregation towards the theme and to prepare them to receive it. Certainly the two lessons should be relevant, together with the hymn expressing our prayer before the sermon and the hymn expressing our response after it. We should not be afraid of simplicity and repetition. This is a further lesson we can learn from the Black experience in the United States. Dr. Henry Mitchell draws an interesting parallel between the Negro spiritual and 'the slow rate characteristic of the Black preaching style':

The Black-culture sermon is the homiletical twin brother to the spiritual. In the case of the sung culture, a whole song can be formed on a very small word base. Haunting choruses are built on as few as four words: 'Remember me, O Lord, remember me.' Where a white-culture hymn has long stanzas full of words delivered at a fairly rapid rate, a Black spiritual might simply say slowly, 'Lord, I want to be a Christian in my heart.' The slow rate of Black preaching, as well as the repetition, is the natural pattern of Black speaking and singing, neither of which is prone to depend on great numbers of words in a brief utterance.[27]

So then, in our sermon preparation, we must not try to by-pass the discipline of waiting patiently for the dominant thought to disclose itself. We have to be ready to pray and think ourselves deep into the text, even under it, until we give up all pretensions of being its master or manipulator, and become instead its humble and obedient servant. Then there will be no danger of unscrupulous text-twisting. On the contrary, the Word of God will dominate our mind, set fire to our hearts, control the development of our exposition and later leave a lasting impression on the congregation.

(4) Arrange your Material to Serve the Dominant Thought

So far, in the process of sermon preparation, we have gathered from our text a lot of miscellaneous ideas, which we have scribbled higgledy-piggledy on a sheet of paper, and we have laboured to isolate its dominant thought. Now we have to knock the material into shape, and particularly into such shape as will best serve the dominant thought. The purpose of this stage is not to produce a literary masterpiece ('fine sermons are one of the most dangerous of the Devil's snares,' writes Charles Smyth[28]), but rather to enable the text's main thrust to make its maximum impact. This chiselling and shaping process has both negative and positive aspects.

Negatively, we have to be ruthless in discarding the irrelevant. This is easier said than done. During our hours of meditation numerous blessed thoughts and scintillating ideas may have occurred to us and been dutifully jotted down. It is tempting to drag them all in somehow. Resist the temptation! Irrelevant material will weaken the sermon's effect. It will come in handy some other time. We need the strength of mind to keep it till then.

Positively, we have to subordinate our material to our theme in such a way as to illumine and enforce it. In order to do so, we need the help of a structure, words and illustrations. Something must be said about each.

First, a *structure*. Most communicators agree that orderly arrangement is necessary. True, we live in an increasingly visual culture. True again, the majority of people in developed nations are more used to being bombarded with images on their television screen than to listening to linear logic. Hence the value, as David Gillett writes, of what has been called the 'blob' teaching method. This 'takes one point as a subject and comes at it from different angles, reinforcing and making clearer the picture that is forming in the person's mind.'[29]

Yet, whether our approach is visual or logical, we still have to organize our thoughts into some structure if they

228

are to be communicable. Borrowing the imagery of the primeval chaos described in Genesis 1:2, W. E. Sangster conceded 'that a sermon can be without form and – such is the grace of God – not utterly void'. Nevertheless, he added, this 'borders on the miraculous. No sermon is really strong which is not strong in structure too.'[30] Just as bones without flesh make a skeleton, so flesh without bones makes a jellyfish. And neither bony skeletons nor jellyfish make good sermons.

We face two main dangers when developing a sermon structure. The first is that the skeleton obtrudes, like the ribs of a skinny human being. They thrust themselves before us; we cannot take our eyes off them. It is the same with too prominent a sermon outline. It distracts from the content by drawing too much attention to the form. This may be because it is too clever (the double and even triple alliterations which some preachers manage to contrive for their headings are the main offenders) or because it is too complicated (like Richard Baxter who, according to Simeon, once reached '"sixty-fifthly", as if any person could remember the sixty-four preceding heads'[31]). Outlines which advertize themselves in these ways are always distracting. Their perpetrators have forgotten that the purpose of the skeleton is to support the body, and in so doing to keep itself largely out of view.

The second danger to which we are exposed when structuring our sermons is that of artificiality. Some preachers impose an outline on their text which neither fits nor illumines it, but rather muddies the clear waters of truth and confuses the listeners. The golden rule for sermon outlines is that each text must be allowed to supply its own structure. The skilful expositor opens up his text, or rather permits it to open itself up before our eyes, like a rose unfolding to the morning sun and displaying its previously hidden beauty. One of the greatest experts at this was Dr. Alexander McLaren, the nineteenth century Baptist preacher at Manchester. William Robertson Nicoll described him as having 'a swift and clear-cutting intellect', and went on to write of his 'extraordinary gift of analyzing a text. He touched it with a silver hammer, and it immediately broke up into natural and memorable divisions.'[32] Spurgeon used the same metaphor. He once spoke to his students about the difficulty he had with some texts. You 'try to break them up,' he said; 'you hammer at them with might and main, but your labour is lost.' Then 'at last you find one which crumbles at the first blow, and sparkles as it falls in pieces, and you perceive jewels of the rarest radiance flashing from within.'[33] All preachers have had that experience, at least from time to time. We need to pray that the Lord will distribute a few more silver hammers among us today.

A discussion of sermon-structure inevitably raises the issue of the popular three-point sermon, and this in its turn usually provokes a wry smile. It is not a modern invention, but has a long history. Charles Smyth goes into great detail about the rigid structure of the medieval 'sermon scheme' which, especially in England, demanded a theme text which was divisible into three, if possible into 'three significant words'.[34] To make the three-point sermon our invariable practice, however, would be to confine ourselves in a strait-jacket. It also does violence to many texts which make only one point or two, or for that matter may be naturally divisible into four and even five. Yet it is strange how often the natural is the triple. I have often wondered if it is because Christians are Trinitarians who easily discern allusions to Father, Son and Holy Spirit, or to God above, for and in us. I was interested, therefore, to discover that this thought occurred to Robert de Basevorn, whose *Forma Praedicandi* was published in 1322. 'This rule may be judged', he wrote, 'by the desire to reverence the Trinity.'[35]

There are many ways of structuring a sermon. W. E. Sangster distinguished five main possibilities which he called 'exposition', 'argument', 'faceting', 'categorizing' and 'analogy'.[36] Halford Luccock was more ambitious in his classification and listed ten types. He also gave them suggestive names, like the 'ladder sermon' (which 'takes one from point to point like the rungs of a ladder'), the 'jewel sermon' (which 'consists in turning one idea around as one might turn a jewel in his fingers, allowing different facets to catch the light'), and the 'sky rocket sermon' (so called 'not because it goes with a fizz or a bang and is a sensational affair' but because 'it begins on the ground, rises to a height, then breaks into pieces and comes down to earth again . . .').[37] Different texts and topics demand different treatment. We need to cultivate diversity and seek deliverance from a single stereotype.

I turn now from structure to *words*. If we preach only once a week for forty years, we shall utter about nine million of them. Words matter. In order to communicate clearly, we have to clothe our thoughts in words. It is impossible to convey a precise message without choosing precise words. Think of the time and trouble we give to composing a message we want to send by cable: because the number of words is severely limited, we go over it again and again, changing a word here, adding or deleting a word there, until we are sure not only that we shall be understood, but also that we shall not be misunderstood. The same should be true of sermons. 'The Preacher sought to find pleasing words, and uprightly he wrote words of truth.' Such 'sayings of the wise,' it is added, especially when they thus combine grace and truth, are 'like goads' to prick the conscience and stimulate the mind, and also 'like nails firmly fixed' because they lodge in the memory and are not easily dislodged. (Eccles. 12:10, 11) So it is worth taking trouble over our words. Not because we shall read our sermons, nor because we shall memorize and recite them, but rather because the discipline of clear thinking demands writing ('writing maketh an exact man' said Bacon), and because if our preparation has extended at least in some parts of the sermon to the words we want to use, it is extraordinary how readily these come back to our mind even when we take only notes into the pulpit. What sort of words, then, shall we use?

231

First, a preacher's words need to be as simple and clear as possible. The famous rendering of 1 Corinthians 13:1, although a misprint, was true: 'Though I speak with the tongues of men and of angels, and have not *clarity*, I am become as sounding brass or a tinkling cymbal.' Sometimes, to be sure, our search for the right word may lead us to an unusual one, but we shall avoid verbiage. Many professional people fall into this trap. There are still politicians who resemble Disraeli's description of Gladstone in 1878 as 'a sophisticated rhetorician, inebriated with the exuberance of his own verbosity'. Lawyers seem to delight in drawing up documents which only legally trained people can interpret. Doctors are sometimes guilty of using quite unnecessary jargon. Dr. K. D. Bardham of Rotherham, South Yorkshire, has given an example from a social services report:

> This elderly geriatric (sic) female has multiple joint problems which limit perambulation. Absence of verbal intercourse aggravates her detachment from reality and reinforces isolationism. She is unable to relate to events at this point in time. Psychogeriatric consideration in the context of conceptual distortion, and paranoia is also a parameter in the total dimensions of her problems.

Dr. Barham goes on to offer his own translation, 'This lady of eighty-three has arthritis, cannot get about, and is lonely, confused and frightened.'[38] His letter was prompted by an article by Christopher Reed about the spread of 'psychobabble' in middle-class America. This is jargon which reduces a genuine psychological understanding of human behaviour to empty slogans.

There is no need, however, for the British to look across the Atlantic to find examples of the misuse of language. There is plenty of it at home, not least in the civil service, and no one has documented it better than Sir Ernest Gowers in his well-known books on *Plain Words*. Their purpose, he explains, is 'to help officials in their use of written English as a tool of their trade',[39] but what he writes is almost equally applicable to spoken English. There is no such thing as style, he maintains, apart from the use of words, and he quotes Matthew Arnold and Dean Swift in support. 'Have something to say and say it as clearly as you can. That is the only secret of style.'[40] 'Proper words in proper places make the true definition of style.'[41] So he urges upon us a careful choice of words, avoiding the superfluous, and choosing the familiar and the precise. Our basic fault is that our speech is complicated. 'Instead of being simple, terse and direct, it is stilted, long-winded and circumlocutory.' He calls it 'gobbledygook'[42] – a word for 'pompous officialese' which was apparently coined by Maury Maverick in the *New York Times Magazine* in May 1944.

Unfortunately, the Church is by no means free of this disease. The late Sir Kenneth Grubb quoted Dr. Gordon Rupp's dictum that the ecumenical movement has been 'the First Murderer of the Queen's English', and went on to give examples of the strange ecclesiastical preference for Latin words instead of Anglo-Saxon:

A meeting becomes a confrontation, a talk a consultation, an aspect a dimension, a display a constellation. These men scorn transitive verbs and the active voice. They despise strong nouns as subjects, and weak adjectives take the place of precise epithets. Nothing happens because the wind is in the west, but only 'within the framework of an occidental circulation'. Thus the good news evaporates in bad language . . .[43]

Over against these examples of diffuse and complex language, preachers have to strive for simplicity and clarity. This will mean using not only straightforward words, but short sentences, with few if any subordinate clauses. One is obliged to do this when being translated into another language, which is good practice for doing it habitually.

'Preach', Bishop J. C. Ryle once said, 'as if you were asthmatical.'

In addition to being simple, the preacher's words should be vivid. That is, they should conjure up images in the mind. I shall have more to say in a moment about illustrations. Meanwhile, we need to acknowledge that stories are not the only type there is; even single words or idioms, if figures of speech, can illumine what we are trying to say. 'The difference between the right word and the nearly right,' commented Mark Twain, 'is the difference between lightning and the lightning bug.'

When we use metaphorical speech, however, we run the risk of mixing our metaphors and so of confusing people by the jumbled images we present to their imagination. Stephen Leacock gives an admirable example, which serves as a salutary warning to all preachers. He is satirizing the Reverend Rupert Drone, Rural Dean of Mariposa, north of Toronto:

> I don't think that at first anybody troubled much about the debt on the church (he writes). Dean Drone's figures showed that it was only a matter of time before it would be extinguished; only a little effort was needed, a little girding up of the loins of the congregation, and they could shoulder the whole debt and trample it under their feet. Let them but set their hands to the plough and they could soon guide it into the deep water. Then they might furl their sails and sit every man under his own olive tree.[44]

If our words are to be simple and vivid, they must also be honest. We have to beware of exaggerations and be sparing in our use of superlatives. Too liberal a supply of these devalues the currency. Besides, Jesus himself has given us some very clear instruction to let our 'yes' be yes, and our 'no' no, without the need for strong language to elaborate our statements (Jas. 5:12, alluding to the Lord's teaching recorded in Matt. 5:33–37).

One recent author who has emphasized this is C. S. Lewis. 'Verbicide' (the murder of words) can be committed, he maintained, in many ways. But one of the commonest is by 'inflation', e.g. saying 'awfully' when we mean 'very', or 'tremendous' when we mean 'great'.[45] It is worth quoting in full the common-sense advice he gave to a child in America in the course of a letter dated 26 June 1956:

What really matters is:
1 Always try to use the language so as to make quite clear what you mean, and make sure your sentence couldn't mean anything else.
2 Always prefer the plain direct word to the long vague one. Don't 'implement' promises, but 'keep' them.
3 Never use abstract nouns when concrete ones will do. If you mean 'more people died', don't say 'mortality rose'.
4 Don't use adjectives which merely tell us how you want us to feel about the thing you are describing. I mean, instead of telling us a thing was 'terrible', descibe it so that we'll be terrified. Don't say it was 'delightful', make *us* say 'delightful' when we've read the description. You see, all those words (horrifying, wonderful, hideous, exquisite) are only saying to your readers 'please will you do my job for me'.
5 Don't use words too big for the subject. 'Don't say 'infinitely' when you mean 'very'; otherwise you'll have no word left when you want to talk about something *really* infinite.[46]

Perhaps these quotations are enough to convince us how important words are to the preacher. When struggling to communicate some message to our listeners, we shall search for simple words which they will understand, vivid words which will help them to visualize what we are saying, and honest words which tell the plain truth without exaggeration. Malcolm Muggeridge has been described as a 'wizard with words'. Yet he confesses in the first volume of his autobiography that, while working as a journalist for the *Manchester Guardian*, he soon found himself becoming glib, facetious and even hypocritical.

> It is painful to me now to reflect (he writes), the ease with which I got into the way of using this non-language; these drooling non-sentences conveying non-thoughts, propounding non-fears and offering non-hopes. Words are as beautiful as love, and as easily betrayed. I am more penitent for my false words – for the most part, mercifully lost for ever in the Media's great slag-heaps – than for false deeds.[47]

Now this penitent has changed ambitions. The epitaph he has himself requested is 'He used words well.'

From a consideration of the structure and words of the sermon, I move on to *illustrations*. I do so with considerable diffidence, because I know how bad I am at using them myself. My friends keep teasing me about it, and I am trying to improve.

I cannot help agreeing that a Christian preacher has no possible excuse for neglecting illustrations, for there is ample divine precedent to encourage him. Cyril Garbett, a former Archbishop of York, used to recount how, when a clergyman wrote to Bishop Mandell Creighton of London, asking him to recommend a book of sermon illustrations, 'he got a reply consisting simply of two words on a post card, "The Bible".'[48] The Bishop was right. The Bible teems with illustrations, particularly similes. Think of the Old Testament. 'As a father pities his children, so the Lord pities those who fear him.' 'The wicked . . . are like the chaff which the wind drives away.' 'I will be as the dew to Israel; he shall blossom as the lily, he shall strike root as the poplar.' 'They shall mount up with wings like eagles.' 'Is not my word like fire, says the Lord, and like a hammer which breaks the rock in pieces?'[49] Or take the New Testament. 'You are the salt of the earth. You are the light of the world.' 'As the lightning flashes and lights up the sky from one side to the other, so will the Son of man be in his day.' 'Woe to you, scribes and Pharisees, hypocrites! for you are like whitewashed tombs, which outwardly appear beautiful, but within they are full of dead men's bones.' 'We were gentle among you, like a mother taking care of her children.' 'What is your life? For you are a mist that appears for a little time and then vanishes.'[50] This is but a random selection; the list could be multiplied many times.

Above all, there are the parables of Jesus. The best-known ones like the Prodigal Son and the Good Samaritan are an integral part of the average person's understanding of Christianity. 'With many such parables he spoke the word to them, as they were able to hear it; he did not speak to them without a parable, but privately to his own disciples he explained everything'. (Mark 4:33, 34) W. E. Sangster was not overstating the case for illustrations when he wrote that, with the example of Jesus before us, 'only a combination of vanity and blasphemy could convince a man that the matter was beneath his notice.'[51] Besides, it is not only the parables of Jesus which demonstrate the importance of illustrating truth, or making it visible, it is Jesus himself. For Jesus is the Word of God made flesh, the visible image of the invisible God, so that he who saw him saw the Father.

It is hardly surprising, therefore, that the use of illustrations in preaching has had a long and honourable record in the history of the Church. The great preachers of the fourth and fifth centuries like Chrysostom, Augustine and Ambrose used them. One of the major characteristics of medieval preaching, writes Charles Smyth, was 'the use of *exempla*, or what we should call "illustrations".'[52] This tradition was further developed in the thirteenth century by Francis of Assisi, Dominic and their friars. At that time collections of *exempla* for preachers were made and circulated (Smyth lists more than fifteen), forerunners of the modern 'treasury of sermon illustrations'. They included Bible stories, anecdotes from classical literature, historical examples, legends of the saints, animal fables and lessons from nature. It was because these *exempla* became used both as vehicles of false teaching and as substitutes for serious biblical exposition that John Wycliffe and his 'Poor Preachers' determined to concentrate rather on the text of Scripture and thus paved the way for the Reformers' emphasis on preaching from the Bible. Charles Smyth concludes this part of his historical survey with what he calls 'The Triumph of Tillotson'. John Tillotson was Archbishop of Canterbury from 1691 to 1694. Though brought up as a Puritan, his later sermons were more essays on moral goodness than gospel addresses. In short sentences and simple language he developed 'the appeal to reason and common sense, the careful, comprehensive argument, solid, unhurried, unadorned'.[53] Yet he seems to have been reacting against speculations, pedantries and elaborate *exempla* of the middle ages, rather than against the Puritans. For, although some Puritan allegorizations were very fanciful, the popularity of Bunyan's great allegory *Pilgrim's Progress* testifies to its strong spiritual influence, and in fact many Puritan preachers depicted the Christian life as a dangerous journey involving struggle and combat. Their sermons were 'sown thick with imagery'; indeed, 'few sermons lacked and many abounded in such allusions to spiritual wayfaring and warfaring.'[54]

To biblical precedent and historical tradition we now add human psychology as another part of the foundation on which the practice of illustration rests. We human beings find it very difficult to handle abstract concepts; we need to convert them either into symbols (as in mathematics) or into pictures. For the power of imagination is one of God's best and most distinctive gifts to mankind.

If I were asked [wrote Professor Macneile Dixon] what has been the most powerful force in the making of history, you would probably judge me of unbalanced mind were I to answer, as I should have to answer, metaphor, figurative expression. It is by imagination that men have lived; imagination rules all our lives. The human mind is not, as philosophers would have you

238

think, a debating hall, but a picture gallery. Around it hang our similes, our concepts. The tyranny of the concept, as, for example, the concept of the universe as a machine . . . is one from which the human mind never escapes . . . Metaphor is the essence of religion and poetry . . . Nor does science escape from this entanglement.[55]

H. W. Beecher applied this principle to our task as preachers. His fifth Yale lecture has a section entitled 'The Power of Imagination'. He wrote: 'The first element on which your preaching will largely depend for power and success, you will perhaps be surprised to learn, is *Imagination*, which I regard as the most important of all the elements that go to make the preacher.' By 'imagination', he went on to explain, he meant 'that power of the mind by which it conceives of invisible things, and is able to present them as though they were visible to others.'[56]

Paul referred to his preaching of the Cross to the Galatians as a 'public portrayal' before their very eyes of Jesus Christ as the one who had been crucified (Gal. 3:1). Now the crucifixion had taken place some twenty years previously, and none of Paul's Galatian readers had been present to witness it. Yet by his vivid proclamation Paul had been able to bring this event out of the past into the present, out of hearsay into a dramatic visual image. Such is the purpose of every illustration, of whatever kind. It is to stimulate people's imagination and to help them to see things clearly in their minds. Illustrations transform the abstract into the concrete, the ancient into the modern, the unfamiliar into the familiar, the general into the particular, the vague into the precise, the unreal into the real, and the invisible into the visible. According to an oriental proverb quoted by J. C. Ryle, 'he is the eloquent man, who turns his hearers' ears into eyes, and makes them see what he speaks of.'[57]

In order to see, we need light. And the word 'illustrate' means to illumine, to throw light or lustre upon an otherwise dark object. It is for this reason that sermon illustrations have sometimes been likened to the windows of a house. In the third series of Spurgeon's *Lectures to My Students*, which is entitled 'The Art of Illustration' and is entirely devoted to this topic, he quotes a saying of 'quaint Thomas Fuller', the seventeenth-century Anglican historian, that 'reasons are the pillars of the fabric of a sermon, but similitudes are the windows which give the best lights.' Declaring this comparison 'happy and suggestive', Spurgeon goes on:

> The chief reason for the construction of windows in a house is, as Fuller says, *to let in light*. Parables, similes and metaphors have that effect; and hence we use them to *illustrate* our subject, or, in other words, to '*brighten it with light*', for that is Dr. Johnson's literal rendering of the word *illustrate*.

A building without windows would be 'a prison rather than a house, . . . and in the same way a discourse without a parable is prosy and dull, and involves a grievous weariness of the flesh.' Why, he continues, 'even the little children open their eyes and ears, and a smile brightens up their faces as we tell a story . . . We dare say they often wish that the sermon were all illustration, even as the boy desired to have a cake made all of plums.'[58] But, of course, a cake cannot be all plums, any more than a house can be all windows. We need to find the happy medium between this and the entire absence of windows and plums. After the publication of my little book *Men Made New* (1966), an attempted exposition of those crucial chapters Romans 5 to 8, a friend wrote me one of those candid epistles which only friends dare write. 'Your book,' he said, 'is like a house without windows, and a pudding without plums!' I cannot help wondering if he had been reading Spurgeon.

From the necessity of illustrations I turn to their dangers. These are principally two. The first is that they can be too prominent, thrusting themselves into the light instead of casting light on some obscurity. W. E. Sangster was surely justified, when criticized for using too many illustrations, in retorting 'My people need lamp posts, John, to light them on their way.'[59] For this is the severely practical function of illustrations; they are not to be 'like pretty drawing-room lamps, calling attention to themselves' but rather 'like street lamps, scarcely noticed, but throwing floods of light upon the road.'[60] We all know the kind of illustration which is too obtrusive. So striking is it that it is remembered in isolation from its context, long after the truth has been forgotten which it was intended to illustrate.

The second danger attached to illustrations applies particularly to analogies which are either improperly or inappropriately applied. In every analogy we have to make it plain at what point the likeness is being suggested. For example, when Jesus told us to 'become like little children', he did not mean that we are to be childlike in every respect. He was not recommending the immaturity or naughtiness or irresponsibility or innocence or ignorance of a child, but only its 'humility'. That is, we are as dependent on grace as a child on its parents. For there are other biblical passages in which we are forbidden, rather than encouraged, to become like children.[61] So it is always dangerous, and often misleading, to 'argue from an analogy', that is to say, to give the false impression that because two objects or events are analogous at one point, they must therefore be analogous in all.

As an example of the inappropriate use of an analogy, I mention another friend of mine who once began a sermon by announcing, with deliberate pauses of immense solemnity: 'Almighty God in Holy Scripture likens himself . . . to a hen.' His assertion was received with amused embarrassment. In a sense, of course, he was quite right. The psalmist delighted to find refuge in the shadow of God's 'wings', and Boaz described Ruth the Moabitess convert as having taken refuge under the 'wings' of the God of Israel.[62] Moreover, there is plain dominical authority for the metaphor. In weeping over Jerusalem, Jesus declared that he had often longed to gather its inhabitants together 'as a hen gathers her brood under her wings'. (Matt. 23:37) It is a beautiful picture, which portrays clearly the loving, tender, protective care of God, and a homely, familiar image to anybody who has visited a farmyard or back garden where chickens are kept. It is vivid too, for one can immediately smell the smell of the farm, hear the cluckings of the mother hen, and see the chicks scurrying towards her.

Why, then, the immediate sense of anomaly when my friend began his sermon? Partly because he introduced his illustration with somewhat pompous language ('Almighty God' and 'Holy Scripture'), and in a pretentious style (the dramatic pauses), so that his hearers were led to expect a noble climax, and instead the word 'hen' came as a comic anticlimax. The second reason for the sense of the ludicrous was that he did not specify at what point he was drawing his analogy. The fact is that Scripture does not liken Almighty God to a hen. What it does is to liken his protective care to the wings of a hen, or, more accurately still (since the image is dynamic, not static), it speaks both of God's grace in terms of his desire to gather us under his wings, and of our responsive faith in terms of taking refuge under them. If, therefore, my friend had kept closer to the Bible, and had said something like 'God in his tender love for us wants to bring us under his saving protection, as a hen gathers her chicks under her wings', there would have been immediate understanding and appreciation without any sense of anomaly.

Illustrations are of many kinds. Some may be no more than a word or two, or a phrase, which nevertheless, because they are striking figures of speech, convey a dramatic visual image. We can talk of God 'breaking through our defences' (so that we visualize people barricading themselves against his assaults), or of the Holy Spirit 'prizing open' our closed minds to new truth (so that we can hear the creaking of the box lid as it reluctantly yields to the pressure of hammer or claw). Some preachers have great

242

skill in re-telling biblical stories and parables in contemporary language, while others are adept at inventing fresh, modern parables. The most effective illustrations, however, are probably anecdotes, culled from history or biography, from current affairs or our own experience. For these help to set biblical truth in the widest possible context, historical, global and personal. Every preacher, therefore, is constantly on the look-out for illustrations, his eye observant and his ear cocked. Not that we read books and listen to people only with the ulterior motive of collecting sermon material. Nevertheless, as Sangster put it, 'all Nature and all life . . . are rich in illustration. As one sails through life with a trawling eye, what fine things come into the net!'[63] And we shall be wise to jot down, either on cards, or in a loose-leaf folder, ideas which come to us and the few best quotations from every book we read.

In this whole matter of using sermon illustrations, we have to find the balance between too many and too few. Theodore Parker Ferris gave some good advice about this. On the one hand, he said, 'one picture is worth ten thousand words. A sermon that is entirely without pictures, without illustrations, is likely to reach only those whose intellectual discipline makes it possible for them to appreciate abstractions.' On the other hand, 'a sermon with too many illustrations is like a woman with too many jewels, and the jewels which are originally intended to enhance the figure, hide it.' In so saying, he practised what he preached.[64]

Having tried to arrange our material (by structure, words and illustrations) in such a way as to serve our text's dominant thought, we are ready for the next stage.

(5) Add the Introduction and Conclusion

It seems essential to prepare the body of the sermon first. If we were to begin with a predetermined introduction or conclusion, we would be almost bound to twist the text to fit. So instead, we start with the body. Only then shall we 'top and tail' the body, that is, supply it with a head and a tail end, an introduction and a conclusion. The old writers on rhetoric and homiletics used to call these the 'exordium' and the 'peroration'.

An introduction is essential, and should be neither too long nor too short. The really lengthy introduction detracts from the sermon itself and steals its thunder. The commoner mistake today, however, is to shorten the introduction too drastically, and even to dispense with it altogether, in order to plunge immediately into the subject. This is unwise. 'Men have a natural aversion to abruptness, and delight in a somewhat gradual approach. A building is rarely pleasing in appearance without a porch or some sort of inviting entrance. An elaborate piece of music will always have a prelude of at least a few introductory notes.'[65] Is this not God's way too? 'Nature herself teaches us the art of preparations and of gradations' by the gentle arrival of both twilight and dawn.[66]

A good introduction serves two purposes. First, it arouses interest, stimulates curiosity, and whets the appetite for more. Secondly, it genuinely 'introduces' the theme by leading the hearers into it. It is comparatively easy to construct an introduction which fulfils one or other of these two functions. Interest can readily be aroused by telling a joke or an arresting story, but, if these do not lead naturally into the subject, the interest gained will be as quickly lost. On the other hand, anyone can introduce a subject in such a way as to lose people's attention before even winning it. The right but hard way is to introduce the topic and arouse interest simultaneously, and so dispose people's minds and hearts towards our message.

The traditional way of introducing a sermon is to announce one's text. The value of this beginning is obvious. It declares from the start that we accept the Christian preacher's responsibility to expound God's Word, rather than ventilate our own opinions. Nevertheless, this opening turns many people off; they find it too traditional, too ecclesiastical, too dull. So at least sometimes we shall be wise to begin situationally instead of biblically, with our topic instead of our text, for then we start where people are, rather than where we hope to take them. I remember, for example, conducting a pastors' seminar on preaching in Guatemala City, soon after the terrible earthquake of 1976 had devastated the country, killed 23,000 people and rendered more than a million homeless. I enquired how many of them had preached about the earthquake the following Sunday, and was glad to discover that some had. Would we have encouraged them to start their sermon on that occasion with 'My text this morning is . . .'? Would it not have been more natural to begin somewhat as follows: 'We have met this morning in great sorrow. Many of us have lost a relative or friend. Others have lost their home and possessions. Why does God allow such disasters? That is the question in all our hearts and minds. How can we still believe in a God of love?' If the text were only now to be announced and read, and if it were to relate directly to the problem of divine providence and/or the assurance of divine love, people's attention would not be lost.

Conclusions are more difficult than introductions. Some preachers seem to be constitutionally incapable of concluding anything, let alone their sermons. They circle round and round, like a plane on a foggy day without instruments, unable to land. Their sermons 'are nothing less than a tragedy of aimlessness'.[67] Others stop too abruptly. Their sermons are like a play without a finale, like music that has neither crescendo nor climax.

The conclusion should not be merely a recapitulation. Recapitulation is valuable. People's memories need to be stimulated. The apostles were not afraid of judicious repetition. 'To write the same things to you is not irksome to me,' said Paul, 'and is safe for you.' Peter was of the same opinion: 'I intend always to remind you of these things, though you know them . . . I think it right, as long as I am in this body, to arouse you by way of reminder . . .'[68] A more recent preacher has described his sermon method in these terms, 'First I tell them what I am going to tell them. Next, I tell them what I have to tell them. Thirdly, I tell them what I have told them.' Thus, his people get told the same message three times, which is fine, especially if he is able to disguise his repetitions a little bit by saying identical things in different words. For how can we lodge a truth in people's minds except (as Luther often put it) by 'dinning it into their heads continually'? Some deft carpenters can drive a nail home with one mighty blow; most find it safer to hammer it in with a series. Just so, truth needs to be driven home by the hammer-blows of repetition.

A true conclusion, however, goes beyond recapitulation to personal application. Not that all application should be left to the end, for our text needs to be applied as we go along. Nevertheless, it is a mistake to disclose too soon the conclusion to which we are going to come. If we do, we lose people's sense of expectation. It is better to keep something up our sleeve. Then we can leave to the end that persuading which, by the Holy Spirit's power, will prevail on people to take action.

This was an essential element in the classical understanding of public speaking. Cicero had said in *The Orator* that 'an eloquent man must so speak as to teach (*docere*), to please (*delectare*) and to persuade (*flectere* or *movere*).' Augustine quoted Cicero's dictum and applied it to the responsibility of Christian preachers to teach the mind, delight or inspire the affections and move the will. 'For,' he went on, 'to teach is a necessity, to please is a sweetness, to persuade is a victory.'[69] Modern communication theory agrees. 'When we learn to phrase our purposes in terms of specific responses from those attending to our messages, we have taken the first step towards efficient and effective communication.'[70] Our expectation, then, as the sermon comes to an end, is not merely that people will understand or remember or enjoy our teaching, but that they will do something about it. 'If there is no summons, there is no sermon.'[71]

The biblical authors were quite clear that this was the purpose of their teaching. Ezekiel was appointed 'a watchman for the house of Israel' in order to warn them of God's judgment and call them to repentance. The great pain of his prophetic ministry was that the people refused to respond to his words. God said to him, 'You are to them like one who sings love songs with a beautiful voice and plays well on an instrument, for they hear what you say, but they will not do it.' (Ezek. 33:30–33) Listening to sermons and listening to concerts, however, should be two very different experiences, for music is to be enjoyed, while Scripture is to be obeyed. The New Testament apostles make it plain that 'truth' brings with it moral demands: it is to be 'done' not merely heard, to be obeyed not merely believed.[72] For Jesus had said to them, 'if you know these things, blessed are you if you do them'. (John 13:17) James expressed the same necessity when he urged his readers to be 'doers of the word, and not hearers only'. (Jas. 1:22–25)

The great preachers in the history of the Church have shared this conviction. The Puritans were a notable example. 'The final characteristic of godly preaching was that every sermon had to have its "use" or application', relating particularly to 'the conversion of souls and their training in holiness'.[73] I have been told (although I cannot find this expression anywhere in their writings) that they used to speak of the need to 'preach through to the heart'. They certainly cannot be accused of by-passing the head, for they preached heavily doctrinal sermons. But they wanted their message to penetrate through the head to the heart, that is, to the decision-making centre of the human personality. Similarly, John Wesley supplies us in his *Journal* with plenty of evidence that he distinguished between 'head-work' and 'heart-work', and that he expected his preaching to get through to the heart. 'I observed none wounded, nor anything more than a calm, dull attention.' 'I cannot find my way to the hearts of the people of Perth.' Again, 'I made a pointed application to the hearts of all that were present.'[74]

Campbell Morgan preferred to speak of the will: 'The preacher is not merely asking a congregation to discuss a situation, and consider a proposition, or give attention to a theory. We are out to storm the citadel of the will, and capture it for Jesus Christ . . . Whether evangelizing or teaching does not matter. The appeal is the final thing.'[75]

Now citadels cannot be stormed without the use of violence. Nor can human hearts and wills. 'If a hardened heart is to be broken, it is not stroking but striking that must do it.'[76] In the same vein, Dr. Paul White, the famous Australian who worked as a Jungle Doctor in Tanzania, tells us in his autobiography what he conceives to be an author's or preacher's secrets of success: 'Hook 'em, hold 'em, hang on to 'em, humour 'em and hit 'em! This last is known as the punch line.'[77]

It is just here that many of us are weak. We would not be comfortable in using these metaphors of 'storming', 'striking', and 'hitting'. They are altogether too violent, too bellicose, for our mood. We have neither the right nor the wish, we say, to intrude into other people's religious privacy. Besides, we are scared of emotionalism. In consequence, we use the pulpit for the reading of harmless little essays, and seldom if ever press home a point which demands decision. R. W. Dale had a section in the first of his Yale lectures called 'Aimless Sermons'. He described how during a summer holiday he had listened to a preacher whose exegesis was sound and scholarly, whose thought was ingenious and fresh, and whose illustrations were admirable. 'But it did not seem to occur to the preacher that there was anybody listening to him . . . I could not make out what truth he wanted to make clearer to us or what neglected duty he wished us to discharge . . .' Dale told him afterwards that it would do him a world of good 'to make twenty or thirty speeches at ward meetings' – political speeches on hotly debated issues.

'To carry the vote and fire the zeal' of our congregations (Dale continued), this, gentlemen, is our true business. If we are to be successful, there must be vigorous intellectual activity, but it must be directed by a definite

248

intention to produce a definite result . . . We shall preach to no purpose unless we have a purpose in preaching. Archbishop Whately said of some preacher that 'he aimed at nothing, and hit it.'[78]

If Dale likened the preacher to a politician in a debating chamber seeking votes, others have likened him to an advocate in a law court, pleading a case before judge and jury, and confidently expecting a favourable verdict. Yet another picture is that of the fisherman, who by his preaching is determined to 'catch men'. (Luke 5:10) He refuses to be like the angler who, responding to an enquiry, confessed that he had not caught any fish, though he thought he had 'influenced' a good many. John Wilkins, the seventeenth-century Bishop of Chester, expressed this point admirably:

> The cheif [sic] end of an Orator is to *perswade* . . . And therefore that Preacher, who in his discourses does only flourish in generall notions, and does not drive at some particular argument, endeavouring to presse upon his auditory the *beleife* or *practise* of some *truth* or *duty*, is like an unwise Fisher, who spreads his net to the empty aire, were he cannot expect any successe of his labours.[79]

Perhaps the most striking metaphor, however, which has been used by a number of authors to illustrate the serious purpose we should have in our sermon applications, is that of gunfire, particularly in hunting or shooting. Bishop J. C. Ryle's comment on the sermons of George Whitefield was that they were 'not like the morning and evening gun at Portsmouth, a kind of formal discharge . . . that disturbs nobody'. On the contrary, 'they were all life and fire. There was no getting away from them . . . There was a holy violence about him which firmly took your attention by storm.'[80]

The person who developed this analogy most graphically was Henry Ward Beecher, in the very first Yale Lectures (1872). He likened his early attempts at preaching to his boyhood shooting escapades:

I used to go out hunting by myself, and I had great success in firing off my gun; and the game enjoyed it as much as I did, for I never hit them or hurt them. I fired off my gun as I see hundreds of men firing off their sermons. I loaded it, and bang! – there was a smoke, a report, but nothing fell; and so it was again and again.[81]

But, as he said in a later lecture, 'A sermon is not like a Chinese firecracker, to be fired off for the noise it makes. It is the hunter's gun, and at every discharge he should look to see his game fall. The power (?a misprint for 'powder') is wasted if nothing be hit.'[82]

Six years later the Yale Lectures were delivered by R. W. Dale of Birmingham (1829–95) and included this:

Mr Beecher said that in the elaborate doctrinal part of Jonathan Edwards' sermons the great preacher was only getting his guns into position; but that in his 'applications' he opened fire on the enemy. There are too many of us, I am afraid (commented Dale), who take so much time getting our guns 'into position' that we have to finish without firing a shot.[83]

As James Black summed it up, 'your business is serious gunfire with a target', and added, 'gentlemen, plenty of fire, but no fireworks!'[84]

Perhaps some of my readers find this gunfire metaphor inappropriate, even offensive, because the imagery is violent and destructive. Yet the analogy is intended to illustrate the preacher's goal (hitting a target), not his means of attaining it (causing a violent death). Jesus' fishing metaphor had a similar purpose. Whether we liken our ministry to fishing or shooting, the same basic point is in mind: we should confidently expect results, namely the catching or capturing of people for Christ.

Spurgeon, as one might expect, embellished the metaphor further, and enlivened it by his wit and wisdom.

It is of no use to fire your rifle into the sky (he said), when your object is to pierce men's hearts. To flourish your sabre finely is a thing which has been done so often that you need not repeat it. Your work is to charge home at the heart and conscience. Fire into the very centre of the foe. Aim at effect . . . effect upon the conscience and upon the heart. Some preachers remind me of the famous Chinese jugglers, who not long ago were everywhere advertized. One of these stood against a wall, and the other threw knives at him. One knife would be driven into the board just above his head, and another close by his ear, while under his armpit and between his fingers quite a number of deadly weapons were bristling. Wonderful art to be able to throw to a hair's breadth and never strike! How many among us have a marvellous skill in missing![85]

It is time to turn from the metaphors to the reality. What exactly do we hope to achieve by our sermons? 'I know what I want to say to my people,' an episcopal clergyman once said to me in Florida, 'but I don't know what I want to do with it.' Yet we must define our object; otherwise the conclusion of every sermon will be an embarrassing anticlimax. One way of summarizing the options is given in the four uses of Scripture, namely that it is profitable 'for teaching the truth and refuting error, or for reformation of manners and discipline in right living'. (2 Tim. 3:16 NEB) But this is too general. More particular was Charles Simeon's aim, by which he wanted his own *Horae Homileticae* (2,536 sermon outlines in twenty-one volumes) to be judged: do they 'uniformly tend to humble the sinner, to exalt the Saviour, and to promote holiness?'[86]

The precise application of our sermon depends, however, on two variables, namely the character of our text and the composition of our congregation. As for our text, we meditated on it until it yielded its dominant thought or theme. It is this, then, which now needs to be enforced in such a way that the people feel its impact and go away

251

determined to act upon it. Does the text call to repentance or stimulate faith? Does it evoke worship, demand obedience, summon to witness, or challenge to service? The text itself determines the particular response we desire.

As for our congregation, we have already emphasized the need to know them and their spiritual condition. Richard Bernard in *The Faithfull Shepheard* (1607), noting that 'no plaster cures when we do but only know it . . . but the particular application to the sore doth good,' listed some of the applications the preacher should have in mind:

> Inform the ignorant, confirm such as have understanding, reclaim the vicious, encourage the virtuous, convince the erroneous, strengthen the weak, recover again the backslider, resolve those that doubt, feed with milk and strong meat continually, in season and out of season.[87]

The only way to do this is to use our God-given imagination. We have been studying our text. Now we try to picture our congregation, and relate the one to the other. There is dear old Lucy, who has recently lost her husband and is experiencing the shock of bereavement and loneliness: what has my text to say to her? Or to Florence, the elderly spinster, who has never come to terms with her singleness? Or to Alan, who is feeling the weight of new responsibilities following his promotion? Or to John and Mary, who have just got married and are setting up their home? Or to those students facing finals and wondering about their career? Or to that Thomas who is full of doubts, that Agrippa who is 'almost persuaded', or that Paul who is newly committed to Christ? It is good to let our mind wander over the church family and ask prayerfully what message God might have for each from our text.

Here is the conclusion of George Whitefield's evangelistic address on *The Kingdom of God*:

I know that many of you come here out of curiosity: though you come only to see the congregation, yet if you come to Jesus Christ, Christ will accept of you. Are there any cursing, swearing soldiers here? Will you come to Christ, and list yourselves under the banner of the dear Redeemer? You are all welcome to Christ. Are there any little boys or little girls here? Come to Christ, and he will erect his kingdom in you . . . you that are old and grayheaded, come to Jesus Christ, and you shall be kings and priests to your God . . . If there be any of you ambitious of honour, do you want a crown, a sceptre? Come to Christ, and the Lord Jesus Christ will give you a kingdom that no man shall take from you.[88]

To give a modern example, this time ethical rather than evangelistic, a young man was invited to preach on the seventh commandment, 'you shall not commit adultery'. His sermon was biblical, brave, direct and practical, and he ended with the following four applications: to single young people (keep yourself pure for your future partner, and learn to be ruthless with the approaches to sin), to people in an adulterous relationship (make up your mind to break it, despite the pain), to married people (work at your marriage and set an example to the many young people who come from broken homes and have no model), and to the local church (have the courage to confront and discipline offenders, in obedience to Jesus' teaching in Matthew 18:15–17).[89]

We need also to be aware that people hear sermons through different 'filters'. Some will be receptive to our message. Others will be resistant to it because they perceive it as a threat to their world view, or culture, or family unity, or personal self-esteem, or sinful way of life, or economic lifestyle. Sensitive to these blocks, we may well need in the conclusion to resort to 'persuasion', a common description of the preaching of the apostles. We may seek to persuade by argument (anticipating and answering people's objections), or by admonition (warning them of the consequences of disobedience), or by indirect conviction (first arousing a moral judgment in them and then turning it upon themselves, as Nathan did with David), or by pleading (applying the gentle pressure of God's love).

Then, as the sermon ends, it is good to invite the people to pray. Although the Anglican tradition is for the congregation to stand while an ascription of praise to God is said, yet after many sermons this is inappropriate, and it is better to pray. Sometimes we will pray aloud and extempore, seeking to express the congregation's response to God's Word. At other times it may be wiser to call the people to silent prayer. For the Holy Spirit may be prompting different responses in different hearts, which a single prayer could never encompass. So why not leave them alone in the silence before God, so that the Holy Spirit may lead each person to crystallize his or her personal response and resolve?

Having added to the sermon its introduction and conclusion, we come to the final stage of our preparation.

(6) Write Down and Pray Over Your Message

The question now arises whether to write the sermon out. Since God has made us all differently, and given us distinct personalities and talents, there can be no fixed rule for everybody. Nevertheless, there seems to be a consensus that we should avoid the two extremes of complete improvisation on the one hand and slavery to a script on the other. Good extempore preaching is very rare. Few people are such clear thinkers and concise talkers that they can express themselves lucidly on their feet without prior written preparation. The great majority would degenerate, as Hensley Henson feared he would have done if he had tried it, 'into the type, so familiar in the religious world, and so deeply repugnant to my conscience and abhorrent to my feelings, which is not unfairly described as a *Windbag*.'[90] One who did try, and failed lamentably, was George Eliot's character the Rev. Amos Barton, the new and evangelical vicar of Shepperton village. A local farmer called Mr. Hackit was extremely uncomplimentary about his attempts:

> Our parson . . . can preach as good a sermon as need be heard when he writes it down. But when he tries to preach wi'out book, he rambles about, and doesn't stick to his text; and every now and then he flounders about like a sheep as has cast itself, and can't get on its legs again.[91]

Doubtless he would have done better if he had heeded Charles Simeon's advice to students not to preach extemporaneously until they have first preached 300–400 written sermons or been three to four years preaching.[92]

The opposite extreme is to read a manuscript word for word. Although this does not at all appeal to our age, we need to recognize that God's signal blessing has rested on some who have done it, notably Jonathan Edwards. His health was poor, his voice languid and his gestures scanty. As for his preaching, 'He *wrote* his sermons; and in so fine and so illegible a hand, that they could be read only be being brought near to the eye. "He carried his notes with him into the desk, and read most that he wrote: still, he was not confined to them." '[93]

To us today, however, if extempore preaching lacks precision, script-reading lacks immediacy. Our generation demands a relationship between preacher and congregation which is face to face and eyeball to eyeball. They approve of preachers like Dick Sheppard, the pacifist Vicar of St. Martin-in-the-Fields 1914–26, who 'always talked to a person' and 'never merely sprayed the solar system with words'.[94]

There seems to be only one way to combine precision of language with immediacy of delivery, and that is for us to write the sermon in our study but decline to read it from the pulpit. Writing is a most salutary discipline. First, it obliges us to think straight. Garrulous preachers can conceal slovenly thinking with clever speech; it is much more difficult to get away with a cover-up on paper. In fact, it is impossible to do so if we want to retain our integrity. Secondly, writing helps us to avoid slipping into the same old clichés; it provokes us to develop new ways of expressing old truths.

So we shall be wise to write the sermon out. But what shall we do with the manuscript? Not recommended is the practice of memorizing it and then leaving it behind, so that, when we are in the pulpit, we can read it off the back of our mind. The labour of such a task is enormous, the risk of forgetting our lines considerable, and the necessary mental energy so great that the preacher has to concentrate on the memorized script instead of on his message and congregation.

A second way is to take the manuscript into the pulpit, but use it for other purposes than reading. One who did this was Joseph Pilmore (1734–1825), who was first commissioned as an itinerant lay preacher by John Wesley and then ordained into the American Episcopal Church by Bishop Seabury, and who retained his evangelical fervour when Rector of Christ Church New York and St Paul's Church Philadelphia. A member of his congregation wrote of him:

He wrote his sermons, and . . . his manuscript was always before him. He began not only by reading, but by reading very deliberately, and with little animation; but he would gradually wax warm, and you would see his eyes begin to kindle, and the muscles of his face to move and expand, until at length his soul would be all on fire, and he would be rushing onward extemporaneously almost with the fury of a cataract. And the only use he would make of his manuscript in such cases would be to roll it up in his hand, and literally shake it at his audience.[95]

The third and best alternative is to reduce the manuscript to notes, and take these into the pulpit with us. It is certainly extraordinary how, if we have prepared carefully and written out the sermon and prayed over it, much of it comes back readily to our minds when we are preaching, while at the same time we have a certain freedom to depart from our notes or elaborate them. Professor James Stewart, himself a wonderfully fluent preacher, has told me that this was his method. 'I did try always to write the morning sermon at least out in full,' he has written, and 'on the Saturday morning I would reduce this to a one- or two-page summary, which then accompanied me to Church on the Sunday.'[96]

After the writing comes the praying. Of course we prayed before we began to prepare, and we have tried to continue throughout our preparation in an attitude of prayer. But now that the sermon is finished and written, we need to pray over it. The best time for this is the half hour before we leave for church on Sunday.

It is on our knees before the Lord that we can make the message our own, possess or re-possess it until it possesses us. Then, when we preach it, it will come neither from our notes, nor from our memory, but out of the depths of our personal conviction, as an authentic utterance of our heart. So, wrote Baxter, 'a minister should take some special pains with his heart before he is to go to the congregation.'[97] 'Get your sermon by heart,' pleaded Cotton Mather, meaning not 'learn it by heart' but 'get your heart suitably touched with what you have prepared.'[98] Every preacher knows the difference between a heavy sermon which trundles along the runway like an overloaded jumbo jet and never gets airborne, and a sermon which has 'what a bird has, a sense of direction and wings'.[99] Which kind any sermon will be is usually settled as we pray over it beforehand. We need to pray until our text comes freshly alive to us, the glory shines forth from it, the fire burns in our heart, and we begin to experience the explosive power of God's Word within us.

Prophets and wise men spoke of this in olden days, 'If I say, "I will not mention him, or speak any more in his name",' said Jeremiah, 'there is in my heart as it were a burning fire shut up in my bones, and I am weary with holding it in, and I cannot.' Job's younger 'comforter' Elihu, angry because the first three speakers had found no answer to Job's predicament, had a similar experience: 'I am full of words, the spirit within me constrains me. Behold, my heart is like wine that has no vent; like new wineskins, it is ready to burst. I must speak, that I may find relief . . .' Then there was the psalmist, who was oppressed by the wicked around him, 'My heart became hot within me. As I mused, the fire burned.'[100] God's message within us should also be like burning fire or fermenting wine. The pressure begins to build up inside us, until we feel we can contain it no longer. It is then that we are ready to preach.

The whole process of sermon preparation, from beginning to end, was admirably summed up by the American Black preacher who said, 'First, I reads myself full, next I thinks myself clear, next I prays myself hot, and then I lets go.'

Postscript

If the process of preparing sermons is so elaborate, I have sometimes been asked by ordination candidates and young preachers, how long does it take to prepare a single sermon? The question has always flummoxed me, because it is impossible to give a simple reply. Probably the best answer is 'your whole lifetime', because every sermon is, in a way, a distillation of everything one has learned hitherto; and is a reflection of the kind of person one has become over the years. The reason it is difficult to calculate the actual hours is that one cannot say precisely when the process began. Shall we include the time spent in background reading? Also, after one has been studying and preparing for a few years, one never comes to a verse or passage which one has not read or pondered before; one comes to it rather with an accumulated fund of ideas. If pressed, however, to say how long it takes from the moment the text is chosen to the moment the sermon is written out, I think that beginners will need ten to twelve hours ('twelve hours' work on a sermon is a good general rule,' said Bonhoeffer),[101] and that experienced preachers are not likely to reduce this to less than a half. A useful rule of thumb is that one needs at least one hour's preparation for every five minutes preached.

Notes

1 Spurgeon, *Lectures*, Second Series, p. 4.
2 Jowett, pp. 113–14.
3 From his treatise *On Preaching*, in Bainton, *Erasmus*, p. 323.
4 Oxford University Press.
5 S.P.C.K. 1969.
6 *The Calendar and Lessons for the Church Year*, p. 7.
7 Morris, p. 143.
8 Stewart, *Heralds*, pp. 110–11.
9 Ford, *Ministry*, p. 210.
10 Morgan, *Preaching*, p. 50.
11 Stalker, p. 166.
12 Tizard, p. 71.
13 Luccock, p. 205.
14 Bosanquet, p. 110.
15 Spurgeon, *Lectures*, First Series, p. 42.
16 Spurgeon, *All-Round Ministry*, p. 124.
17 Hirsch, p. 1.
18 Dale, p. 91.
19 This account is taken from a personal communication dated 7 December 1979.
20 Carus, p. 717.
21 Simeon, *Horae*, pp. vi, vii. The italics and capitals are Simeon's own.
22 ibid., Vol. XXI.
23 Hopkins, p. 59.
24 Baxter, *Reformed Pastor*, p. 160.
25 Jowett, p. 133.
26 Pitt-Watson, p. 65.
27 Mitchell, *Black Preaching*, p. 175.
28 Smyth, *The Art*, p. 27.
29 Gillett, p. 12.

30 Sangster, *The Craft*, p. 90.
31 Smyth, *The Art*, p. 177.
32 Nicoll, pp. 245, 249.
33 Spurgeon, *Lectures*, First Series, pp. 88–9.
34 Smyth, *The Art*, pp. 19–54.
35 ibid., p. 22.
36 Sangster, *The Craft*, pp. 53–94.
37 Luccock, pp. 134–47.
38 The *Guardian Weekly*, 29 January 1978.
39 Gowers, p. 1.
40 Arnold, in Gowers, p. 3.
41 Swift, in Gowers, p. 119.
42 Gowers, p. 47.
43 Grubb, pp. 153, 155.
44 Leacock, p. 109.
45 Lewis, C. S., *Studies*, pp. 6–7.
46 Lewis, W. H., *Letters*, p. 271.
47 Muggeridge, *Chronicles*, *The Green Stick*, p. 171.
48 Smyth, *Garbett*, p. 172.
49 Ps. 103:13; Ps. 1:4; Hos. 14:5; Isa. 40:31; Jer. 23:29.
50 Matt. 5:13, 14; Luke 17:24; Matt. 23:27; 1 Thess. 2:7; Jas. 4:14.
51 Sangster, *The Craft*, p. 211.
52 See the chapter entitled 'The Exemplum' in Smyth, *The Art*, pp. 55–98.
53 Smyth, *The Art*, p. 146.
54 Haller, pp. 140, 142.
55 From Chapter 3 of *The Human Situation* (1937), in Keir, pp. 65–66.
56 Beecher, pp. 127, 134.
57 Ryle, *Light*, p. 408.
58 Spurgeon, *Lectures*, Third Series, 'pp. 1–3.
59 Sangster, P., *Dr. Sangster*, p. 275.
60 Jowett, p. 141.
61 e.g. Jer. 1:6; I Cor. 3:1, 2; 14:20; Heb. 5:11–14.
62 Ps. 36:7; Ruth 2:12.
63 Sangster, W., *The Craft*, p. 239.
64 Ferris, p. 93.
65 Broadus, p. 101.
66 Vinet, p. 269.
67 Bull, p. 131.
68 Phil. 4:1; 2 Pet. 1:12, 13 cf. 3:1, 2.
69 *On Christian Doctrine*, IV.12, in Schaff, Vol. III, p. 583.

70 Berlo, p. 12.
71 Broadus, p. 210.
72 e.g. John 3:18–21; Rom. 1:18–23; 2 Thess. 2:10–12; 1 John 1:6, 8; 2 John 4; 3 John 3, 4.
73 Morgan, I., *Godly Preachers*, p. 28.
74 See the entries for 13 May 1769, 21 May 1774 and 13 June 1779.
75 Jones, p. 289 and Gammie, p. 198.
76 Baxter, *Reformed Pastor*, p. 160.
77 White, P., *Jungle Doctor*, p. 129.
78 Dale, pp. 22–4.
79 Wilkins, p. 25.
80 Ryle, *Christian Leaders*, p. 53.
81 Beecher, pp. 23–5.
82 ibid., p. 236.
83 Dale, p. 146.
84 Black, p. 62.
85 Spurgeon, *All-Round Ministry*, pp. 117–18.
86 Simeon *Horae*, Vol. 1, p. xxi.
87 Bernard, pp. 11 and 72. Similarly, Chapter VII of John Perkins's *The Art of Prophecying* (1631) is entitled 'Of the wayes how to use and apply doctrines'. He lists different categories of people and how to relate our message to them (pp. 664–8).
88 Dargan, Vol. II, pp. 314–15.
89 This was the conclusion of a sermon preached in All Souls Church by Roger Simpson.
90 Henson, *Retrospect*, Vol. III, pp. 312–13.
91 Eliot, p. 48.
92 Smyth, *The Art*, p. 178.
93 Dwight, Vol. I, p. 605.
94 *The Best of Dick Sheppard* ed. H. E. Luccock 1951, p. xix, in Davies, pp. 103–4.
95 Chorley, pp. 34–5.
96 From a private communication dated 30 September 1978.
97 Baxter, *Reformed Pastor*, p. 158.
98 Mather, p. 192.
99 Luccock, p. 12.
100 Jer. 20:9; Job 32:18–20; Ps. 39:3.
101 Fant, *Bonhoeffer*, p. 148.

CHAPTER SEVEN

Sincerity and Earnestness

Sincerity

Nothing is more nauseating to contemporary youth than hypocrisy, and nothing more attractive than sincerity. In this, moreover, they reflect the mind of Christ, who reserved his most scathing denunciations for hypocrites. Young people hate our adult shams and subterfuges. They have a very sensitive nose, with which they can smell the faintest odour of religious humbug from a considerable distance. They are especially suspicious of us preachers and of our loud pretensions; they sniff round us to see what inconsistencies they can discover, like dogs after a rat which has gone to ground. Not that they are invariably honest and consistent themselves; what fallen human being has ever been? Nevertheless, they are right to expect high standards of integrity in us. For preachers are not lecturers, who may discourse on topics remote from their own experience, concern and belief, but are personally committed to their message. So preachers must of all people be sincere.

The sincerity of a preacher has two aspects: he means what he says when in the pulpit, and he practises what he preaches when out of it. In fact, these things belong inevitably together since, as Richard Baxter put it, 'he that means as he speaks will surely do as he speaks.'[1]

The very first and most elementary application of this principle to the preacher is that he who proclaims the gospel must himself have embraced the gospel, and he who preaches Christ must know Christ. What shall we say, then, of the oddity of an unconverted preacher, or unevangelized evangelist? With customary forcefulness Spurgeon portrays him. 'A graceless pastor is a blind man elected to a professorship of optics, philosophizing upon light and vision . . . while he himself is absolutely in the dark! He is a dumb man elevated to the chair of music; a deaf man fluent upon symphonies and harmonies! He is a mole professing to educate eaglets; a limpet elected to preside over angels . . .'[2] We smile at his graphic imagery, but not at the grotesque anomaly he describes. Yet such people are still found in the pulpits of some churches.

No more remarkable instance can be cited than that of the Rev. William Haslam. Ordained into the Church of England ministry in 1842, he served conscientiously in a parish of North Cornwall. He was a Tractarian clergyman with a hearty dislike for dissenters, and an authority in things antiquarian and architectural. But he was not satisfied, having no spring of living water within him. Then in 1851, nine years after his ordination, while preaching from the gospel of the day on the text, 'What think ye of Christ?', the Holy Spirit (in answer no doubt to many prayers) opened his eyes to see the Christ of whom he was speaking, and his heart to believe in him. The change which came over him was so obvious that a local preacher, who happened to be in church, jumped up and shouted, 'The parson is converted! Hallelujah!', at which his voice was drowned by the praises of 300 or 400 of the congregation. As for Haslam himself, he 'joined in the outburst of praise, and, to make it more orderly . . . gave out the Doxology . . . and the people sang it with heart and voice, over and over again.' The news spread like wildfire 'that the parson was converted, and that by his own sermon, in his own pulpit!' His conversion was the beginning of a great revival in his parish, which lasted for nearly three years, with a vivid sense of God's presence, and conversions almost daily, while in later years God called him into the most unusual ministry of leading many of his fellow clergy to a personal knowledge of Jesus Christ.[3]

Church members have a right to expect, however, that the Holy Spirit has done more in the life of their pastors than bring them to conversion. They naturally look for the fruit of the Spirit as well, that is, the ripening of Christian character. Paul told Timothy and Titus to be models of Christian behaviour. Peter similarly instructed the elders, instead of domineering, to be 'examples to the flock'.[4] The emphasis is plain. Communication is by symbol as well as speech. For 'a man cannot only preach, he must also live. And the life that he lives, with all its little peculiarities, is one of two things: either it emasculates his preaching or it gives it flesh and blood.'[5] We cannot hide what we are. Indeed, what we are speaks as plainly as what we say. When these two voices blend, the impact of the message is doubled. But when they contradict each other, even the positive witness of the one is negatived by the other. This was the case with the man Spurgeon describes as a good preacher but a bad Christian: he 'preached so well and lived so badly, that when he was in the pulpit everybody said he ought never to come out again, and when he was out of it they all declared he never ought to enter it again.'[6]

It is at this point that a practical problem presents itself to us. Pastors are told to be models of Christian maturity. The congregation tend to view us as such, to put us on a pedestal, and to idealize, even idolize, us. We know, however, that the reputation they give us is at least partly false, because, although indeed the grace of God has been and continues to be at work in us, we are not the paragons of virtue they sometimes seem to think. So what should we do? Does not the very sincerity we are discussing require us to destroy the myth they have created and to divulge the truth about ourselves? What degree of self-disclosure is appropriate in the pulpit? My response to these important questions is that once again we should avoid extreme reactions. On the one hand, to turn the pulpit into a confessional would be inappropriate, unseemly, and helpful to nobody. Yet, on the other, to masquerade as perfect would be both dishonest in us and discouraging to the congregation. So certainly we should admit the truth that like them we are human beings of human frailty and fallenness, vulnerable to temptation and suffering, struggling with doubt, fear and sin, and needing continuously to depend on God's forgiving and liberating grace. In this way the preacher can remain a model – but a model of humility and truth.

The Preacher as a Person
From all this it is again evident that preaching can never be degraded into the learning of a few rhetorical techniques. A whole theology lies beneath it, and a whole lifestyle behind it. The practice of preaching cannot be divorced from the person of the preacher.

Hence the New Testament emphasis on the self-discipline of the pastor. 'Take heed to yourselves' was the admonition Paul addressed to the presbyters of the Ephesian church, before adding 'and to all the flock in which the Holy Spirit has made you overseers'. (Acts 20:28) He wrote similarly to Timothy: 'take heed to yourself and to your teaching'. (1 Tim. 4:16) The order is vital. We pastors have God-given responsibilities both to the congregation we serve and to the doctrine we teach, for both have been committed to us. Yet our prior responsibility is to ourselves, to guard our personal walk with God and our loyalty to him. Nobody can be a good pastor or teacher of others who is not first a good servant of Jesus Christ. Disciplined habits, of pastoral visitation and counselling on the one hand, and of theological study and sermon preparation on the other, become barren exercises unless they are supported by disciplined habits of personal devotion, especially in biblical meditation and prayer. Every pastor knows how exacting his ministry is. We may encounter misunderstanding and even opposition; we shall certainly grow weary in mind and body; we may also have to endure loneliness and discouragement. Even the strongest personalities collapse under the weight of these pressures, unless the power of God is being revealed in our weakness, and the life of Jesus in our mortal bodies, so that 'inwardly we are being renewed day by day. (2 Cor. 4:7–11 and 16)

The indissoluble link between preacher and preaching is reflected in many of the definitions of preaching. One of the most widely known was given by Phillips Brooks, who for twenty-two years was Rector of Trinity Church in Boston (1869–91), delivered the 1877 Lyman Beecher lectures at Yale Divinity School, and for the last two years of his life (1891–1893) was Bishop of Massachusetts. His first lecture was entitled 'The Two Elements in Preaching', and in it he gave this definition:

> Preaching is the communication of truth by man to men. It has in it two essential elements, truth and personality. Neither of those can it spare and still be preaching . . . Preaching is the bringing of truth through personality . . . The truth is in itself a fixed and stable element; the personality is a varying and growing element.[7]

Perhaps Phillips Brooks was consciously echoing Henry Ward Beecher, who gave the first Yale lectures in 1872 in memory of his father. 'A preacher', he said, 'is, in some degree, a reproduction of the truth in personal form. The truth must exist in him as a living experience, a glorious enthusiasm, an intense reality.'[8]

A somewhat similar emphasis may be discerned in the definition of preaching offered by the Congregational layman, Bernard Lord Manning (1892–1941), namely 'a manifestation of the Incarnate Word, from the Written Word, by the Spoken Word'. He went on to say that preaching is 'a most solemn act of worship, in which the thing given – the Gospel of the Son of God – overshadows and even transfigures the preacher by whom it is declared.'[9] It is certainly inconceivable that a preacher could remain unmoved by what he preaches. It is the message which makes the preacher, controlling his thoughts and inspiring his deeds. Hence James Black's exuberant definition: 'To us, preaching is the natural overflow of our religion. We have received good news, and we long to tell it to others. Our religion is like joy we cannot suppress or contain. It bubbles over like a brimming cup . . . Preaching is not a duty in any sense, but a sheer, inevitable joy. It is a spontaneous passion, like the coming of love into a young man's heart.'[10] These four definitions all emphasize that there is an indispensable link between the preacher and the act of preaching.

Arguments for Sincerity
To most people sincerity is a self-evident virtue; it hardly needs to be commended. Yet the ease with which all of us decline from strict honesty and slip into some degree of pretense or hypocrisy suggests that we shall be wise to arm ourselves with arguments. They are not far to seek; the New Testament deploys at least three.

First, it warns us of the dangers inherent in being a teacher. To be sure, teaching is a spiritual gift, and its ministry a great privilege. At the same time, it is a ministry fraught with peril. For teachers who instruct others cannot plead ignorance of their own curriculum. As Paul wrote of a Jewish rabbi, 'if you are sure that you are a guide to the blind, a light to those who are in darkness, a corrector of the foolish, a teacher of children, having in the law the embodiment of knowledge and truth – you then who teach others, will you not teach yourself?' (Rom. 2:17–21) The reason why hypocrisy is particularly unpleasant in teachers is that it is inexcusable. Hence the harshness of Jesus' judgment on the Pharisees, 'for they preach but do not practise.' (Matt. 23:1–3) Hence also James's surprising advice, 'let not many of us become teachers, my brethren.' Why not? 'For you know that we who teach shall be judged with greater strictness.' (Jas. 3:1)

Secondly, hypocrisy causes great offence. Without doubt many people have been alienated from Christ by the hypocritical behaviour of some who claim to follow him. Paul knew this, and was determined not to be a stumbling block to other people's faith: 'we put no obstacle in any-one's way, so that no fault may be found with our ministry, but as servants of God we commend ourselves in every way.' (2 Cor. 6:3, 4) He then proceeded to list his endurance and his character as evidence of the reality of his faith. There was no dichotomy between his message and his behaviour.

With other preachers it is different. We make great claims for Christ and his salvation while up in the pulpit, but when we descend from it we deny him and give no more evidence of being saved than anybody else. Then our message lacks credibility. People will no more accept our Christian message if our life contradicts it than they would take a cold cure recommended by a salesman who coughs and sneezes between each sentence.[11] We greatly hinder our own work, says Baxter, if for an hour or two on Sunday we build up with our mouths, and then during the rest of the week pull down with our hands:

> It is a palpable error in those ministers that make such disproportion between their preaching and their living, that they will study hard to preach exactly and study little or not at all to live exactly. All the week long is little enough to study how to speak two hours; and yet one hour seems too much to study how to live all the week . . . We must study as hard how to live well as how to preach well.[12]

William Golding is a contemporary novelist who has vividly illustrated the negative power of hypocrisy. In his book *Free Fall* he tells the story of Sammy Mountjoy, an illegitimate child brought up in a slum, who became a famous artist. During his school days he was torn between two teachers and between the two worlds they represented. On the one hand there was Miss Rowena Pringle, a Christian who taught Scripture, and on the other Mr. Nick Shales, an atheist who taught science. Hers was the world of 'the burning bush', of supernatural mystery, his of a rationally explicable universe. Instinctively, Sammy was drawn to the burning bush. Unfortunately, however, the advocate of this Christian interpretation of life was a frustrated spinster who had her knife into Sammy because he had been adopted by the clergyman she had hoped to marry. She took her revenge by being cruel to the boy. 'But how,' Sammy later asked himself, 'could she crucify a small boy . . . and then tell the story of that other crucifixion with every evidence in her voice of sorrow for human cruelty and wickedness? I can understand how she hated, but not how she kept on such apparent terms of intimacy with heaven.'[13] It was this contradiction which kept Sammy from Christ.

Miss Pringle vitiated her teaching. She failed to convince, not by what she said but by what she was. Nick persuaded me to his natural scientific universe by what he was, not by what he said. I hung for an instant between two pictures of the universe; then the ripple passed over the burning bush and I ran towards my friend. In that moment a door closed behind me. I slammed it shut on Moses and Jehovah.[14]

The third argument for sincerity concerns the positive influence of being a real person. This was evident in the case of Paul. He had nothing to hide. Having decisively 'renounced disgraceful, underhanded ways', his policy was to make an 'open statement of the truth' and so commend himself 'to every man's conscience in the sight of God'. (2 Cor. 4:2) Guile and deception were abhorrent to him. He exercized his ministry in the open, and could appeal to both God and man as his witnesses (e.g. 1 Thess. 2:1–12). His personal conviction, consistency of conduct and rejection of all subterfuge provided a strong base for his whole ministry. There was nothing in his life or lifestyle which hindered his hearers from believing or which they could have made an excuse for not believing. They believed him because he was believable. What he said and what he was were all of a piece.

A strangely fascinating power is exerted by those who are utterly sincere. Such believers attract unbelievers, as with the case of David Hume, the eighteenth-century British deistic philosopher who rejected historic Christianity. A friend once met him hurrying along a London street and asked him where he was going. Hume replied that he was going to hear George Whitefield preach. 'But surely,' his friend asked in astonishment, 'you don't believe what Whitefield preaches, do you?' 'No, I don't,' answered Hume, 'but he does.'[15]

I am convinced that in our day simple sincerity has not lost any of its power to appeal or to impress. It was in 1954 that Billy Graham first hit the headlines in Britain, with his Greater London Crusade. Approximately 12,000 people came to the Haringay Arena every night for three months. Most nights I was there myself, and as I looked round that vast crowd, I could not help comparing it with our half-empty churches. 'Why do these people come to listen to Billy Graham,' I asked myself, 'when they don't come to listen to us?' Now I am sure that many answers could have been justly given to that question. But the answer I kept giving myself was this: 'There is an incontrovertible sincerity about that young American evangelist. Even his fiercest critics all concede that he is sincere. I really believe he is the first transparently sincere Christian preacher many of these people have ever heard.' Today, twenty-five years later, I have found no reason to change my mind.

Sincerity has become an even more vital quality in the television age. John Poulton has written about this in his perceptive little book *A Today Sort of Evangelism*:

The most effective preaching comes from those who embody the things they are saying. They *are* their message . . . Christians . . . need to look like what they are talking about. It is *people* who communicate primarily, not words or ideas . . . Television has drilled us all to watch for the hesitancies, the over-quick response . . . Television has played havoc with the politician's trade. It has revealed the unrealities, the case-pleading, the artificial furies . . . Authenticity (on the other hand) gets across from deep down inside people . . . A momentary insincerity can cast doubt on all that has made for communication up to that point . . . What communicates now is basically personal authenticity.[16]

Thus, hypocrisy always repels, but integrity or authenticity always attracts.

One of the chief evidences of authenticity is a willingness to suffer for what we believe. Paul spoke of his afflictions as his credentials.[17] The insincere preacher soft-pedals the gospel of free grace, in order that he 'may not be persecuted for the cross of Christ'. (Gal. 5:11; 6:12) The true servant of God, on the other hand, commends himself by his endurance of opposition. (2 Cor. 6:4, 5) His sufferings may be internal too. For the preacher is particularly vulnerable to doubt and depression. It is often through a dark and lonely struggle that he has emerged into the light of a serene faith. His hearers can discern it, and will give heed to him the more attentively. Colin Morris has expressed this well:

> It is not from a pulpit but a cross that power-filled words are spoken. Sermons need to be seen as well as heard to be effectual. Eloquence, homiletical skill, biblical knowledge are not enough. Anguish, pain, engagement, sweat and blood punctuate the stated truths to which men will listen.[18]

Personal sincerity is probably the best context in which to mention the practical matters of voice production and gesture, which cause anxiety to most young and inexperienced preachers. It is understandable that they should be apprehensive about their speech ('what do I sound like?') and their bearing ('what do I look like?'). In consequence, some determine to find out. They stand before the mirror, strike a variety of poses and watch themselves gesticulate; they also listen to themselves on a cassette recorder. Indeed, nowadays sight and sound have been combined in the video recorder, which is already in regular use by American seminarians who are learning to preach, and in some other countries. Well, I do not want to rule out

271

altogether the use of these devices, for I do not doubt their helpfulness. And certainly audio- and video-tape are preferable to the mirror, since before the mirror one is bound to be acting, whereas tape permits the later and objective evaluation of a sermon which during its actual delivery was entirely artless. Nevertheless, I still want to warn you of the dangers. If you look at yourself in the mirror, and listen to yourself on tape, or do both simultaneously on video-tape, I fear you may find that you continue to look at yourself and listen to yourself when you are in the pulpit. In that case you will condemn yourself to the cramping bondage of preoccupation with yourself just at the time when, in the pulpit, it is essential to cultivate self-forgetfulness through a growing awareness of the God for whom and the people to whom you are speaking. I know actors make use of glass and tape, but preachers are not actors, nor is the pulpit a stage. So beware! It may be more valuable to ask a friend to be candid with you about your voice and mannerisms, especially if they need correction. An Indian proverb says 'he who has a good friend needs no mirror.' Then you can be yourself and forget yourself.

I can myself testify to the great value of having one or more 'lay critics'. When I began to preach at the end of 1945, I requested two medical student friends to act as mine. (Medical people are excellent because they are trained in the art of observation!) Although I remember being devastated by some of the letters they wrote me, their criticisms were always salutary. Both are now eminent medical men.[19] A preacher who belongs to a team ministry should certainly ask his colleagues for their comments. Indeed, an occasional group evaluation, either by the staff team or by a specially convened group which includes lay people, has proved immensely valuable to preachers. The evaluation will then go beyond speech and gesture, manner and mannerisms, to the content of the sermon, including our use of Scripture, our dominant thought and aim, our structure, words and illustrations, and our introduction and conclusion.

Spurgeon has two lectures in his *Second Series* on 'Posture, Action and Gesture' in the delivery of sermons, illustrated by cartoons of grotesquely gesticulating clerics. These lectures contain a lot of sensible and amusing advice, yet he is obviously concerned lest he make his students too self-conscious. He would prefer them to be clumsy and even eccentric rather than start 'posturing and performing'.[20]

> I hope we have foresworn the tricks of professional orators (he writes), the strain for effect, the studied climax, the prearranged pause, the theatric strut, the mouthing of words, and I know not what besides, which you may see in certain pompous divines who still survive upon the face of the earth. May such become extinct animals ere long, and may a living, natural, simple way of talking out the gospel be learned by us all; for I am persuaded that such a style is one which God is likely to bless.[21]

'Gentlemen', he said to his students in another lecture, 'I return to my rule – use your own natural voices. Do not be monkeys, but men; not parrots, but men of originality in all things . . . I would repeat this rule till I wearied you if I thought you would forget it: be natural, be natural, be natural evermore.'[22]

Such naturalness is the twin of sincerity. Both forbid us to ape other people. Both tell us to be ourselves.

Earnestness

Earnestness goes one step beyond sincerity. To be sincere is to *mean* what we say and to *do* what we say; to be earnest is, in addition, to *feel* what we say. Earnestness is deep feeling, and is indispensable to preachers. 'No man can be a great preacher without great feeling' wrote James W. Alexander of Princeton.[23] For 'it is a matter of universal observation that a speaker who would excite deep feeling must feel deeply himself.'[24]

Not that the need for earnestness is restricted to Christian communication, or even to speech. Every serious attempt to communicate requires us to put feeling into it. This is certainly true of music. As an example, let me take José Hernandez' classic nineteenth-century poem *The Gaucho*, the name given to an Argentinian descendant from the original Spanish settlers, who earns his living by raising cattle and horses. It is a long ballad, which tells the story of a gaucho called Martin Fierro, his varied experiences and the injustices done to him. In the penultimate chapter he gives fatherly advice to his sons. They must trust in God, be wary of men, work hard, not quarrel and avoid drink. Then he goes on to their music-making by guitar and song:

> If you want to be singers, feel it first –
>   And you won't have to watch your style:
>   Don't ever tune up your strings, my boys,
>   Just to hear yourselves, and to make a noise,
> But get in the habit, that when you sing,
>   It's always of things worth while.[25]

It sounds obvious that worthwhile song and worthwhile speech will both give expression to deep feeling. Yet it has been a regular complaint in many Christian traditions that the pulpit offers preaching without feeling. 'We have loud and vehement, we have smooth and graceful, we have splendid and elaborate preaching, but very little that is earnest.'[26] Mark Twain gave a graphic account of a Sunday morning service: 'The minister gave out his text and droned along monotonously through an argument that was so prosy that many a head by and by began to nod – and yet it was an argument that dealt in limitless fire and brimstone, and thinned the predestined elect to a company so small as to be hardly worth the saving.' Young Tom Sawyer found it so boring (despite the solemnity of the subject) that he produced a large black beetle from his pocket, whose adventures both with Tom and with a vagrant poodle dog created a hilarious diversion. At last, however, the sermon and the service ended. 'It was a genuine relief to the whole congregation when the ordeal was over, and the benediction pronounced.'[27]

It is true that the amount of feeling we either have or express is due to a large extent to our natural temperament. Some have a more lively disposition, others a more lethargic. Nevertheless, to handle issues of eternal life and death as if we were discussing nothing more serious than the weather, and to do so in a listless and lackadaisical manner, is to be inexcusably frivolous. 'We must not talk to our congregations,' said Spurgeon to his students, 'as if we were half asleep. Our preaching must not be articulate snoring.'[28] For one thing is certain: if we ourselves grow sleepy over our message, our listeners can hardly be expected to stay awake.

It should not be necessary to develop an apologetic for earnestness. Yet I fear that it is. Earnestness is the quality of Christians who care. First and foremost, they care about God, about his glory and his Christ. When Paul in Athens was 'provoked' because he saw the city smothered by its idols, he was feeling indignant over Athenian idolatry, and jealous for the honour of the one, living and true God. (Acts 17:16) He cared about the glory of God. And when he told the Philippians that many were living 'as enemies of the cross of Christ', he could do so only 'with tears'. (3:18) To think that people were contradicting the purpose of Christ's death, by trusting in their own righteousness instead of his, and by living in self-indulgence instead of holiness, made him weep. He cared about the glory of Christ. So should we.

We should also care about people and their lostness. Jesus wept over the impenitent city of Jerusalem because its inhabitants were resistant to his love and ignorant of their true welfare. (Matt. 23:37; Luke 19:41, 42) In the evangelistic ministry of the apostle Paul as well, preaching and weeping went hand in hand. For three years in Ephesus he 'did not cease night or day to admonish every one with tears'. (Acts 20:31; cf. v; 19 and v. 37) We must not imagine, however, that weeping died out with the New Testament. To be sure, Anglo-Saxon inheritance and contemporary British culture would frown, even scowl on any such outward display of emotion. But what does this say about our ability to care? Authentic Christian evangelists, bearing the good news of salvation and fearing that some may reject it and so condemn themselves to hell, have never been far from tears. George Whitefield is a good example. People always sensed that he loved them, writes his biographer John Pollock.

> His tears – and he could seldom manage a sermon without weeping – were totally unaffected. 'You blame me for weeping,' he would say, 'but how can I help it when you will not weep for yourselves, although your immortal souls are on the verge of destruction, and for aught I know, you are hearing your last sermon and may never more have another opportunity to have Christ offered to you?'[29]

D. L. Moody is a yet more modern example. We are told that Dr. R. W. Dale, who for thirty-six years was pastor of Carr's Lane Congregational Church in Birmingham, was inclined at first to look on Mr. Moody with disfavour. But then 'he went to hear him, and his opinion was altered. He regarded him ever after with profound respect, and considered that he had a right to preach the gospel "because he could never speak of a lost soul without tears in his eyes".'[30]

I constantly find myself wishing that we twentieth-century preachers could learn to weep again. But either our tear-springs have dried up, or our tear-ducts have become blocked. Everything seems to conspire together to make it impossible for us to cry over lost sinners who throng the broad road which leads to destruction. Some preachers are so preoccupied with the joyful celebration of salvation that they never think to weep over those who are rejecting it. Others have been deceived by the devil's lie of universalism. Everybody will be saved in the end, they say, and nobody will be lost. Their eyes are dry because they have closed them to the awful reality of eternal death and outer darkness of which both Jesus and his apostles spoke. Yet others are faithful in warning sinners of hell, but do so with a glibness and even a sick pleasure, which are almost more terrible than the blindness of those who ignore or deny its reality. To these intolerable attitudes the weeping of Jesus and Paul, of Whitefield and Moody, provides a healthy alternative.

The Puritans also shared this perspective, notably Richard Baxter. What Broadus aptly terms 'his tremendous earthshaking earnestness'[31] was due to his sense of urgency in the face of approaching death and eternity. He expressed it in his poem 'Love Breathing Thanks and Praise':

> This called me out to work while it was day;
> And warn poor souls to turn without delay:
> Resolving speedily thy Word to preach,
> With Ambrose I at once did learn and teach.
> Still thinking I had little time to live,
> My fervent heart to win men's souls did strive.
> *I preached as never sure to preach again,*
> *And as a dying man to dying men!*
> O how should preachers men's repenting crave
> Who see how near the Church is to the grave?
> And see that while we preach and hear, we die,
> Rapt by swift time to vast eternity![32]

More eloquent still are those passages in *The Reformed Pastor* (1656) in which Richard Baxter both bemoaned his own lack of earnestness and exhorted his fellow-pastors to bestir themselves. He wrote of himself in the following terms:

I marvel how I can preach . . . slightly and coldly, how I can let men alone in their sins, and that I do not go to them and beseech them for the Lord's sake to repent, however they take it, and whatever pains or trouble it should cost me. I seldom come out of the pulpit but my conscience smiteth me that I have been no more serious and fervent. It accuseth me not so much for want of human ornaments or elegance, nor for letting fall an uncomely word; but it asketh me: 'how could'st thou speak of life and death with such a heart? Should'st thou not weep over such a people, and should not thy tears interrupt thy words? Should'st not thou cry aloud and show them their transgressions, and entreat and beseech them as for life and death?'[33]

Because he was thus critical of his personal failings in this area, Baxter was well-qualified to exhort his colleagues in the pastorate to greater earnestness:

How few ministers do preach with all their might? . . . Alas, we speak so drowsily or gently, that sleeping sinners cannot hear. The blow falls so light that hard-hearted persons cannot feel it . . . What excellent doctrines some ministers have in hand, and let it die in their hands for want of close and lively application . . . O Sirs, how plainly, how closely and earnestly should we deliver a message of such nature as ours is, when the everlasting life or death of men is concerned in it . . . What! speak coldly for God and for men's salvation? . . . Such a work as preaching for men's salvation should be done with all our might – that the people can *feel* us preach when they hear us.[34]

So far I have concentrated on the appropriateness of deep feelings to grave subjects. How can we deliver a solemn message in a flippant manner, or refer to the eternal destinies of men and women as if we were discussing where they will spend their summer holidays? No, topic and tone, matter and manner must match one another, or the anomaly will be deeply offensive. A congregation learns the seriousness of the gospel by the seriousness with which their pastors expound it. But this fact leads to a further aspect of the subject, namely that earnestness of manner is one of the surest ways of arousing and holding people's attention.

The ninth address in Spurgeon's first series of *Lectures to my Students* has the arresting title *Attention!* It concerns 'how to obtain and retain the attention of our hearers', and contains that combination of common sense and good humour which we have come to associate with this giant of a man. His first piece of advice could hardly be more practical: 'The next best thing to the grace of God for a preacher is oxygen. Pray that the windows of heaven may be opened, but begin by opening the windows of your meeting-house . . . A gust of fresh air through the building might be to the people the next best thing to the gospel itself; at least it would put them into a fit frame of mind to receive the truth.'[35] Next after oxygen 'the first golden rule' he establishes is 'always say something worth hearing,'[36] and moreover something which the people recognize to be of importance to themselves. Mourners do not fall asleep while the will is being read, if they expect to be beneficiaries of it, nor do prisoners go to sleep while the judge is summing up and their life or freedom are at stake. 'Self-interest quickens attention. Preach up on practical themes, pressing, present, personal matters, and you will secure an earnest hearing.'[37]

Spurgeon's next counsel is 'be interested yourself and you will interest others.' He quotes William Romaine, the eighteenth-century evangelical leader, that it is infinitely more important to know the *heart* of preaching than its *art*, by which he meant putting one's whole heart and soul into it. 'Have something to say, and say it earnestly, and the congregation will be at your feet.'[38] By contrast,

nothing will avail if you go to sleep yourself while you are preaching. Is that possible? Oh, possible! It is done every Sunday. Many ministers are more than half-asleep all through the sermon; indeed, they never were awake at any time, and probably never will be unless a cannon should be fired off near their ear: tame phrases, hackneyed expressions and dreary monotones make the staple of their discourses, and they wonder that the people are so drowsy: I confess I do not.[39]

Mind and Heart

Sleepy preaching sounds so ludicrous, and is such a contradiction in terms, that we need to enquire into its origins. Why is it, for example, that the pulpit tradition of the Episcopal Church, particularly in England, is to exhibit a gentle sweet reasonableness and never to show any emotion? I suspect it is because Anglicanism has always valued scholarship and cherished the ideal of the educated minister, and then supposed that any kind of emotional display is incompatible with them.

I choose Parson James Woodforde as my example, who has delighted generations of English readers by the five volumes of his *Diary of a Country Parson 1758–1802*. Ministering for nearly thirty years in the village of Weston in Norfolk, the keynote of his life was 'tranquillity'. He loved sport, animals, country life, and above all good food and drink. Searching his five volumes I learned a great deal about his favourite dishes and wines, but nothing at all about his favourite texts. Some years ago, however, Professor Norman Sykes gained access to forty of Woodforde's unpublished sermons and was thus able to look behind the 'laconic entries' in the diary. He discovered that James Woodforde preached from the Bible, and that reasonableness was the hallmark of his exposition. In one sermon he warned his flock 'against the contemporary bugbear of "enthusiasm"', against 'religious phrensy, by which men have been led into the greatest and wildest extravagancies'. True, he went on to warn them against the opposite danger of 'a culpable languor and insensibility of spirit in matters of religion'. Nevertheless, it is evident that Parson Woodforde was more frightened of 'enthusiasm' than of barren orthodoxy.[40]

This was certainly the prevalent fear of eighteenth-century ecclesiastical leaders, who made sweeping generalizations about the excesses of 'Methodism', had refused to come to terms with the evangelical revival, and were relieved that the Methodists had taken themselves outside the Established Church. 'Enthusiasm' was to them a dirty word, and it is typical of those days that a church bell could be inscribed (or so it is said) with the paradoxical doxology 'Glory to God and damnation to enthusiasts'. Hence the stir created by Charles Simeon when in 1782 he became Vicar of that Church, and began preaching his expository sermons with much emotion. Hugh Evan Hopkins, his latest biographer, writes,

> Abner Brown remembers sitting next to a married undergraduate and his family in Trinity Church and overhearing their small daughter, intrigued by the antics of the demonstrative man in the pulpit, whispering to her mother, 'O Mama, what is the gentleman in a passion about?' . . . As his curate Carus wrote in his *Memoirs*, 'The intense fervour of his feelings he cared not to restrain; his whole soul was in his subject, and he spoke and acted exactly as he felt.'[41]

Simeon himself, when towards the end of his life the gout limited his activity, wrote to Thomas Thomason, 'I compare myself to bottled small beer; being corked up, and opened only twice a week, I make a good report; but if I were opened every day I should soon be as ditch-water.'[42]

Simeon's influential ministry at Holy Trinity, Cambridge, which lasted for fifty-four years, offers us a model of the reconciliation of emotion with reason in preaching. He was certainly emotional, as his hearers have testified, but nobody could accuse him of the kind of 'enthusiasm' which denigrates the intellect or despises theology. On the contrary, a perusal of his collected sermons in *Horae Homileticae* reveals his painstaking thoughtfulness in analysis, exegesis and application. In fact, his outlines look a little dull today, and one sometimes wonders what he got himself into a passion about.

Nevertheless, the combination of mind and heart, the rational and the emotional, was obviously present in Simeon's preaching, and for this combination there is ample precedent in the New Testament. I have already alluded to Paul's tears. But what about his mighty intellect which has kept scholars studying his thoughts ever since? The same apostle who reasoned with people out of the Scriptures, and sought to convince them by the power of argument and of the Holy Spirit, also wept over them like his Master before him. Consider how exposition and exhortation blend with one another in his letters. For example, he gives at the end of 2 Corinthians 5 one of the major explanations of the doctrine of reconciliation in the New Testament. He handles the tremendous themes that God was in Christ reconciling the world to himself, that he determined not to count against sinners their sins, but that for our sake he actually made Christ to be sin who knew no sin in order that in him we might become God's righteousness. Here are tightly packed assertions about God and his initiative, about Christ and his cross, and about sin, reconciliation and righteousness, which commentators are still struggling to unpack and explain. Yet Paul is not content with a profound theological statement. He goes beyond the fact of reconciliation to the ministry and message of reconciliation, beyond what God did in Christ to what he now does in us, beyond the affirmation of Christ's apostles that 'God was in Christ reconciling' to the appeal of Christ's ambassadors 'be reconciled to God'. If he did not stop with the exposition but went on to the appeal, he equally did not issue the appeal until he had first given the exposition. In his ministry affirmation and appeal were inseparable.

The contemporary Church urgently needs to learn Paul's lesson and follow his example. To be sure, some preachers have no fear of enthusiasm. In evangelistic preaching they make interminable appeals for decision or conversion.

Their sermons are sometimes nothing but one, long, protracted appeal. Yet their listeners are bewildered, because they have not grasped (or even been helped to grasp) either the nature or the ground of the appeal. The request for decision without doctrine is an offence to human beings, for it is little less than a mindless manipulation.

Other preachers make the opposite mistake. Their exposition of the central biblical doctrines of the gospel is impeccable. They are faithful to Scripture, lucid in explanation, felicitous in language, and contemporary in application. It would be hard to find fault with their content. Yet somehow they appear cold and aloof. No note of urgency is ever heard in their voice, and no suspicion of a tear is ever seen in their eyes. They would never dream of leaning over the pulpit in order to beg sinners in the name of Christ to repent, come to him and be reconciled with God. They resemble the preacher of whom Spurgeon wrote, 'It is dreadful work to listen to a sermon, and feel all the while as if you were sitting out in a snowstorm, or dwelling in a house of ice, clear but cold, orderly but killing . . .'[43] No wonder he pleaded instead for 'much heavenly fire', and declared that 'even fanaticism is to be preferred to indifference.'[44] 'Give us more of the speech which comes of a burning heart,' he cried, 'as lava comes of a volcanic overflow . . .'[45]

What is needed today then is the same synthesis of reason and emotion, exposition and exhortation, as was achieved by Paul. Writing of Isaac Barrow, the seventeenth-century Professor of Greek at Cambridge, whom he describes as 'a traveller, a philologist, a mathematician and a divine', J. W. Alexander goes on to call him 'the eloquent reasoner' and adds that 'he abounds in high argument, which is . . . inflamed by passion.'[46] Earlier in his book Alexander has made a plea for 'theological preaching'. What interests people, he says, is 'argument made red-hot', for 'argument admits of great vehemence and fire'.[47]

A British preacher of this century who made a plea for the same combination was Dr. George Campbell Morgan, minister of Westminster Chapel, London, from 1904 to 1917 and again from 1933 to 1943. At Cheshunt College, Cambridge, which trained men for the Congregational ministry and of which he was President from 1911–1914, he lectured on preaching. The three essentials of a sermon, he said, are 'truth, clarity and passion'.[48] On 'passion' he told a tale of the great English actor, Macready. A preacher once asked him how he could draw such crowds by fiction, while he was preaching the truth and not getting any crowd at all. 'This is quite simple,' replied the actor. 'I can tell you the difference between us. I present my fiction as though it were truth; you present your truth as though it were fiction.'[49] Then Campbell Morgan added his own comment. Given the preacher with his Bible, he said, 'I cannot personally understand that man not being swept sometimes right out of himself by the fire and the force and the fervour of his work.'[50]

Dr. Martyn Lloyd-Jones, Campbell Morgan's successor in the pulpit of Westminster Chapel, shared his conviction that truth and passion are essential ingredients of Christian preaching. In his moving book *Preaching and Preachers*,[51] he asks 'What is preaching?' and then supplies his own definition.

> Logic on fire! Eloquent reason! Are these contradictions? Of course they are not. Reason concerning this truth ought to be mightily eloquent, as you see it in the case of the Apostle Paul and others. It is theology on fire. And a theology which does not take fire, I maintain, is a defective theology, or at least the man's understanding of it is defective. Preaching is theology coming through a man who is on fire.[52]

Moreover, he elaborates this theme in *The Christian Warfare*, his exposition of Ephesians 6:10–13, with reference to the work of the Holy Spirit:

> Do not quench the fire, do not quench the Spirit . . . Christianity means warmth, it means a glow . . . 'Yes,

of course,' you say, 'but if you have true scholarship you will not be animated; you will be dignified. You will read a great treatise quietly and without passion.' Out with the suggestion! That is quenching the Spirit! The Apostle Paul breaks some of the rules of grammar; he interrupts his own argument. It is because of the fire! We are so decorous, we are so controlled, we do everything with such decency and order that there is no life, there is no warmth, there is no power! But that is not New Testament Christianity . . . Does your faith melt and move your heart? Does it get rid of the ice that is in you, the coldness in your heart, and the stiffness? The essence of New Testament Christianity is this warmth that is invariably the result of the presence of the Spirit . . .[53]

I think Dr. Lloyd-Jones has put his finger on a crucial point. Fire in preaching depends on fire in the preacher, and this in turn comes from the Holy Spirit. Our sermons will never catch fire unless the fire of the Holy Spirit burns in our own hearts and we are ourselves 'aglow with the Spirit'. (Rom. 12:11) A story is told of W. E. Sangster of Westminister Central Hall which is not in *Dr. Sangster*, the biographical sketch written by his son Paul, but which I believe and hope is true. He was once a member of a selection panel who were interviewing applicants for the Methodist ministry, when a rather nervous young man presented himself. Given an opportunity to speak, this candidate said he felt he ought to explain that he was rather shy and was not the sort of person who would ever set the River Thames on fire, that is, create a stir in the city. 'My dear young brother,' responded Dr. Sangster with consummate wisdom, 'I'm not interested to know if you could set the Thames on fire. What I want to know is this: if I picked you up by the scruff of your neck and dropped you into the Thames, would it sizzle?' In other words was the young man himself on fire? That was the important question.

How, then, can we remarry what should never have been

divorced, namely truth and eloquence, reason and passion, light and fire? Some preachers serve out excellent theology from the pulpit, but it seems to have come out of the freezer. There is no warmth, no glow, no fire. Other pulpits catch fire all right, and threaten to set the church ablaze, but precious little theology goes with it. It is the combination which is almost irresistible in its power, namely theology on fire, passionate truth, eloquent reason. But how? What is the secret of this blend? Two answers may be given. First, the Holy Spirit is the Spirit of both. Jesus called him 'the Spirit of truth', and he appeared on the Day of Pentecost in 'tongues of fire'. Since the two are not separated in him, they will not be in the Spirit-filled Christian either. Once we allow him his freedom, both in the preparation and in the delivery of our sermons, the light and the fire, the truth and the passion, will again be reunited.

The second secret was learned by the two disciples with whom Jesus walked to Emmaus on the first Easter afternoon. When he had vanished, they said to one another, 'Did not our hearts burn within us while he talked to us on the road, while he opened to us the Scriptures?' (Luke 24:32) There can be no doubt that the heartburn they felt was an emotional experience. They were deeply moved. Fire had broken out inside them. When did it begin? It began when he talked to them and opened up the Scriptures to them. It was when they glimpsed new vistas of truth that the fires began to burn. It is still truth – Christ-centred, biblical truth – which sets the heart on fire.

Humour in the Pulpit

The acknowledged need for earnestness in our preaching inevitably prompts the question whether it is ever appropriate for the preacher to make the congregation laugh. At first sight seriousness and laughter appear to be incompatible, and we find ourselves in agreement with Richard Baxter when he wrote, 'Whatever you do, let the people see that you are in good earnest . . . You cannot break men's hearts by jesting with them . . .'[54]

The issue is not so simply settled, however. For 'there is . . . a time to weep and a time to laugh'. (Eccles. 3:4) We have seen that weeping is not necessarily to be banned from the pulpit; so maybe laughing should not be banned either?

The place to begin our enquiry is the teaching of Jesus, for it seems to be generally agreed that humour was one of the weapons in the armoury of the Master Teacher. Dr. Elton Trueblood, Professor of Philosophy at Earlham College, the distinguished American Quaker, wrote his book *The Humour of Christ* in 1965. He tells us that the germ of the idea was planted in his mind when he was reading Matthew 7 (about specks and logs in people's eyes) at family prayers, and his four-year-old child starting laughing. So he lists thirty humorous passages in the Synoptic Gospels and challenges 'the conventionalized picture of a Christ who never laughed',[55] but was always sombre, dull and gloomy. At the same time, Professor Trueblood is at pains to show that the commonest form of humour used by Jesus was *irony* ('a holding up to public view of either vice or folly'), not *sarcasm* (which is cruel and wounds its victims).

It is very important to understand (he writes), that the evident purpose of Christ's humour is to clarify and increase understanding, rather than to hurt. Perhaps some hurt is inevitable, especially when . . . human pride is rendered ridiculous, but the clear aim is something other than harm . . . Truth, and truth alone, is the end . . . The unmasking of error and thereby the emergence of truth.[56]

Another scholar who clearly demonstrated the humorous element in the teaching of Jesus was T. R. Glover in his best-selling *The Jesus of History*.[57] A good example is Jesus' caricature of the Scribes and Pharisees who were conscientious in minute duties, while altogether neglecting 'the weightier matters of the law'. Their lack of proportion was like people drinking, who would 'strain out a gnat and swallow a camel'. (Matt. 23:23, 24) Glover gets us laughing by making us imagine a man attempting to swallow a camel:

> How many of us have ever pictured the process, and the series of sensations, as the long hairy neck slid down the throat of the Pharisee – all that amplitude of loose-hung anatomy – the hump – two humps – both of them slid down – and he never noticed – and the legs – all of them – with the whole outfit of knees and big padded feet. The Pharisee swallowed a camel and never noticed it.[58]

Even if Jesus only used the expression and attempted no description, he must have had his listeners in fits of laughter.

Because of the precedent set by Jesus, it is hardly surprising that the use of humour in preaching and teaching has had a long and honourable tradition. It particularly flourished during the sixteenth-century Reformation, for both Martin Luther on the Continent and Hugh Latimer in England used their earthy descriptive powers to the full. They drew cartoons with words, which still have the power to make us laugh today.

So humour is legitimate. Nevertheless, we have to be sparing in our use of it and judicious in the topics we select for laughter. It is always inappropriate for finite and fallen human beings to laugh about God, whether the Father, the Son or the Holy Spirit. It is equally unfitting for sinners to laugh about the cross or resurrection of Jesus by which their salvation has been achieved, or about the solemn realities of the last things, namely death, judgment, heaven and hell. These topics are not in themselves amusing, and are trivialized if we try to make them funny. People may also stop taking us seriously. Our ministry then will be as ineffective as Lot's who urged his sons-in-law to escape from Sodom because the Lord was about to destroy it, but 'he seemed to his sons-in-law to be jesting' (Gen. 19:14). Phillips Brooks was entirely justified in his Yale lectures in expressing contempt for 'the clerical jester' who 'lays his hands on the most sacred things, and leaves defilement upon all he touches.'[59] An irresponsible buffoon like that, he says, has never grasped that 'humour is something very different from frivolity'.[60]

What, then, is the value of humour if used in the right places and about the right things? First, it breaks tension. Most people find it hard either to maintain mental concentration or to endure the build-up of emotional pressure for a prolonged period. They need to relax for a few moments, and one of the simplest, quickest and healthiest ways to secure their relaxation is to tell a joke and make them laugh.

Secondly, laughter has extraordinary power to break down people's defences. A man comes to church in a stubborn and rebellious frame of mind. He is determined not to respond to a missionary appeal or to change his mind over some issue. You can tell it from his face. See those pursed lips and that furrowed brow; they are symbols of his unyielding resistance. Then suddenly he laughs, in spite of himself, and his resistance collapses. James Emmau Kwegyir Aggrey (1875–1927) knew this power of humour. Born in what used to be known as the Gold Coast, he was educated in the United States, became the first Vice-Principal of Achimota College, and was deeply concerned for racial harmony. When he helped to make an educational survey of West, South and East Africa, people were afraid that his outspokenness might provoke antagonism. But they need not have feared. 'I get their mouths open in a laugh,' he said, 'and then ram the truth down.'[61] Or, as Christopher Morley aptly expressed it, 'after the mirth-quake the still small voice'.[62]

The third and greatest benefit of humour is that it humbles us by pricking the bubble of human pomposity. I know no better elaboration of this than the first chapter in Ronald Knox's *Essays in Satire*.[63] Called by Horton Davies 'The Merry Monsignor, a fountain of gaiety and grace',[64] he sought in his introduction to distinguish between wit, humour, satire and irony.

The sphere of humour is, predominantly, Man and his activities, considered in circumstances so incongruous, so unexpectedly incongruous, as to detract from their human dignity . . . A man falling down on a frosty day is funny, because he has unexpectedly abandoned that upright walk which is man's glory as a biped . . . There is nothing at all funny about a horse falling down . . . Only Man has dignity; only Man, therefore, can be funny . . . In all humour there is loss of dignity somewhere, virtue has gone out of somebody. For there is no inherent humour in things; wherever there is a joke it is Man, the half-angel, the half-beast, who is somehow at the bottom of it.[65]

So then, to laugh at somebody's foibles is a back-handed compliment. It recognizes the innate dignity of human beings. It cannot take seriously their deviations from authentically human behaviour, their pride, pretence and pettiness. These things are funny because they are incongruous. Moreover humour can be directed against oneself; one laughs at one's own idiosyncracies, at one's ludicrous lapses from humanness.

'Satire,' however, Ronald Knox continued, '. . . is born to scourge the persistent and even recurrent follies of the human creature as such . . . Laughter is a deadly explosive which was meant to be wrapped up in the cartridge of satire, and so, aimed unerringly at its appointed target, deals its salutary wound.'[66]

To sum up Knox's point, laughter – especially of the satirical variety – by poking fun at our human eccentricities bears witness to our fallenness and shames us into repentance. So we preachers ought to use satire more skilfully and more frequently, ensuring always that in laughing at others we are also laughing at ourselves within the solidarity of human pomp and folly. Mark Twain in *The Mysterious Stranger*[67] has Satan himself reminding us that the human race in its poverty 'has unquestionably one really effective weapon – laughter.' How, for example, can some 'colossal humbug' be destroyed? 'Only laughter can blow it to rags and atoms in a blast. Against the assault of laughter nothing can stand.'[68]

One of our contemporaries who uses this weapon to great effect is Malcolm Muggeridge. As a former editor of what he dubs 'an allegedly humorous magazine called *Punch*', he has had good reason to meditate on the meaning of laughter which, 'next to mystical enlightenment is the most precious gift and blessing that comes to us on earth.' More than that, he has come to see laughter as 'the converse face of mysticism', since the mystic reaches upwards towards God, while the humourist recognizes our human inability to find him. This paradox he sees illustrated in the great cathedrals of medieval Europe which have both 'a steeple climbing into the sky' and 'a gargoyle grinning down at the earth'. For these are not ill-assorted but complementary, 'the steeple straining to reach up to the glories of eternity in heaven' and 'the gargoyle laughing at the antics of mortal men'. Together they help us to define humour as 'an expression, in terms of the grotesque, of the inexorable disparity between human aspiration and human performance'.[69] Some readers of Malcolm Muggeridge have found his rather caustic criticisms of others upsetting, but we need to remember that he does not spare himself. The steeple and the gargoyle exemplify his own life, for he confesses the gulf he finds between his heavenly vision and his earthly attainment. He seeks to be true to the reality of Christ he has perceived, but adds with melancholy, 'I hate to think how many hundreds of thousands of miles this ridiculous carcass of mine has been carted about the world for one reason and another.'[70]

So humour should definitely not be prohibited in the pulpit. On the contrary, provided that we are laughing at the human condition, and therefore at ourselves, humour helps us to see things in proportion. It is often through laughter that we gain clear glimpses both of the heights from which we have fallen and of the depths to which we have sunk, leading to a wistful desire to be 'ransomed, healed, restored, forgiven'. Thus humour can be a genuine preparation for the gospel. Since it can contribute to the awakening within human hearts of shame over what we are and of longing for what we could be, we should press it gladly into service in the cause of the gospel.

The Length of Sermons

I have often been asked how long I think a sermon ought to be. It is an impossible question to answer because there are so many imponderables. It depends on the occasion and the topic, on the preacher's gift and the congregation's maturity. Yet it seems right to raise the issue in this chapter on sincerity and earnestness because, at least in principle, I think every sermon should last just as long as the preacher needs in which to deliver his soul. Basically, it is not the length of a sermon which makes a congregation impatient for it to stop, but the tedium of a sermon in which even the preacher himself appears to be taking very little interest. 'The true way to shorten a sermon,' said H. W Beecher, 'is to make it more interesting.'[71]

The apostle Paul remains a permanent warning to wordy preachers, because of the fate of that poor young man Eutychus who first fell asleep and then fell out of the window, and was taken up dead. On that occasion Paul's sermon was in two parts, the first lasting from sundown until midnight, and the second from midnight until daybreak. (Acts 20:7–12) Even that is not a record. According to the 1980 *Guinness Book of Records*[72] the longest sermon ever preached lasted twenty-three hours. It was preached between 18 and 22 September 1978 by the Rev. Donald Thomas of Brooklyn, New York. Leaving aside that rather meaningless competition, there have been many instances of sermons lasting several hours. John Wesley notes in his journal on 19 October 1739 how he preached at the Shire Hall of Cardiff with 'such freedom of speech' as he had seldom experienced. 'My heart was so enlarged,' he added, 'I knew not how to give over, so that we continued three hours.' The first sermon preached by Jonathan Edwards in

Princeton Chapel after his appointment as President in 1758 was on 'the unchangeableness of Christ'. 'It was upwards of two hours in the delivery; but is said to have been listened to with such profound attention and deep interest by the audience that they were unconscious of the lapse of time, and surprised that it closed so soon.'[73] Richard Channing Moore (1762–1841), who later became Bishop of Virginia and Presiding Bishop of the American Episcopal Church, drew vast congregations when he was Rector of St. Andrew's, Staten Island.

> At the close of a Sunday afternoon service a member of the congregation rose and said, 'Dr. Moore, the people are not disposed to go home; please give us another sermon.' He complied. Still they remained hungry for the Word of life. A third sermon followed, at the close of which the preacher said: 'My beloved people, you must now disperse – for, although I delight to proclaim the glad tidings of salvation, my strength is exhausted, and I can say no more.'[74]

I give these three examples – John Wesley's three hours, Jonathan Edwards' two hours and Richard Channing Moore's three consecutive sermons – partly because they belong to the same leisurely century and partly because they were all responses to the unusual spiritual hunger of particular congregations. Although in the Victorian era forty-five minutes was the norm, and often the full hour which it took for the hour glass to empty, only the most mature congregations would endure, let alone welcome, such long sermons today. Besides, even in those days some congregations grew restless. Spurgeon tells of a farmer who bitterly complained to him of a young man who went on for too long:

> 'Sir, he ought to have given over at four o'clock, but he kept on till half-past, and there were all my cows waiting to be milked! How would he have liked it if he had been a

cow?' There was a great deal of sense in that question (commented Spurgeon). The Society for the Prevention of Cruelty to Animals ought to have prosecuted that young sinner. How can farmers hear to profit when they have cows-on-the-brain?[75]

It is sad, however, that in reaction against Victorian expansiveness many preachers have reduced their sermons to a ten-minute homily. Congregations will not grow spiritually healthy on an inadequate diet like that. 'Sermonettes breed Christianettes', as both Campbell Morgan of Westminster Chapel and Stuart Holden of St. Paul's, Portman Square, who were contemporaries, have been credited with saying. P. T. Forsyth commented similarly, 'Brevity may be the soul of wit, but the preacher is not a wit . . . A Christianity of short sermons is a Christianity of short fibre.'[76] I am thankful that this is being increasingly recognized. In an article in *The Times* on 6 August 1977 Bishop R. P. C. Hanson of Manchester University complained about 'an absence of depth and seriousness' in the church, and attributed it largely to short sermons. 'The angel Gabriel himself', wrote the Bishop, 'could not convert anyone in ten minutes.' The sermons of Bishop William Connor Magee were described as 'sustained exercises in the practice of clear thinking on religious matters', but 'no sermon lasting only ten minutes could be called a sustained exercise in anything: this lack of attention to the preaching of the Word is a sign of superficiality in religion.'

No hard and fast rules can be laid down about the length of sermons, except perhaps that ten minutes are too short and forty minutes too long. It has been wisely said that every sermon should 'seem like twenty minutes', even if it is actually longer. On arrival at a new church a preacher will be well advised to begin by giving the congregation what they have been accustomed to. Gradually, however, as the Word of God quickens their appetite, they will ask for more.

*　　*　　*

This has been a somewhat subjective chapter, but necessarily so, for preaching can never be isolated from the preacher. Ultimately it is who he is that determines both what he says and how he says it. He may glimpse the glory of preaching and grasp its theology. He may study hard and prepare well. He may see the need to relate the Word to the world, and genuinely desire to be a bridge-builder. Yet still he may lack the vital ingredient (for lack of which nothing can compensate) of personal spiritual reality. Sincerity and earnestness are not qualities which can be attached to us from the outside, like the decorations we tie to our Christmas trees. They are the fruit of the Spirit. They simply describe a person who believes and feels what he says.

As E. M. Bounds wrote at the beginning of the century, 'the man, the whole man, lies behind the sermon. Preaching is not the performance of an hour. It is the outflow of a life. It takes twenty years to make a sermon, because it takes twenty years to make the man.'[77] James Black put it similarly, 'the best preaching is always *the natural overflow* of a ripe mind and the expression of a growing experience. A good sermon is never worked up but worked out.'[78]

I like those two words 'outflow' and 'overflow'. They express succinctly that true preaching is never a superficial activity; it wells up out of the depths. Jesus himself laid much emphasis on this principle. Without the perennial spring of the Holy Spirit's life within us, he said, the rivers of living water can never flow forth from us. Again, it is out of the abundance of the heart that the mouth speaks. (See John 4:14; 7:37–39; Matt. 12:34.)

Notes

1 Baxter, *Reformed Pastor*, p. 162.
2 Spurgeon, *Lectures*, First Series, p. 4.
3 Haslam, pp. 48–9.
4 1 Tim. 4:12; Titus 2:7; 1 Pet. 5:3.
5 Bavinck, p. 93.

6 Spurgeon, *Lectures*, First Series, pp. 12, 13.

7 Brooks, *Lectures*, pp. 5, 28.

8 Beecher, p. 16.

9 Manning, p. 138.

10 Black, p. 6.

11 cf. Spurgeon, *Lectures*, Second Series, p. 45.

12 Baxter, *Reformed Pastor*, p. 162.

13 Golding, p. 210.

14 ibid., p. 217.

15 Black, p. 23.

16 Poulton, pp. 60–1, 79.

17 e.g. 2 Cor. 11:21–33; 1 Thess. 2:1–4; 2 Tim 3:10–12.

18 Morris, pp. 34, 35.

19 One is Tony Waterson, Professor of Virology at the Royal Post-graduate Medical School, Hammersmith. He is modest enough to say that, on reflection, his comments were 'probably brash, ill-considered and immature', and that they concerned technicalities of structure and delivery rather than the really important questions whether God was anointing the message, Jesus was being exalted, and people were being blessed. But I think he underestimates the help and challenge which he gave me.

20 Spurgeon, *Lectures*, Second Series, p. 132.

21 ibid., p. 29.

22 Spurgeon, *Lectures*, First Series, p. 131.

23 Alexander, p. 20.

24 Broadus, *Preparation and Delivery*, p. 218.

25 Hernandez, p. 241.

26 Alexander, p. 6.

27 Twain, pp. 50, 51.

28 Spurgeon, *Lectures*, Second Series, p. 46.

29 Pollock, *Whitefield*, p. 263.

30 David Smith on 2 John 12 in the *Expositor's Greek Testament*.

31 Dargan, Vol. II, p. 174.

32 Baxter, *Poetical Fragments*, pp. 39–40.

33 Baxter, *Reformed Pastor*, p. 110.

34 ibid., p. 106.

35 Spurgeon, *Lectures*, First Series, pp. 138–9.

36 ibid., p. 140.

37 ibid., p. 149.

38 ibid., p. 146.

39 ibid., p. 148.

40 For two articles on Woodforde by Norman Sykes see *Theology*, Vol. 38, No. 224, February 1939, and No. 227, May 1939.

41 Hopkins, p. 65.

42 ibid., p. 162; Carus, p. 445.

43 Spurgeon, *All-Round Ministry*, p. 175.

44 ibid., p. 173.

45 ibid., p. 224.

46 Alexander, p. 266.

47 ibid., p. 25.

48 Morgan, G. C., *Preaching*, pp. 14, 15.

49 ibid., p. 36.

50 ibid., p. 37.

51 1971.

52 Lloyd-Jones, *Preaching*, p. 97.

53 Lloyd-Jones, *Warfare*, pp. 273–4.

54 Baxter, *Reformed Pastor*, p. 145.

55 Trueblood, p. 10. Lentulus, made a Roman consul in 14 B.C., is said to have given the Senate a description of Jesus which included the statement, 'It cannot be remembered that any have seen him laugh.' But this cannot be traced back earlier than A.D. 1680 and is certainly not authentic.

56 ibid., pp. 49–53.

57 1917.

58 Glover, p. 44.

59 Brooks, *Lectures*, p. 55.

60 ibid., p. 57.

61 *Men Who Served Africa*, p. 154.

62 Luccock, p. 192.

63 1928.

64 Davies, p. 116.

65 Knox, pp. 13–15.

66 ibid., pp. 26–7.

67 1916.

68 *The Portable Mark Twain*, p. 736.

69 The quotations are taken from a report of the 1979 Commencement Address which Malcolm Muggeridge gave at Gordon College, Wenham, Massachusetts, although in a personal letter dated 24 September 1979 he told me that he had used the 'Gargoyle and Steeple' image many times in writing and speaking. 'To the best of my memory,' he said 'the notion first struck me at Salisbury, noting that exquisite steeple climbing with crazy audacity into the sky, and then

the little gargoyle faces grinning so malevolently down at the earth.'

70 Muggeridge, *Chronicles, The Green Stick*, p. 98.
71 Beecher, *Lectures*, p. 257.
72 *Guinness Book of Records*, 1980, p. 228.
73 Dwight, p. 577.
74 Chorley, p. 39.
75 Spurgeon, *Lectures*, First Series, pp. 144–5.
76 Forsyth, *Positive Preaching*, pp. 109–10.
77 Bounds, p. 11. See also Martin's tract for the times, *What's Wrong with Preaching Today?*
78 Black, p. 37.

CHAPTER EIGHT

Courage and Humility

Courage

There is an urgent need for courageous preachers in the pulpits of the world today, like the apostles in the early Church who 'were all filled with the Holy Spirit and spoke the word of God with boldness'. (Acts 4:31, cf. v. 13) Neither men-pleasers nor time-servers ever make good preachers. We are called to the sacred task of biblical exposition, and commissioned to proclaim what God has said, not what human beings want to hear. Many modern churchmen suffer from a malady called 'itching ears', which induces them to 'accumulate for themselves teachers to suit their own likings'. (2 Tim. 4:3) But we have no liberty to scratch their itch or pander to their likings. Rather are we to resemble Paul in Ephesus who resisted this very temptation and twice insisted that he 'did not shrink from declaring' to them what had to be declared, namely 'anything that was profitable' for them and indeed 'the whole counsel of God'. (Acts 20:20, 27) We have to beware of selecting our texts and topics – even unconsciously – according to personal prejudice or popular fashion. The medicine of the gospel has been prescribed by the Good Physician; we may neither dilute it nor add ingredients to make it more palatable; we must serve it neat. Nor need we fear that people will not take it. To be sure, some may leave, but most will respond. 'People are driven from the Church,' commented George Buttrick, 'not so much by stern truth that makes them uneasy as by weak nothings that make them contemptuous.'[1]

'Courage,' said Phillips Brooks in his 1877 Yale Lectures,

> . . . is the indispensable requisite of any true ministry . . . If you are afraid of men and a slave to their opinion, go and do something else. Go and make shoes to fit them. Go even and paint pictures which you know are bad but which suit their bad taste. But do not keep on all your life preaching sermons which shall say not what God sent you to declare, but what they hire you to say. Be courageous. Be independent.[2]

Truly, 'the fear of man lays a snare' (Prov. 29:25), and many preachers get caught in it. But once ensnared, we are no longer free; we have become the obsequious servants of public opinion.

The Tradition of Courageous Preaching

The Christian preacher who seeks God's grace to be faithful today can derive much inspiration from a long tradition of predecessors, beginning even in Old Testament times. Although one may look right back to Moses as the first prophet who heard, believed, obeyed and taught the Word of God, in spite of opposition and consequent loneliness, yet the distinctive tradition of Hebrew prophecy belonged to the period of the monarchy and may be said to have begun with Elijah. True, his arithmetic was sadly awry, when he complained that all the people of Israel had forsaken God's covenant and that 'I, even I only, am left.' For the faithful remnant was much larger than he had supposed, seven thousand in fact, who had 'not bowed to Baal'. (2 Kgs. 19:9–18) Nevertheless, we cannot help admiring the courage with which he opposed the whole national establishment, in the double cause of religious truth and social justice. He challenged the prophets of Baal to a public show-down and condemned the king and queen for murdering Naboth and seizing his vineyard. In both protests he stood alone. It was a fine precedent, and the confrontation of prophet and king, divine word and royal authority, became a regular feature of the prophetic witness. Nathan dared to rebuke King David for his adultery with Bathsheba and his murder of her husband. Amos fulminated against evil even in the king's sanctuary at Bethel, and predicted a horrible fate for the royal chaplain Amaziah for trying to silence him. (7:10–17)

Jeremiah was another lonely voice. From the beginning of his prophetic ministry God warned him of the opposition which his message of national doom would provoke, and promised to make him 'a fortified city, an iron pillar and bronze walls against the whole land, against the kings of Judah, its princes, its priests, and the people of the land'. They would fight against him, but they would not prevail against him. (1:17–19) Although we cannot condone Jeremiah's outbursts of self-pity and despair, or his occasional longings for personal revenge, yet his courageous and solitary stand wins our profound respect. He was a true patriot, knowing that only heartfelt repentance could save the nation; yet he was called to announce God's judgment through the Babylonians, and in consequence was accused of hating his own country and even of deserting to the enemy.

The prophetic testimony of the Old Testament culminated in that 'voice crying in the wilderness', John the Baptist, whom Jesus characterized as neither a reed blown by public opinion, nor a soft-living courtier indulging the desires of the flesh, but a true prophet, controlled by the Word of God, indeed as the greatest man who had yet lived. (Matt. 11:7–11) He was the new Elijah, in whose ministry the same two strands of witness – religious and social – reappeared, as he both announced the arrival of God's reign and denounced the adultery of the king. His courage cost him his life. Indeed, he was the last of the long line of martyr-prophets whom Israel rejected and killed (cf. 2 Chr. 36:15, 16; Matt. 23:29–36; Acts 7:52), though of course they went on to kill their Messiah and oppose his apostles as well (cf. 1 Thess. 2:15).

Jesus himself gained a reputation for fearless and uncompromising speech. Towards the end of his life the Pharisees sent a deputation to him, who said, 'Teacher, we know that you are true, and teach the way of God truthfully, and care for no man; for you do not regard the position of men.' (Matt. 22:16) It is small wonder, then, that his Galilean popularity lasted only a year or so, and that the hostility of the authorities increased until they determined to do away with him. At the same time, he warned his followers that the disciple was not greater than his teacher, and that if the teacher was persecuted, the disciples would be also. And so it happened. Luke describes in the Acts how first Peter and John were arrested and imprisoned, next Stephen and James were martyred, and then Paul suffered all manner of indignities at the hands of the opponents of the gospel. This persecution was a direct consequence of the *parrēsia*, the freedom and boldness of speech, or outspokenness, with which those early Christians bore witness to Jesus. This was the quality which Paul desired above all others in his ministry. From prison he wrote to ask his friends to pray for him, that he might be given 'utterance' in opening his mouth 'boldly' to proclaim the gospel. (Eph. 6:19, 20) Far from silencing him, his imprisonment would afford him fresh opportunities for courageous testimony. Luke takes leave of him under house arrest in Rome, still welcoming all who visited him, and still preaching and teaching 'quite openly (literally, "with all boldness", *parrēsia*) and unhindered'. (Acts 28:30, 31)

This tradition of courageous witness and consequent suffering, in the Old and New Testaments, by prophets and apostles and by the Lord of both, is consistent and unremitting. It established a pattern which has continued throughout Church history. A few examples may be given as illustration, to inspire us with the readiness to follow suit, and to cure us of the perverse ambition to be a 'popular preacher'. I begin with Chrysostom at the very end of the fourth century, who preached with great eloquence and courage first in Antioch, and then as Archbishop of

Constantinople for six years, until he offended the Empress and was deposed and banished. He bravely denounced the vices of the city, and 'rebuked without fear or favour all classes and conditions of men'.[3] Take, for instance, his seventeenth homily on Matthew's Gospel, in which he expounded Jesus' prohibition of false swearing. (Matt. 5:33–37) He was determined that the congregation would take their Lord's instruction with due seriousness, and obey it:

> If I see you persisting [he said], I will forbid you for the future to set foot on this sacred threshold, and partake of the immortal mysteries; as we do fornicators and adulterers, and persons charged with murder . . . Let me have no rich man, no potentate, puffing at me here, and drawing up his eyebrows; all these are to me a fable, a shade, a dream.

Every one of them, he emphasized, would have to stand before God and give an account of himself.[4]

Let me now jump nearly a thousand years to John Wycliffe, the precursor of the English Reformation. It was no light task for him to oppose the ecclesiastical establishment almost single-handed with his forthright criticisms. He attacked the worldliness of the clergy, likening them to the scribes and Pharisees, the corruptions of the papacy and the errors of transubstantiation. Several times he was brought to trial, but his friends defended him and he escaped condemnation. Many of his followers, the Lollards, however, were burned to death for heresy.

With Martin Luther the full light of the Reformation shone over Europe. Whether attacking the sale of indulgences or defying the authority of the Pope or taking his stand on the Word of God, his courage was phenomenal. Open his published works at random, and on almost every page may be found examples of uncompromising outspokenness. As he put it in his commentary on the Sermon on the Mount, 'I am a preacher. I have to have teeth in my

mouth. I have to bite and salt and tell them the truth.'[5]
Again,

> Whoever wants to do his duty as a preacher and perform
> his office faithfully must retain the freedom to tell the
> truth fearlessly, regardless of other people. He must
> denounce anyone that needs to be denounced – great or
> small, rich or poor or powerful, friend or foe. Greed
> refuses to do this, for it is afraid that if it offends the
> bigwigs or its good friends, it will be unable to find bread.
> So greed puts its whistle into its pocket and keeps
> quiet . . .[6]

No Christian preacher can have shown more courage, however, than the Scottish reformer, John Knox. His contemporaries described him as little and frail, but he had a
fiery disposition and a vehement way of speaking. After his
return to Scotland in 1559 from his exile in Geneva, his
audacious biblical preaching put new heart into the Scots
who longed for deliverance from the Catholic French and
for a reformed kirk. As Randolph, the English envoy, said
in a dispatch to Queen Elizabeth, 'the voice of one man is
able in one hour to put more life in us than 500 trumpets
continually blustering in our ears.'[7] When Mary Queen of
Scots was contemplating marriage with Don Carlos, son
and heir of King Philip of Spain, which would have brought
the Pope's power (political as well as religious) and the
Spanish Inquisition to Scotland, Knox preached publicly
against it. Such a union, he cried, would 'banish Christ
Jesus from this realm'. The Queen was deeply offended,
sent for him, protested, burst into tears, and vowed that she
would get her revenge. Knox replied,

> Without [sc. outside] the preaching place, Madam, I
> think few have occasion to be offended at me; but there,
> Madam, I am not master of myself, but maun [sc. must]
> obey him who commands me to speak plain, and to
> flatter no flesh upon the face of the earth.

Knox died in 1572, and was buried with national mourning in the churchyard behind St. Giles', Edinburgh. The Regent (the Earl of Morton) said at his grave, 'Here lies one who never feared the face of man.'[8]

Preachers continued to maintain a brave witness in the following three centuries and to suffer for it, and in our twentieth century many instances could be given not only under Nazi, Marxist, Moslem and Hindu opposition to the gospel, but in the so-called Christian West also. Here too there have been courageous preachers, who have refused to edit their message in order to make it more popular. I content myself with only one example, the Rev. Martin Luther King Senior, father of the black American civil rights leader who was later assassinated. In her book *My Life with Martin Luther King Jr.*, Coretta Scott King describes her late husband's father in these words, he 'had by that time (viz. 1964) been pastor of Ebenezer Baptist Church on Auburn Avenue in Atlanta for thirty-three years. He is a big man, physically and spiritually. He stands strong and broad in his pulpit, afraid of no man, white or black, telling it like it is, preaching the Word to his congregation and giving them his overflowing love.'[9]

To Comfort and Disturb

So consistent is this tradition of unpopular preaching, both in Scripture and in Church history, and so contrary to the preacher's natural inclination to be popular, and to comfort people rather than disturb them, that we are prompted to enquire into its origin. We do not have far to look. The only possible explanation is that preachers like prophets believe themselves to be bearers of a Word from God and are therefore not at liberty to deviate from it. In Old Testament days even heathen soothsayers like Balaam, whatever his association with Israel may have been, knew that he was not a free man. His liberty was curtailed by revelation. Although the Moabite King Balak hired him to curse Israel, he persisted in blessing them. To the exasperated Balak he explained, 'Have I now any power at all to speak

305

anything? The word that God puts in my mouth, that must I speak.' (Num. 22:38) If Balaam could thus express his lack of independent utterance and his obligation to submit to God's Word, how much more did the prophets of Israel? To each of them God gave the same commission that he gave to Jeremiah, 'Behold I have put my words in your mouth . . . say to them everything that I command you', with its negative corollary, 'do not hold back a word.' (Jer. 1:9, 17; 26:2)

It is in contrast to this acknowledged obligation to receive and relay God's Word that the other tradition of false prophecy appears so despicable. Israel's false prophets refused the discipline of submitting to revelation, and the loss of liberty this entailed; they felt free to speculate, to dream their own dreams, and to concoct their own messages. In consequence, God said, 'They speak visions of their own minds, not from the mouth of the Lord.' Again, 'Let the prophet who has a dream tell the dream, but let him who has my word speak my word faithfully. What has straw in common with wheat?' (Jer. 23:16, 28; cf. Ezek. 13:2, 3)

The tragedy was that their dreams and visions were 'vain hopes', the fantasy of peace in place of the reality of judgment. To be sure, this was what the people wanted to hear. 'The prophets prophesy falsely, . . . and my people love to have it so.' (Jer. 5:31) They said 'to the seers "see not", and to the prophets "prophesy not to us what is right; speak to us smooth things, prophesy illusions, leave the way, turn aside from the path, let us hear no more of the Holy One of Israel."' (Isa. 30:9–11. Cf. Mic. 2:6–11) Israel thus preferred the comfort of lies to the disturbance of truth. And alas! the false prophets were glad, even eager, to oblige. 'They say continually to those who despise the word of the Lord "It shall be well with you"; and to everyone who stubbornly follows his own heart they say "no evil shall come upon you."' (Jer. 23:17. Cf. 5:12, 13; Lam. 2:14) Their stock-in-trade was 'smooth things' and their refrain 'Peace, peace', even when there was no peace. As a result, they 'healed the wound of God's people lightly'. (Jer. 6:14;

8:11) Like quack doctors they merely applied a dressing, when what was needed was radical surgery. Or, changing the imagery from doctors to builders, 'when the people build a wall, these prophets daub it with whitewash.' That is, they gave official religious sanction and an aura of religious respectability to everything the people wanted to do, however contrary to God's will. But human beings cannot build a wall to protect them against the wrath of God, and prophetic whitewash cannot conceal its cracks. Before the wind and rain of divine judgment it will collapse. (Ezek. 13:10–16; 22:28) Both metaphors convey the same message. Unrepentant sinners are in deep trouble from the judgment of God. Their wound festers, their wall totters. Superficial remedies (a bandage on the wound, whitewash on the wall) are useless, and those who apply them are criminally irresponsible, for they shield people from the reality they ought to face. As Father Mapple cried in *Moby Dick*, drawing a lesson for preachers from the story of Jonah, 'Woe to him who seeks to pour oil upon the waters when God has brewed them into a gale!'[10]

The situation is made worse for preachers who are seeking courage to be faithful to God's Word by the fact that they find themselves alienated not only from the people but from other preachers as well. Today there is controversy in the Church even over fundamental questions of doctrine and ethics on which Scripture speaks unequivocally, and the layman is treated to the unedifying spectacle of supposed experts in theology disagreeing sharply with one another on television or in the newspapers. Yet this phenomenon is not new; it is in principle the same as the clash between true and false prophets in the Bible. The prototype in this conflict was Micaiah, the son of Imlah. Judah's King Jehoshaphat and Israel's King Ahab (who were related by marriage) decided to join forces to recover Ramoth Gilead from Syrian occupation. Before setting out on their military expedition, however, they thought it prudent to 'inquire for the word of the Lord'. (It is still a common ploy today first to reach a decision and then to

seek divine endorsement in order to make it respectable.)
The 400 court prophets, who were consulted, at once responded, 'Go up to Ramoth Gilead, for the Lord will give it
into the hand of the king.' The prophet Zedekiah, who
seems to have been a bit of an exhibitionist, even paraded
in a set of iron horns and said, 'Thus says the Lord, with
these you shall push the Syrians until they are destroyed.'
But Jehoshaphat was uneasy. He somehow suspected that
there was another prophet who might express a different
message. Ahab conceded that there was another, by name
Micaiah the son of Imlah, 'But I hate him,' he added, 'for
he never prophesies good concerning me, but evil.'
Nevertheless, he was fetched, and the messenger who went
to find him, said to him, 'The words of the prophets with
one accord are favourable to the king. Let your word be
like the word of one of them, and speak favourably.' It was
surely meant to be friendly advice for Micaiah's own protection, yet in fact it was devilish. For which was more
important: the majority view with the favour of the king, or
the word of the Lord without it? Micaiah does not seem to
have hesitated, 'As the Lord lives, what the Lord says to
me, that I will speak.' And when he stood before the two
kings, 'sitting on their thrones, arrayed in their robes', he
was not dazzled by their magnificence. He courageously
declared, 'I saw all Israel scattered upon the mountains, as
sheep that have no shepherd.' This was not only a predic-
tion of Ahab's death in battle, but also a contradiction of
the court prophets, whose counsel he attributed to 'a lying
spirit' in their mouths. One of them slapped him in the face
for his candour. (1 Kgs. 22:1–29)

Micaiah could not avoid the dilemma which faced him.
He was compelled to choose. Either he must toe the popular line, find favour with the king and be false to his God, or
he must stand alone against the establishment view, in
order to be faithful to his God, even though it would mean
losing the royal favour. To his eternal credit he preferred
the praise of God to the praise of men. He appears in the
biblical record only in this one incident, but he deserves to

be more widely known and acclaimed. He is one of the unsung heroes of Scripture. Moreover, the choice between truth with unpopularity and falsehood with popularity regularly confronts Christian preachers. I wish each of us could endorse what Hensley Henson wrote just after he had been elected Head of Oxford House, Bethnal Green, in 1887, 'I do not care one straw about popularity, for I know that it is generally purchased by a sacrifice of the truth.'[11] It is surely for this reason that Jesus uttered his warning, 'Woe to you, when all men speak well of you, for so their fathers did to the false prophets.' (Luke 6:26) He seems to have taken it for granted that, as with prophets so with preachers, popularity can be achieved only at the price of integrity. Yet few church members or leaders seem to believe this any more, or at least to be willing to bear the cost of believing it.

The fact is that the authentic gospel of the New Testament remains extremely offensive to human pride, and nobody who preaches it faithfully can expect to escape at least some degree of opposition. Paul found in his day that the message of Christ crucified was both folly to Greek intellectuals and a stumbling block to self-righteous Jews. Nobody can reach God by his own wisdom or by his own morality. Only at the cross can God be known. And this is doubly offensive to men and women of culture. They resent the exclusiveness of the Christian claim, and even more the humiliation implicit in it. Christ from his cross seems to say to us, 'I am here because of you. If it were not for your sin and pride, I would not be here. And if you could have saved yourself, I would not be here either.' The Christian pilgrimage begins with bowed head and bent knee; there is no way into the kingdom of God except by the exaltation of those who have humbled themselves.

I have often thanked God that he taught me this truth very early in my Christian experience, partly through glimpses into the pride of my own heart and partly through a glimpse into somebody else's. It was when I was an undergraduate at Trinity College, Cambridge. Only recently I had come to Christ myself, and now – clumsily, I am sure – I was trying to share the good news with a fellow student. I was endeavouring to explain the great doctrine of justification by grace alone, that salvation was Christ's free gift, and that we could neither buy it nor even contribute to its purchase, for Christ had obtained it for us and was now offering it to us gratis. Suddenly, to my intense astonishment, my friend shouted three times at the top of his voice, 'Horrible! Horrible! Horrible!' Such is the arrogance of the human heart that it finds the good news not glorious (which it is) but horrible (which it is not).

Alexander Whyte came to a crisis towards the end of his ministry in Edinburgh on this very point. He knew that some regarded him as 'little short of a monomaniac about sin', and he was tempted to muffle that note in his preaching. But one day while walking in the Highlands – he could ever after remember the exact spot –

What seemed to me to be a Divine Voice spoke with all-commanding power in my conscience, and said to me as clear as clear could be: 'No! Go on, and flinch not! Go back and boldly finish the work that has been given you to do. Speak out and fear not. Make them at any cost to see themselves in God's holy law as in a glass. Do you that, for no one else will do it. No one else will so risk his life and his reputation as to do it. And you have not much of either left to risk. Go home and spend what is left of your life in your appointed task of showing my people their sin and their need of my salvation.'

He did. He was not disobedient to the heavenly vision. It gave him 'fresh authority and fresh encouragement' to finish his course.[12]

Preachers cannot then escape the duty of disturbing the complacent. We all know that Christ spoke many 'comfortable words', and in the Church of England we rehearse some of them at every Communion service. But not all his words were comforting. Some were deeply disturbing. We

310

must be faithful, therefore, in expounding his 'uncomfortable words' as well. This will mean preaching God's wrath as well as his love, grace and mercy (indeed, these shine all the more brightly against that dark background), his judgment as well as his salvation, hell as well as heaven (however tentative we may deem it wise to be about the details of both, in our anxiety not to go beyond the plain teaching of Scripture), death with Christ as well as resurrection with him, repentance as well as faith, Christ's Lordship as well as his Saviourhood, the cost as well as the compensations of Christian discipleship, self-denial as the road to self-discovery, and the yoke of Christ's authority under which we find our rest.

It is not only in gospel preaching, but also in teaching about the Christian life, that we need courage not to neglect the less palatable aspects of the New Testament message, but rather to find the biblical balance. For example, the apostles write of the 'unutterable and exalted joy' of knowing Christ, but add that we also have to endure a certain 'heaviness' as a result of various trials and Satanic pressures. (1 Pet. 1:6–8) They describe the rest of faith in Christ's finished work and the Spirit's indwelling, but also portray us as soldiers, athletes, farmers and boxers – metaphors which all imply strong exertion. They emphasize the exhilarating freedom into which Christ has liberated us, but add that this is also a new slavery to Christ and his will. They assure us that we are no longer 'under the law' in the sense that God's acceptance of us depends on his grace and not on our works, but add that obedience is still expected of us, indeed that Christ died for us precisely 'in order that the just requirement of the law might be fulfilled in us, who walk not according to the flesh but according to the Spirit.' (Rom. 8:3, 4)

So high moral standards are set before us. Moreover, the apostles go beyond vague generalizations to precise applications, and many a congregation would be startled if a course of sermons were preached on, for example, Ephesians 4:25–5:21, or Titus 2:1–15, or the Letter of James, or indeed the Sermon on the Mount. Are we faithful in teaching what the apostles taught about relations between husbands and wives, parents and children, masters and servants? that covetousness is idolatry, wealth is dangerous, and generous mutual responsibility is to mark God's new society? that lifelong heterosexual marriage is the only context which God has ordained for sexual fulfilment, so that divorce (even if sometimes permitted as a concession to human frailty) is always a declension from God's ideal, and that both heterosexual adultery and fornication on the one hand and homosexual practices on the other are contrary to his will? that work is a consequence of the creation not the fall, and is intended by God as a means to a partnership with him, the service of others and self-fulfilment, which emphasizes the tragedy of unemployment?

If we are faithful in our preaching about 'sin, righteousness and judgment', we must at the same time be careful to avoid any imbalance. It has to be admitted that some preachers enjoy thundering forth God's judgments. They find a morbid satisfaction in seeing their audience writhe under the lash of their whip. Whether it is a form of verbal sadism, or gives them what Americans call an 'ego trip', it is always sick to derive pleasure from other people's pain. Anthony Trollope in *Barchester Towers* very evidently despised his character, the Rev. Obadiah Slope, for this very thing. Although he was 'gifted with a certain kind of pulpit eloquence', yet, Trollope wrote, 'in his sermons he deals greatly in denunciations.' Indeed, 'his looks and tones are extremely severe . . . As he walks through the streets, his very face denotes his horror of the world's wickedness; and there is always an anathema lurking in the corner of his eye . . . To him the mercies of our Saviour speak in vain . . .'[13] In a neat phrase of Colin Morris, he used the pulpit 'to purvey Good Chidings rather than Good Tidings'.[14]

The more we feel it necessary, especially in days of moral laxity, to dwell on the judgment of God upon sin, the more we need also to dwell on his mercy towards sinners. Jesus's own woes against the scribes and Pharisees for their hypocrisy are among the fiercest denunciations in the whole Bible, yet he was called 'the friend of sinners', they flocked round him and listened to him gladly, he invited them to come to him with their burdens and promised to give them rest, he accepted the demonstrative affection of a forgiven prostitute, and he said to the woman caught in adultery 'neither do I condemn you; go and do not sin again.'

It is significant that Paul appealed to the Corinthians 'by the meekness and gentleness of Christ'. (2 Cor. 10:1) He could be severe. He expected the churches to discipline offenders and even excommunicate the unrepentant. But it is very obvious that he found no pleasure in these things. On the contrary, he showed the gentleness, affection and self-giving love of a parent. Indeed, he likened himself, in his dealings with the Thessalonians, both to 'a mother taking care of her children' and to 'a father with his children'. (1 Thess. 2:7, 11)

Every Christian pastor today has the same feelings of tender love towards those who have been committed to his care. As he speaks to them every Sunday, he knows something of the burdens they are bearing. One has soon to face major surgery, another has recently been told he has an incurable illness, yet another has just been bereaved. Then there is that couple whose marriage is falling apart, that man whose wife has been unfaithful, that woman whose husband is cruel to her, that single person who has been frustrated in love, those young people who are finding it hard to maintain Christian standards in their non-Christian environment. As he looks at their faces, there seems to be tragedy behind every brave façade. Almost everybody has been bruised by life, and is feeling the pressure of temptation or defeat, depression, loneliness or despair. It is true that some need to be disturbed from their complacency, but others need above all else the comfort of God's love. J. H. Jowett wrote,

I have been greatly impressed in recent years by one refrain which I have found running through many biographies. Dr. Parker repeated again and again, 'Preach to broken hearts!' And here is the testimony of Ian Maclaren: 'The chief end of preaching is comfort . . .' And may I bring you an almost bleeding passage from Dr. Dale: 'People want to be comforted . . . They need consolation – really need it, and do not merely long for it.'[15]

Somehow then we have to strike the balance, and need to pray for sensitivity if we are to succeed in doing it. Chad Walsh, the American Episcopalian, gave an excellent definition of preaching in his early book *Campus Gods on Trial*, 'the true function of a preacher is to disturb the comfortable and to comfort the disturbed.'[16] A century earlier John Newton, the converted slave-trader, 'used to say that the point in all his preaching was "to break a hard heart and to heal a broken heart." '[17] It is this combination which seems so rare. Some preachers are great comforters. Their every sermon soothes. But they have omitted first to disturb those whom they are so busy comforting. Others make the opposite mistake. They are great disturbers of the congregation's peace, as they preach on human sin and divine holiness, but they forget to go on to comfort those whom they have so effectively disturbed. Chad Walsh's definition, which brings the two functions together, can be well illustrated from John Wesley's *Journal*. For example, on 21 June 1761 he preached in the churchyard of Osmotherley, which is in Yorkshire, 'I believe many were wounded,' he wrote, 'and many comforted.'[18] Then on 17 August 1787 he preached to a large congregation near the Governor's House on the Isle of Alderney in the Channel Islands, 'I believe many were cut to the heart this hour,' he wrote, 'and some not a little comforted.'[19]

A more modern example is given by Dr. Horton Davies in *Varieties of English Preaching 1900–1960*. Having dedicated the book to his father, a Congregational preacher, he begins his Preface with these words,

As a son of the Manse, it was a great privilege to hear the lively Word of God preached and applied with insight and compassion to a variety of families and callings . . . Sunday was always the peak of the week, and its climax was reached when the congregation settled back into their pews to hear one who might be a son of thunder (Boanerges) or a son of consolation (Barnabas), and was often both in the same sermon . . .[20]

Every preacher needs to be both a Boanerges (having the courage to disturb) and a Barnabas (having the charity to console).

The Value of Systematic Exposition
In the context of the preacher's need for courage I commend the practice of systematic exposition, that is to say, of working steadily through a book of the Bible or a section of a book, either verse by verse or paragraph by paragraph. The first benefit of this scheme is that it forces us to take passages which we might otherwise have overlooked, or even deliberately avoided. I well remember some years ago preaching through the Sermon on the Mount, and coming in due course to Matthew 5:31, 32, in which our Lord deals with the subject of divorce. I have to confess that, although I had been in the pastoral ministry for twenty-five years, I had never previously preached on this topic. I am ashamed to have to admit this, since divorce is a burning contemporary issue and many people are wanting help in this area, but it is true. Of course I could have made a number of cogent excuses. 'It's a very complex subject, and I do not have the necessary expertise.' 'It's also controversial, and I don't want to stir up strife.' 'Besides, I'd be sure to offend somebody.' So, because of the difficulties, I had steered clear of the topic. But now I was leading the congregation through the Sermon on the Mount, and here staring me in the face were Matthew 5, verses 31 and 32. What should I do? I could not possibly skip those verses and begin my sermon, 'Last Sunday my text was Matthew 5:30; today it is

Matthew 5:33.' No, I was obliged to do what I had so long shirked, and I clearly recall the hours I had to spend in study and thought before I dared attempt to handle those verses.

The second benefit of systematic exposition is that people's curiosity is not aroused as to why we take a particular text on a particular Sunday. If I had suddenly, out of the blue, preached on divorce, church members would inevitably have wondered why. They would have asked themselves, 'Who is he tilting at today?' But as it happened, their attention was not distracted by such questions. They knew that I was seeking to expound Matthew 5:31, 32 only because they were the next consecutive verses in the sermon series.

The third benefit is probably the greatest. It is that the thorough and systematic opening up of a large portion of Scripture broadens people's horizons, introduces them to some of the Bible's major themes, and shows them how to interpret Scripture by Scripture. P. T. Forsyth put this point well,

> We need to be defended from his (sc. the preacher's) subjectivity, his excursions, his monotony, his limitations. We need, moreover, to protect him from the peril of preaching himself or his age. We must all preach *to* our age, but woe to us if it is our age we preach, and only hold up the mirror to the time.[21]

Again,

> One of the great tasks of the preacher is to rescue the Bible from the textual idea in the mind of the public, from the Biblicist, atomist idea which reduces it to a religious scrap book, and uses it only in verses and phrases . . . He must cultivate more the free, large and organic treatment of the Bible, where each part is most valuable for its contribution to a living, evangelical whole, and where that whole is articulated into the great course of human history.[22]

316

Whether or not they would have expressed their reasons in this way, the fact is that some of the greatest preachers in the history of the Church have expounded Scripture in a conscientious, thorough, systematic fashion. The most notable example in the first four centuries of the Church was John Chrysostom, whom I have already mentioned in this chapter in connection with his courage. During approximately the last two decades of the fourth century, he expounded the Book of Genesis and the Psalms from the Old Testament, and from the New the Gospels of Matthew and John, the Acts, and all the Pauline letters.

It is the sixteenth-century Reformers, however, in their anxiety to expose their congregations to the pure and powerful Word of God, who most effectively developed the practice of systematic exposition. Luther and Calvin were different in many respects. Luther was German and Calvin French; Luther's physique was burly and strong, Calvin's slender and weak; Luther's style depended on his vivid, even fiery imagination, Calvin's on cool and lucid analysis. Yet both handled the Scriptures with a diligence and a profundity which put us moderns to shame. In Wittenberg the Reformers (Luther and his clergy colleagues),

. . . undertook an extensive campaign of religious instruction through the sermon. There were three public services on Sunday: from five to six in the morning on the Pauline epistles, from nine to ten on the Gospels, and in the afternoon at a variable hour on a continuation of the theme of the morning or on the catechism . . . On Mondays and Tuesdays there were sermons on the catechism, Wednesdays on the Gospel of Matthew, Thursdays and Fridays on the apostolic letters, and Saturday evening on John's Gospel. No one man carried this entire load, . . . but Luther's share was prodigious. Including family devotions he spoke often four times on Sundays, and quarterly undertook a two-week series four days a week on the catechism. The sum of his extant sermons is 2,300.

317

The highest count is for the year 1528, for which there are 195 sermons distributed over 145 days.[23]

Calvin's method was similar to Luther's, although perhaps he was more systematic still. From 1549 he preached in Geneva twice every Sunday and in alternate weeks at a daily evening service. He tended to handle the Old Testament on weekdays, and the New Testament or Psalms on Sundays. A paid stenographer took down his sermons as he preached, and later transcribed them. In the fifteen-year period from 1549 until he died, he expounded from the Old Testament Genesis, Deuteronomy, Judges, Job, some Psalms, 1 and 2 Samuel, 1 Kings, and all the major and minor prophets, and from the New Testament a harmony of the Gospels, the Acts, 1 and 2 Corinthians, Galatians, Ephesians, 1 and 2 Thessalonians, and the three Pastoral Epistles.

Other Swiss Reformers followed the same custom. Zwingli, for example, at the beginning of his ministry in Zürich, 'announced his intention to preach, not simply upon the church lessons, but upon the whole Gospel of Matthew, chapter after chapter. Some friends objected that it would be an innovation, but he just said, "it is the old custom. Call to mind the homilies of Chrysostom on Matthew and of Augustine on John."'[24] The same conviction was shared by Henry Bullinger, who succeeded Zwingli at Zürich. According to E. C. Dargan, he was 'tall of form, with a flowing beard, a benevolent and intelligent expression, a pleasing voice, a dignified yet animated bearing'. Dargan goes on to say that between 1549 and 1567 he preached 100 sermons on Revelation, 66 on Daniel, 170 on Jeremiah, 190 on Isaiah, and many more besides.[25]

A century later Matthew Henry supplies a splendid example of faithful, biblical preaching. During his twenty-five year ministry as a dissenting preacher in Chester (1687–1712), by focussing on the Old Testament each Sunday morning and on the New Testament each Sunday afternoon, he worked through the whole Bible twice, and during his midweek lectures expounded the whole Psalter no less than five times. These expositions form the substance of his famous commentary.

The pulpit giants of the last century continued the tradition established by Augustine and Chrysostom, and developed by Luther and Calvin, the other Reformers and the Puritans. For example, Charles Simeon's expositions, published in the twenty-one volumes of *Horae Homileticae*, number 2,536; he pointed out that, if we were to read one a day, they would last us seven years.

Joseph Parker, minister of the City Temple in London for thirty-three years from 1869, preached regularly to 3,000 people. In 1884 he announced his intention to preach through the whole Bible. Preaching twice on Sundays and once on Thursdays at midday, he accomplished his task in seven years. His sermons were published as *The People's Bible* in twenty-five volumes, the last one appearing in 1895.

Alexander Maclaren, the Baptist minister who attracted very large crowds to Union Chapel in Manchester for nearly half a century (1858–1903) and was sometimes called 'the prince of expositors', covered virtually the entire Bible in the thirty-two volumes of his *Expositions of Holy Scripture*, published during the last six years of his life (1904–10).

In our own century it is interesting that William Temple, while Rector of St. James's, Piccadilly, during the First World War, preached through the Gospel of John in nearly four years, and later published his expositions as *Readings from St John's Gospel*.

For the health of the Church (which lives and flourishes by the Word of God) and for the help of the preacher (who needs this discipline), it is urgent to return to systematic exposition. In doing so, however, we shall need to take due account of the characteristics of our age, and not ape our forebears with unimaginative literalism. There are not many congregations spiritually mature and hungry enough to digest the lengthy expositions for extended periods which were traditional in a bygone era. Dale mentions, for example, a 'German exegetical professor who, after lecturing on the Book of Isaiah for rather more than twenty years, had reached the middle of the second chapter'.[26] Even Dr. Martyn Lloyd-Jones's remarkable exposition of Romans which took him up to chapter 14 verse 17, and which he continued for twelve years until he retired from Westminster Chapel, could hardly be repeated in any British church. But if we make due allowances for contemporary people, and take a paragraph rather than a verse as our text, and continue the consecutive exposition for a few months rather than a few years, modern congregations will lap it up.[27] It will also help us preachers to grow in the courage we need to unfold the whole counsel of God.

Humility

Unfortunately, the resolve to be courageous in the pulpit can result in our becoming headstrong and arrogant. We may succeed in being outspoken, but spoil it be becoming proud of our outspokenness. Truth to tell, the pulpit is a perilous place for any child of Adam to occupy. It is 'high and lifted up', and thus enjoys a prominence which should be restricted to Yahweh's throne. (Isa. 6:1) We stand there in solitude, while the eyes of all are upon us. We hold forth in monologue, while all sit still, silent and subdued. Who can endure such public exposure and remain unscathed by vanity? Pride is without doubt the chief occupational hazard of the preacher. It has ruined many, and deprived their ministry of power.

In some it is blatantly obvious. They are exhibitionists by temperament and use the pulpit as the stage on which they show off. Dr. Lloyd-Jones is surely right to call such people 'pulpiteers rather than preachers', since they are experts in professional showmanship.[28] In Henry Ward Beecher's ninth lecture at Yale (1872), entitled 'Sermon-making', he spoke of 'Nebuchadnezzar sermons'. He was referring by this unusual expression to rhetorical discourses 'over which the vain preacher stands', repeating in effect the boastful words of Nebuchadnezzar, 'Is not this great Babylon, which I have built by my mighty power . . . for the glory of my majesty?' 'Would to God,' continued Beecher, 'that these preachers, like Nebuchadnezzar, might go to grass for a time if, like them, they would return sane and humble.'[29] The analogy is telling. For there is something fundamentally 'obscene' about pride, something offensive to the Christian sense of what is decent, something calculated to disgust. What is perhaps most noteworthy about Nebuchadnezzar's downfall and restoration is that his pride issued in madness, while his sanity returned when he humbled himself.

Other preachers are not Nebuchadnezzars, however, for their pride does not take the form of blatant boastfulness. It is more subtle, more insidious, and even more perverse. For it is possible to adopt an outward demeanour of great meekness, while inside our appetite for applause is insatiable. At the very moment when in the pulpit we are extolling the glories of Christ, we can in reality be seeking our own glory. And when we are exhorting the congregation to praise God, and are even ostensibly leading them in praise, we can be secretly hoping that they will spare a bit of praise for us. We need to cry out with Baxter, 'O what a constant companion, what a tyrannical commander, what a sly, subtle and insinuating enemy is this sin of pride!'[30]

In order to expose, combat and defeat this enemy, I think the best and most positive procedure will be to make an analysis of what the preacher's humility should be.

The Word of God
First of all, we need the humility to submit to the Word of God. That is, we must resist the temptation to avoid the unfashionable truths of Scripture and to ventilate our own more trendy opinions instead. 'A fool finds no pleasure in understanding, but delights in airing his own opinions.' (Prov. 18:2, NIV)

Christian humility begins as *tapeinophrosunē*, 'lowliness

321

of mind'. It has to do with how we think, both in relation to others (esteeming them more important than ourselves, and so gladly serving them, Phil. 2:3, 4; 1 Pet. 5:5) and in relation to God ('walking humbly with your God', Mic. 6:5), especially the latter. The humble mind is neither closed nor uncritical, but it acknowledges its limitations. Its language is 'O Lord, my heart is not lifted up, my eyes are not raised too high; I do not occupy myself with things too great or too marvellous for me.' (Ps. 131:1) Again, in reference to God's omniscience, 'Such knowledge is too wonderful for me; it is high, I cannot attain it.' (Ps. 139:6) This is not obscurantism, nor even anti-intellectualism. It is merely a humble, sane, sober recognition that God's infinite being is beyond our apprehension, that his thoughts and ways are as much higher than ours as the heavens are higher than the earth (Isa. 55:8, 9), that apart from his self-disclosure we could never know him, and indeed that 'the foolishness of God is wiser than men'. (1 Cor. 1:25) If then, God's judgments are unsearchable and his ways inscrutable, it is ludicrous to suppose that we could ever know his mind by ourselves, let alone instruct him or offer him advice. (Rom. 11:33, 34) We have no liberty, therefore, to contradict his revelation or criticize his plan of salvation. To be sure, the message of the cross may seem stupid to our finite and fallen minds and we may even wish to propose alternative ways of salvation which we deem preferable. But God says, 'I will destroy the wisdom of the wise,' and determines instead to save us through the 'folly' of the gospel which, in fact, is his wisdom (1 Cor. 1:18–25; cf. 3:18–20). It is our responsibility, therefore, to do everything we can, both in ourselves and in others, to 'destroy arguments and every proud obstacle to the knowledge of God, and take every thought captive to obey Christ'. (2 Cor. 10:5)

How will the humble mind's submission to God's revelation in Christ find expression in preachers? Humble preachers will avoid either adding to Scripture according to their own speculations or substracting from Scripture according to their own predilections. The first often takes the form of a craze for originality. Some preachers find the Bible flat, so they try to freshen it up with their own effervescence. Others find it insipid, so they try to season it with a little of their own relish. They are unwilling to take it as it is; they are for ever trying to improve it with bright ideas of their own. But this is not the preacher's task. We have to be 'original' in the sense that we take old truths and seek creatively to restate them in modern terms and re-apply them to modern conditions. But to be biblically 'creative' in these ways is not to be 'inventive' of new and unbiblical notions. Nor are we vain or foolish enough to imagine that our attempted reinterpretations possess the authority which belongs to the Word of God we are striving to reinterpret.

The preacher with a humble mind will avoid omissions as much as additions. He must refuse to manipulate the biblical text in order to make it more acceptable to our contemporaries. For the attempt to make 'it' more acceptable really means to make 'ourselves' more acceptable, and this is the lust for popularity.

Adding to God's Word was the fault of the Pharisees, and subtracting from it the fault of the Sadducees. Jesus criticized them both, insisting that the Word of God must be allowed to stand by itself, without plus or minus, without amplification or modification, supreme and sufficient in its authority. The modern Pharisees and Sadducees in the Church, who tamper with Scripture, discarding what they wish was not there and inserting what they wish was, should heed these criticisms of Jesus. There is, I am afraid we have to say, a certain arrogance about the theological liberalism which deviates from historic biblical Christianity. For any-one who refuses to submit to God's Word, and 'does not agree with the sound words of our Lord Jesus Christ and the teaching which accords with godliness' is 'puffed up with conceit', and 'insubordinate'. (1 Tim. 6:3, 4; Titus 1:9, 10) The Christian preacher is to be neither a speculator who invents new doctrines which please him, nor an editor who excises old doctrines which displease him, but a steward, God's steward, dispensing faithfully to God's household the truths committed to him in the Scriptures, nothing more, nothing less and nothing else. For this ministry a humble mind is necessary. We need to come daily to the Scriptures, and to sit like Mary at Jesus' feet, listening to his Word.

Such 'listening' is what Bonhoeffer had in mind when he emphasized the need for 'silence'. He was not advocating (as some imagine) that the Church should give up preaching because its failures in the area of responsible action had robbed it of its right to speak. On the contrary, what he condemned was not a 'proclaiming' Church but a 'chattering' Church. He longed that the Church would become respectfully silent before the Word of God. 'The Church's silence is silence before the Word . . . The proclamation of Christ is the Church speaking from a proper silence.'[31]

Such a receptive and expectant mood before God's revelation is not only proper; it is also productive. For, as Jesus plainly stated, God hides his secrets from the wise and erudite, and reveals them instead to little children, that is, to humble, open-hearted seekers for the truth. (Matt. 11:25)

The Glory of Christ
Humility of mind is to be accompanied by humility of motive. Why do we preach? What do we hope to accomplish by our preaching? What incentive impels us to persevere? I fear that too often our motives are selfish. We desire the praise and the congratulations of men. We stand at the door after the Sunday services and feast our ears on the commendatory remarks which some church members, especially in the United States, seem to have been schooled to make, 'Fine sermon, pastor!' 'You really blessed my heart today!' To be sure, genuine words of appreciation can do much to boost a discouraged preacher's morale. But idle flattery, and the hypocritical repetition of stock phrases (irrespective of the real quality of the sermon) are damag-

324

ing to the preacher and repugnant to God. Congregations should be encouraged to repent of this tradition, and to be more sparing and more discerning in their expressions of encouragement.

The main objective of preaching is to expound Scripture so faithfully and relevantly that Jesus Christ is perceived in all his adequacy to meet human need. The true preacher is a witness; he is incessantly testifying to Christ. But without humility he neither can nor wants to do so. James Denney knew this, and had these words framed in the vestry of his Scottish church, 'No man can bear witness to Christ and to himself at the same time. No man can give the impression that he himself is clever and that Christ is mighty to save.'[32] Something very similar was spoken by John Watson, the 'Ian Maclaren' who wrote the best-selling novel *Beside the Bonnie Brier Bush*, 'the chief effect of every sermon should be to unveil Christ, and the chief art of the preacher to conceal himself.'[33] But the preacher's purpose is more than to unveil Christ; it is so to unveil him that people are drawn to come to him and to receive him. It is this which led Ronald A. Ward to call his book on preaching *Royal Sacrament*. He perceived a parallel between the ministry of the Word and the ministry of the sacrament which he expressed in these terms, 'As in the Holy Communion we give bread and wine, and the faithful receive Christ, so in preaching we give words and the faithful receive Christ.'[34] Thus, in both the Lord's Supper and the exposition of Scripture there is an outward sign (bread and wine, or words) and an inward and spiritual grace (Christ received by faith).

Another way of putting the same truth is to say that 'preaching is in the nature of personal encounter.' Or at least its purpose is to facilitate an encounter. 'The great encounter, however, is not between the preacher and the people. It is between God and the people.'[35] Donald G. Miller puts it even more strongly. Taking up P. T. Forsyth's dictum that 'a true sermon is a real deed,' he writes, 'No man has really preached until the two-sided encounter between him and his congregation has given way to a three-sided encounter, where God himself becomes one of the living parties to it.'[36]

I find myself in complete accord with these statements. The most privileged and moving experience a preacher can ever have is when, in the middle of the sermon, a strange hush descends upon the congregation. The sleepers have woken up, the coughers have stopped coughing, and the fidgeters are sitting still. No eyes or minds are wandering. Everybody is attending, though not to the preacher. For the preacher is forgotten, and the people are face to face with the living God, listening to his still, small voice. Dr. Billy Graham has often described this experience. I remember hearing him address about 2,400 ministers in the Central Hall, Westminster, on 20 May 1954, at the conclusion of the Greater London Crusade. The third of his twelve points emphasized the power of the Holy Spirit, and the liberty in preaching which he had felt as a result. 'I have often felt like a spectator,' he said, 'standing on the side, watching God at work. I have felt detached from it. I wanted to get out of the way as much as I could, and let the Holy Spirit take over . . .'[37] It is precisely here that humility of motive comes in. 'I wanted to get out of the way.' For it is all too easy to get in the way, to intrude ourselves between the people and their Lord. Two helpful images have been used to illustrate this.

The first concerns a wedding. The desire of the best man is to do all he can to facilitate the marriage of the bride to the bridegroom, and to do nothing to come between them. Now Jesus took over the Old Testament imagery of the marriage between Yahweh and Israel, and boldly proclaimed himself the Bridegroom (e.g. Mark 2:19, 20). In some way John the Baptist seems to have understood this. He knew he was not himself the Christ and said so plainly. He was his forerunner, sent ahead of him. He went on, 'The bride belongs to the bridegroom. The friend who attends the bridegroom waits and listens for him, and is full of joy when he hears the bridegroom's voice. That joy is mine, and it is now complete. He must become greater; I

326

must become less.' (John 3:28–30, NIV) In this respect the preacher's ministry resembles that of the Baptist, preparing Christ's way, rejoicing in his voice, leaving him with his bride, and constantly decreasing in order that he may increase. The great apostle Paul clearly saw his ministry in these self-effacing terms. 'I betrothed you to Christ,' he wrote to the Corinthians, 'to present you as a pure bride to her one husband.' He even felt jealous on behalf of Christ, because his bride was showing signs of unfaithfulness. (2 Cor. 11:2, 3) Every Christian preacher understands this language and has felt this jealousy. 'We are to be the friends of the Bridegroom,' said J. H. Jowett, 'winning men, not to ourselves but to him, match-making for the Lord, abundantly satisfied when we have brought the bride and the Bridegroom together.'[38] Moreover, he meant it. At the beginning of a certain service at which he was to preach, a prayer was offered for him which opened with what he called 'this inspired supplication', 'O Lord, we thank thee for our brother. Now blot him out!' And the prayer continued, 'Reveal thy glory to us in such blazing splendour that he shall be forgotten.' 'He was absolutely right,' commented Jowett, 'and I trust the prayer was answered.'[39]

The second image which illustrates the need for the preacher to get out of the way is that of the conductor of an orchestra. I take Otto Klemperer as my example, the distinguished German conductor, particularly famed for his interpretations of Brahms and Beethoven, who died in 1973 at the age of eighty-eight. One of his biographers summed up his gift by the simple expression 'he let the music flow.'[40] And in an article which celebrated his eightieth birthday and hailed him as 'the foremost living conductor', Neville Cardus the music critic wrote, 'He has never been a prima-donna conductor; never in his long life has he thrust himself between the music and the listeners. He has maintained a sort of visible invisibility on the rostrum, a classic anonymity.'[41] I very much like that expression 'visible invisibility'. It applies equally to the conductor and the preacher. Neither can help being seen, the one on the rostrum, the other in the pulpit, but neither should seek to draw attention to himself. A concert audience does not come to watch the conductor but to listen to the music; a church congregation should not come to watch or hear the preacher, but to listen to God's Word. The function of the conductor is to draw the music out of the choir or orchestra, in order that the audience may enjoy the music; the function of the preacher is to draw the Word of God out of the Bible, in order that the congregation may receive his Word with joy. The conductor must not come between the music and the audience; the preacher must not come between the Lord and his people. We need the humility to get out of the way. Then the Lord will speak, and the people will hear him; the Lord will manifest himself, and the people will see him; and, hearing his voice and seeing his glory, the people will fall down and worship him.

The Power of the Holy Spirit
The third ingredient in my analysis of a preacher's humility I will call the humility of dependence. Every preacher desires to be effective. He hopes the people will listen to his sermons, understand them and respond to them in faith and obedience. But on what does he rely for this effect?

Many rely on themselves. They are extroverts by temperament, and have a strong as well as an outgoing personality. They may also have a keen intellect. So they make an impression on everybody they meet, for they are born leaders. They naturally expect to use these gifts while they are in the pulpit. Are they right to do so? Yes and no. Certainly, they should recognize the powers of their mind and personality as coming from God. They should neither pretend that they lack these gifts, nor try to obliterate them, nor neglect to use them either in their preparation in the study or in their delivery in the pulpit. They should be themselves. But they should not imagine that even God-given talents can bring people to Christ without the addition of God-given blessing.

In all our ministry we need to remember both the pitiable

spiritual condition of people without Christ and the fright-ening strength and skill of the 'principalities and powers' arrayed against us. Jesus himself illustrated human lostness by the language of physical disability. By ourselves we are blind to God's truth and deaf to his voice. Lame, we cannot walk in his ways. Dumb, we can neither sing to him nor speak for him. We are even dead in our trespasses and sins. Moreover, we are the dupes and slaves of demonic forces. Of course, if we think this exaggerated or 'mythical' or frankly false, then we shall see no need for supernatural power; we shall consider our own resources adequate. But if human beings are in reality spiritually and morally blind, deaf, dumb, lame and even dead, not to mention the pris-oners of Satan, then it is ridiculous in the extreme to suppose that by ourselves and our merely human preaching we can reach or rescue people in such a plight. Let Spur-geon express it with his usual wit and force,

> I shall not attempt to teach a tiger the virtues of veg-etarianism; but I shall as hopefully attempt that task as I would try to convince an unregenerate man of the truth revealed by God concerning sin, and righteousness, and judgment to come.[42]

Only Jesus Christ by his Holy Spirit can open blind eyes and deaf ears, make the lame walk and the dumb speak, prick the conscience, enlighten the mind, fire the heart, move the will, give life to the dead and rescue slaves from Satanic bondage. And all this he can and does, as the preacher should know from his own experience. Therefore, our greatest need as preachers is to be 'clothed with power from on high' (Luke 24:49), so that, like the apostles, we may 'preach the gospel . . . by the Holy Spirit sent down from heaven' (1 Pet. 1:12), and the gospel may come to people through our preaching 'not only in word, but also in power and in the Holy Spirit and with full conviction'. (1 Thess. 1:5) Why, then, does the power of the Spirit seem to accompany our preaching so seldom? I strongly suspect that the main reason is our pride. In order to be filled with the Spirit, we have first to acknowledge our own emptiness. In order to be exalted and used by God, we have first to humble ourselves under his mighty hand. (1 Pet. 5:6) In order to receive his power, we have first to admit, and then even to revel in, our own weakness.

It is this last paradox which, I confess, has struck me most among all the varied ways in which the New Testament authors express the same truth. 'Power through weakness': it is a recurring theme, perhaps even the dominant theme, in Paul's Corinthian correspondence. The Corinthians badly needed it too. For they were proud people, boastful of their own gifts and attainments on the one hand, and boastful of their leaders on the other, indulging in a disgraceful personality cult, playing one apostle off against another, in a way which horrified Paul. They were giving him a deference which was due to Christ alone. 'Was Paul crucified for you?' he cries out in dismay. 'Or were you baptized in the name of Paul?' (1 Cor. 1:13) He will not allow them to go on boasting either of themselves or of any human leaders. 'Let no one boast of men,' he insists. Rather, 'Let him who boasts, boast of the Lord.' (1 Cor. 3:21; 1:31)

It is against this background of Corinthian conceit that Paul's 'power through weakness' theme stands out in clear relief. There are three main passages in which it recurs.

And I was with you in weakness and in much fear and trembling; and my speech and my message were not in plausible words of wisdom, but in demonstration of the Spirit and power, that your faith might not rest in the wisdom of men but in the power of God. (1 Cor. 2:3–5)

But we have this treasure in earthen vessels, to show that the transcendent power belongs to God and not to us. (2 Cor. 4:7)

And to keep me from being too elated by the abundance of revelations, a thorn was given me in the flesh, a messenger of Satan, to harass me, to keep me from being too elated. Three times I besought the Lord about this, that it should leave me; but he said to me, 'My grace is sufficient for you, for my power is made perfect in weakness.' I will all the more gladly boast of my weaknesses, that the power of Christ may rest upon me. For the sake of Christ, then, I am content with weaknesses, insults, hardships, persecutions, and calamities; for when I am weak, then I am strong. (2 Cor. 12:7–10)

Apart from the power-weakness contrast, divine power in and through human weakness, there is something else very important which unites these three passages. It is the occurrence of the Greek word *hina*, 'in order that'. Perhaps I could paraphrase Paul's statements in my own words. First, 'I was with you in personal weakness, and therefore relied on the Holy Spirit's powerful demonstration of the truth of my message, *in order that* your faith might rest in God's power alone.' Secondly, 'We have the treasure of the gospel in fragile earthenware pots (that's how weak and brittle our bodies are), *in order that* it may be plainly seen that the tremendous power which sustains us and converted you comes from God and not from ourselves.' Thirdly, 'Because Jesus told me that his power is made perfect in human weakness, therefore I will gladly boast about my weaknesses, *in order that* Christ's power may rest upon me . . . For it's only when I'm weak that I'm strong.' It is difficult to avoid the significance of this repeated 'in order that', or to resist the conclusion to which it points. In these cases human weakness was deliberately permitted to continue, in order to be the medium through which divine power could operate and the arena in which it could be displayed. Certainly Paul is explicit about his 'thorn in the flesh', whatever physical (or possibly psychological) infirmity it was. True, it was 'a messenger of Satan'. Nevertheless, the Lord Jesus Christ rejected Paul's three entreaties that it might be removed. It was given to humble him, and it was allowed to remain in order that in his very weakness Christ's power might rest on him and be perfected in him.

We cannot, however, restrict this principle to Paul; it has a universal application. One of the aphorisms attributed to Hudson Taylor, founder of the China Inland Mission, is that 'all God's giants have been weak men,' who (he must have meant) needed on that account to depend on the power of God. His assertion cannot be proved, for in some men and women whom God has greatly used no weakness is known. May there not, then, have been hidden, secret weaknesses? I think so. At all events, the number of outstanding preachers simply in the last century or so who are known to have had infirmities is remarkable. Take Dr. James Macgregor, who for nearly forty years was minister of St. Cuthbert's Church in Edinburgh. He was not only small of stature but had been seriously deformed since childhood. On one occasion a pastoral theology lecturer had been insisting, as something indispensable to ministers, on 'a big strong physical frame'. At that very moment, 'the door opened, and he who was affectionately known as "wee Macgregor" entered, as though in challenge of the statement . . . For that figure, with short twisted legs that dwarfed him, was the triumphant vindication of the transcendent independence of the spirit over the handicap of the body.'[43]

The infirmity of others has been more psychological than physical. F. W. Robertson (1816–53), sometimes called 'the preacher's preacher', whose sermons delivered in Trinity Chapel, Brighton, had great influence in his lifetime and are still read today, suffered not only from bad health throughout his short life of thirty-seven years, but also from introspection and melancholy. He felt a failure and was often in deep darkness of soul. Surely it was out of these very weaknesses that the courage and power of his preaching were born. Many are astonished to hear that Joseph Parker, who preached for twenty-eight years in the City Temple, London, with commanding authority and widespread appeal was tormented with feelings of inferior ity because he was the son of a Northumbrian stonemason and had received but a scanty theological education. To some the most surprising disclosure of all is that the great C. H. Spurgeon, invariably known as 'the prince of preachers', who was mighty in the Scriptures, confident, articulate, eloquent and witty, said of himself in a sermon preached in 1866, 'I am the subject of depressions of spirit so fearful that I hope none of you ever get to such extremes of wretchedness as I go to.'[44]

I hesitate to mention myself in this connection, for I certainly do not belong to the class of pulpit masters to whom I have just referred. Nevertheless, although I do not have their power, I think I know something of their weakness. Indeed, I have had several experiences during the thirty-five years of my ordained ministry which have corroborated Paul's Corinthian instruction about power through weakness. I will mention only one. It was in Australia in June 1958. I was leading a week's mission in the University of Sydney, and we had come to the last day, a Sunday. With daring faith the students had booked the imposing Great Hall of the University for the final evening meeting. But what Australians call a 'wog', and the rest of us call a 'bug', had made a vicious assault upon me and deprived me of my voice. I was speechless. All through the afternoon I had been on the point of telephoning somebody to the effect that they must find a substitute preacher. But I was persuaded not to. At seven-thirty, half an hour before the final meeting was due to begin, I was waiting in a side room. Some students were with me, and I whispered a request to the mission committee chairman to read the 'thorn in the flesh' verses from 2 Corinthians 12. He did. The conversation between Jesus and Paul came alive.

Paul: 'I beg you to take it away from me.'
Jesus: 'My grace is sufficient for you, for my power is made perfect in weakness.'
Paul: 'I will all the more gladly boast of my weaknesses,

that the power of Christ may rest upon me . . .
for when I am weak, then I am strong.'

After the reading, he prayed over me and for me, and I walked to the platform. When the time came for the address, all I can say is that I croaked the gospel through the microphone in a monotone. I was utterly unable to modulate my voice or exert my personality in any way. But all the while I was crying to the Lord to fulfil his promise to perfect his power through my weakness. Then at the end, after a straightforward instruction on how to come to Christ, I issued an invitation and there was an immediate and reasonably large response. I have been back to Australia seven or eight times since then, and on every occasion somebody has come up to me and said, 'Do you remember that final service of the 1958 mission in the University Great Hall, when you had lost your voice? I came to Christ that night.'

All of us who are Christian preachers are finite, fallen, frail and fallible creatures, in biblical language 'pots of earthenware' (2 Cor. 4:7 NEB) or 'jars of clay' (NIV). The power belongs to Christ and is exerted through his Spirit. The words we speak in human weakness the Holy Spirit carries home by his power to the mind, heart, conscience and will of the hearers. 'It were better to speak six words in the power of the Holy Ghost,' said Spurgeon once, 'than to preach seventy years of sermons without the Spirit.'[45] I have before me, as I write, a photograph of the massive central pulpit from which Spurgeon preached in the Metropolitan Tabernacle. The photograph is reproduced in the second volume of his *Autobiography*. Fifteen steps led up to it on each side, in a great sweeping curve, and I have heard it said (but been unable to confirm) that as Spurgeon mounted those stairs, with the measured tread of a heavily built man, he muttered to himself on each one, 'I believe in the Holy Ghost.' We may be quite sure that, after fifteen repetitions of this credal affirmation, by the time he entered his pulpit, he *did* believe in the Holy Spirit. He also urges us to do the same:

The gospel is preached in the ears of all; it only comes with power to some. The power that is in the gospel does not lie in the eloquence of the preacher; otherwise men would be converters of souls. Nor does it lie in the preacher's learning; otherwise it would consist in the wisdom of men. We might preach till our tongues rotted, till we should exhaust our lungs and die, but never a soul would be converted unless there were mysterious power going with it – the Holy Ghost changing the will of man. O Sirs! We might as well preach to stone walls as preach to humanity unless the Holy Ghost be with the word, to give it power to convert the soul.[46]

*   *   *

A humble mind (being submissive to the written Word of God), a humble ambition (desiring an encounter to take place between Christ and his people), and a humble dependence (relying on the power of the Holy Spirit) – this is the analysis of a preacher's humility which we have made. It indicates that our message must be God's Word not ours, our aim Christ's glory not ours, and our confidence the Holy Spirit's power, not ours. It is, in fact, a Trinitarian humility, as in 1 Corinthians 2:1–5, where the apostle writes that in Corinth he had proclaimed the Word or 'testimony' of God about the cross of Christ in demonstration of the Spirit and of power.

I do not think I can conclude this chapter better than by quoting some anonymous words which were found by the Rev. Basil Gough in the vestries of St. Mary-at-Quay Church in Ipswich, Suffolk, and in Hatherleigh Parish Church in Devon. They were given to me by him, and have been hanging in my bedroom ever since:

> When telling thy salvation free,
> Let all-absorbing thoughts of thee
>   My heart and soul engross:
> And when all hearts are bowed and stirred
> Beneath the influence of thy word,
>   Hide me behind thy cross.

Notes

1 Buttrick, p. 133.
2 Brooks, *Lectures*, p. 59.
3 Dargan, Vol. I. p. 90.
4 *The Works of St Chrysostom*, in Schaff, Vol. X, p. 123.
5 Works, Vol. 21, p. 124.
6 Works, Vol. 21, pp. 201–2.
7 Whitley, p. 147.
8 ibid., pp. 199, 235.
9 King, p. 18.
10 Melville, p. 142.
11 Henson, *Retrospect*, Vol. I, p. 27.
12 Nicoll, p. 320.
13 Trollope, pp. 26, 27.
14 Morris, p. 11.
15 Jowett, p. 107.
16 Walsh, p. 95.
17 Pollock, *Amazing Grace*, p. 155.
18 Wesley, *Journal*, p. 250.
19 ibid., p. 401.
20 Davies, p. 13.
21 Forsyth, p. 5.
22 ibid., p. 19.
23 Bainton, *Here I Stand*, pp. 348–9.
24 Broadus, *History*, Vol. 1, p. 115.
25 ibid., pp. 414–15.
26 Dale, p. 231
27 I have given in Chapter Six some examples of what, under Michael Baughen's leadership, we have tried to do at All Souls Church.
28 Lloyd-Jones, *Preaching*, p. 13.
29 Beecher, p. 249. Beecher was referring to the incident recorded in Dan. 4:28–37.
30 Baxter, *Reformed Pastor*, p. 95.
31 From his *Christology*, in Fant, *Bonhoeffer*, p. 64.
32 Turnbull, p. 41.
33 Tizard, pp. 40–1.
34 Ward, p. 25.
35 Terwilliger, pp. 112, 114.
36 Miller, D. G., *Fire*, p. 18.
37 Colquhoun, p. 164.
38 Jowett, *The Preacher*, p. 24.

39 ibid., pp. 150–1.
40 Beavan, p. 2.
41 The *Guardian Weekly*, 20 May 1965.
42 Spurgeon, *All-Round Ministry*, p. 322.
43 Gammie, p. 24.
44 Wiersbe, p. 263. See also Spurgeon on 'The Minister's Faint-
    ing Fits', *Lectures*, First Series, Lecture XI, pp. 167–79.
45 Spurgeon, *Twelve Sermons*, p. 122.
46 This moving exhortation was sent to me perhaps thirty years
    ago by Canon Fred Pickering, at that time Vicar of Christ
    Church, Southport. It is not to be found in any of the three
    volumes of his *Lectures to my Students*, however. Nor is it in
    An All-Round Ministry or in his *Twelve Sermons* on the Holy
    Spirit. I have been unable to trace the reference.

Epilogue

I Believe in Preaching. The words are more than the title of this book; they also affirm a strong personal conviction. I do believe in preaching, and I further believe that nothing is better calculated to restore health and vitality to the Church or to lead its members into maturity in Christ than a recovery of true, biblical, contemporary preaching. Certainly there are strong objections, which we have tried to face. But there are even stronger theological arguments, which we have tried to grasp. Certainly too, the task of preaching today is extremely exacting, as we seek to build bridges between the Word and the world, between divine revelation and human experience, and to relate the one to the other with integrity and relevance. So God's call comes to us freshly to give ourselves more time in which both to study and to prepare, and to determine to preach with sincerity, earnestness, courage and humility.

The question which immediately springs to our lips is: who is sufficient for these things? The privilege is great, the responsibility is taxing, the temptations are many, and the standards are high. How can we hope to make an adequate response?

I would like to share with you, in reply, a simple secret. I struggle myself to remember it, and whenever I am enabled to do so, I find it extremely helpful. It begins with the negative fact of Psalm 139 that, wherever we go, we cannot escape from God, and it continues with the positive counterpart that, wherever we are, 'even there' his right hand leads and holds us. More than that. His eye as well as his hand is upon us, and his ears are open to our words and prayers. (Ps. 32:8; Ps. 34:15 = 1 Pet. 3:12) This truth is

338

important for every Christian, but it has special significance for the preacher. As examples I choose Jeremiah in the Old Testament and Paul in the New.

Jeremiah: What passes my lips is open before you. (Jer. 17:16 NIV)

Paul: As men of sincerity, as commissioned by God, in the sight of God, we speak in Christ. It is in the sight of God that we have been speaking in Christ. (2 Cor. 2:17; 12:19)

True, when we preach, we speak in the sight and the hearing of human beings, and they challenge us to be faithful. But how much more challenging is the awareness that we preach in the sight and the hearing of God? He sees what we do; he listens to what we say. Nothing will more quickly rid us of laziness and coldness, of hypocrisy, cowardice and pride than the knowledge that God sees, hears and takes account. So may God grant us a more constant and more vivid awareness of his presence, to whom all hearts are open and from whom no secrets are hidden! God grant that, when we preach, we may become even more conscious that *he* sees and hears than that the congregation sees and hears, and that this knowledge will inspire us to faithfulness!

Handley Moule, who was later to become the first Principal of Ridley Hall Cambridge and then Bishop of Durham, was ordained in 1867 to serve under his father at Fordington in Dorset. This explains the title of his poem 'Fordington Pulpit – a preacher's weekday thoughts'. Although it can hardly claim to be great poetry, it contains the fruit of his own self-examination. Referring to God as 'this Great Listener', who stands at the preacher's side and hears his sermons, it ends with these searching questions:

Has he found thy message true?
Truth, and truly spoken too?
Uttered with a purpose whole
From a self-forgetful soul,

339

Bent on nothing save the fame
Of the great redeeming Name,
And the pardon, life and bliss
Of the flock he bought for his?[1]

Self-forgetfulness is an unattainable goal, except as the by-product of preoccupation with Another's presence, and with his message, his power and his glory. It is for this reason that, for a number of years now, I have found it helpful before preaching to pray this prayer in the pulpit:

Heavenly Father, we bow in your presence.
May your Word be our rule,
    your Spirit our teacher,
and your greater glory our supreme concern,
through Jesus Christ our Lord.

Note

1 Harford and Macdonald, p. 63.

Select Bibliography

(For quotation references see the notes following each chapter; full details of books quoted are given only here.)

1. Books on Ministry and Preaching

Alexander, James W., *Thoughts on Preaching* (1864; Banner of Truth reprint, 1975).

Allmen, Jean-Jacques von, *Preaching and Congregation* (French original 1955; Lutterworth, 1962).

Bavinck, J. H., *An Introduction to the Science of Missions* (Presbyterian and Reformed Publishing Co., 1960).

Baxter, Richard, *The Reformed Pastor* (1656; Epworth second edition revised by John T. Wilkinson, 1950).

Beecher, Henry Ward, *Lectures on Preaching: Personal Elements in Preaching*, the 1872 Yale Lectures (Nelson, 1872).

Bernard, Richard, *The Faithfull Shepheard* (London 1607).

Black, James, *The Mystery of Preaching*, the 1923 Warrack and Sprunt Lectures (James Clarke, 1924; revised edition, Marshall, Morgan & Scott, 1977).

Blackwood, Andrew W., *The Preparation of Sermons* (Abingdon, 1948; Church Book Room Press, 1951).

Brilioth, Bishop Yngve, *Landmarks in the History of Preaching*, the 1949 Donellan Lectures in Dublin (S.P.C.K., 1950).

Broadus, John A., *On the Preparation and Delivery of Sermons* (1870; new and revised edition by J. B. Weatherspoon, Harper, 1944).

Lectures on the History of Preaching (1876; Armstrong, New York, 1899).

Brooks, Phillips, *Lectures on Preaching*, the 1877 Yale Lectures (Dutton, 1877; Allenson, 1895; Baker, 1969).

Essays and Addresses, religious, literary and social, ed. John Cotton Brooks (Macmillan, 1894).

Brunner, Emil, *The Word and the World* (S.C.M., 1931).

Buttrick, George A., *Jesus Came Preaching*, Christian Preaching in the New Age, the 1931 Yale Lectures (Scribner, 1931).

Bull, Paul B., *Lectures on Preaching and Sermon Construction* (S.P.C.K., 1922).

Coggan, F. Donald, *Stewards of Grace* (Hodder & Stoughton, 1958).

 On Preaching (S.P.C.K., 1978)

Crum, Milton, *Manual on Preaching*, a new process of sermon development (Judson, 1977).

Dale, R. W., *Nine Lectures on Preaching*, the 1876 Yale Lectures (Hodder & Stoughton, 1877; Barnes, 1878; Doran, New York, 1900).

Dargan, Edwin Charles, *A History of Preaching, Vol. 1 A.D. 70–1572* (Hodder & Stoughton and G. H. Doran, 1905), *Vol. II A.D. 1572–1900* (Hodder & Stoughton and G. H. Doran 1912).

Davies, Horton, *Varieties of English Preaching 1900–1960* (S.C.M. and Prentice-Hall, 1963).

Davis, H. Grady, *Design for Preaching* (Fortress, 1958).

Fant, Clyde E., *Bonhoeffer: Worldly Preaching* (Nelson, 1975. Includes Bonhoeffer's Finkenwalde Lectures on Homiletics 1935–39).

Ferris, Theodore Parker, *Go Tell the People*, the 1950 George Craig Stewart Lectures on Preaching (Scribner, 1951).

Ford, D. W. Cleverley, *An Expository Preacher's Notebook* (Hodder & Stoughton, 1960).

 A Theological Preacher's Notebook (Hodder & Stoughton, 1962).

 A Pastoral Preacher's Notebook (Hodder & Stoughton, 1965).

 Preaching Today (Epworth and S.P.C.K., 1969).

 The Ministry of the Word (Hodder & Stoughton, 1979).

Forsyth, P. T., *Positive Preaching and the Modern Mind* (Independent Press, 1907).

Gillett, David, *How Do Congregations Learn?* (Grove Booklet on Ministry and Worship No. 67, 1979).

Hall, Thor, *The Future Shape of Preaching* (Fortress, 1971).

Herbert, George, *A Priest to the Temple* or *The Country Parson, his Character and Rule of Holy Life* (written 1632, published 1652; ed. H. C. Beeching, Blackwell, 1898).

Horne, Charles Silvester, *The Romance of Preaching*, the 1914 Yale Lectures (James Clarke and Revell, 1914).

Huxtable, John, *The Preacher's Integrity and other lectures* (Epworth, 1966).

Jowett, J. H., *The Preacher: his life and work*, the 1912 Yale Lectures (G. H. Doran, New York, 1912).

Keir, Thomas H., *The Word in Worship* (O.U.P., 1962).

Lloyd-Jones, D. Martyn, *Preaching and Preachers* (Hodder & Stoughton, 1971; Zondervan, 1972).

   The Christian Warfare, an Exposition of Ephesians 6:10–13 (Banner of Truth, 1976; Baker, 1976).

Mahaffy, Sir John Pentland, *The Decay of Modern Preaching* (Macmillan, 1882).

Martin, Al, *What's Wrong with Preaching Today?* (Banner of Truth, 1968).

Mather, Cotton, *Student and Preacher*, or *Directions for a Candidate of the Ministry* (1726; Hindmarsh, London, 1789).

McGregor, W. M., *The Making of a Preacher*, the 1942–3 Warrack Lectures (S.C.M., 1945).

McWilliam, Stuart W., *Called to Preach* (St. Andrew Press, 1969).

Miller, Donald G., *Fire in Thy Mouth* (Abingdon, 1954).

Mitchell, Henry H., *Black Preaching* (1970; second edition Harper & Row, 1979).

   The Recovery of Preaching (Harper & Row, 1977; Hodder & Stoughton, 1979).

Morgan, G. Campbell, *Preaching* (1937; Baker Book House reprint 1974).

Morris, Colin, *The Word and the Words* (Epworth, 1975).

Neill, S. C., *On the Ministry* (S.C.M., 1952).

Perkins, William, *The Art of Prophecying* or 'A Treatise concerning the sacred and onely true manner and methode of preaching', being Vol. II (1631) of *The Workes of that Famous and Worthy Minister of Christ in the Universitie of Cambridge, Mr. William Perkins* (John Legatt and John Haviland, London, 3 Vols. 1631–5).

Perry, Lloyd M., *Biblical Preaching for Today's World* (Moody Press, 1973).

Phelps, Austin, *Men and Books* or *Lectures Introductory for the Theory of Preaching* (Dickinson, 1882).

Pitt-Watson, Ian, *A Kind of Folly*, Toward a Practical Theology of Preaching, the 1972–5 Warrack Lectures, (St. Andrew Press, 1976; Westminster, 1978).

Poulton, John, *A Today Sort of Evangelism* (Lutterworth, 1972).

Quayle, William A., *The Pastor-Preacher* (1910; Baker 1979).

Rahner, Karl, (ed.). *The Renewal of Preaching* – theory and practice, Vol. 33 of *Concilium*, (Paulist Press, New York, 1968).

Ramsey, Michael, *The Christian Priest Today* (Mowbray, 1972).

Read, David H. C., *The Communication of the Gospel*, the 1951 Warrack Lectures (S.C.M., 1952).

Reid, Clyde, *The Empty Pulpit*, a Study in Preaching as Communication (Harper & Row, 1967).

Robinson, Haddon W., *Biblical Preaching*, the development and delivery of expository messages (Baker, 1980).

Sangster, W. E., *The Craft of Sermon Illustration* (1946; incorporated in *The Craft of the Sermon*, Epworth, 1954).
 The Craft of Sermon Construction (1949; incorporated in *The Craft of the Sermon*, Epworth, 1954).
 The Approach to Preaching (Epworth, 1951).
 Power in Preaching (Epworth, 1958).

Simpson, Matthew, *Lectures on Preaching* (Phillips & Hunt, New York, 1879).

Smyth, Charles, *The Art of Preaching*, a Practical Survey of Preaching in the Church of England 747–1939 (S.P.C.K., 1940).

Spurgeon, C. H., *An All-Round Ministry*, a collection of addresses to ministers and students, 1900 (Banner of Truth, 1960).
 Lectures to My Students in 3 Vols., first series 1881; second series 1882; third series 1894 (Passmore and Alabaster; Zondervan, 1980).

Stalker, James, *The Preacher and his Models*, the 1891 Yale Lectures (Hodder & Stoughton, 1891).

Stewart, James S., *A Faith to Proclaim*, the 1953 Yale Lectures (Scribner's, 1953).
 Heralds of God, the 1946 Warrack Lectures (Hodder & Stoughton, 1946).

Sweazey, George E., *Preaching the Good News* (Prentice-Hall, 1976).

Terwilliger, Robert E., *Receiving the Word of God* (Morehouse-Barlow, 1960).

Tizard, Leslie J., *Preaching* – The Art of Communication (George Allen & Unwin, 1958).

Turnbull, Ralph G., *A Minister's Obstacles* (1946; Baker Book House edition, 1972).

Vinet, A., *Homiletics* or *The Theory of Preaching* (English translation from French, T. and T. Clark, 1853).

Volbeda, Samuel, *The Pastoral Genius of Preaching* (Zondervan, 1960).

Wand, William, *Letters on Preaching* (Hodder & Stoughton, 1974).

Ward, Ronald A., *Royal Sacrament*, The Preacher and his Message (Marshall, Morgan & Scott, 1958).

Welsh, Clement, *Preaching in a New Key*, studies in the psychology of thinking and listening (Pilgrim Press, 1974).

White, R. E. O., *A Guide to Preaching*, a practical primer of homiletics (Pickering & Inglis, 1973).

Wilkins, John, Bishop of Chester, *Ecclesiastes* or 'A discourse concerning the gift of Preaching, as it falls under the Rules of Art, showing the most proper Rules and Directions, for Method, Invention, Books, Expression whereby a Minister may be furnished with such abilities as may make him a Workman *that need not to be ashamed*' 1646, third edition, 1651.

Williams, Howard, *My Word*, Christian Preaching Today (S.C.M., 1973).

Wingren, Gustaf, *The Living Word* (1949, English translation S.C.M., 1960).

2. Books on Communication and the Media

Berlo, David K., *The Process of Communication*, an introduction to theory and practice (Holt, Rinehart & Winston, 1960).

Broadcasting, Society and the Church, report of the Broadcasting Commission of the General Synod of the Church of England (Church Information Office, 1973).

Children and Television, a national survey among 7–17 year olds (1978) commissioned by Pye Limited, Cambridge.

Evans, Christopher, *The Mighty Micro*, the Impact of the Microchip Revolution (1979, Hodder & Stoughton Coronet edition, 1980).

Freire, Paulo, *Pedagogy of the Oppressed* (Penguin, 1972).

The Future of Broadcasting, the Annan Report (H.M.S.O., London 1977).

Gowers, Sir Ernest, *The Complete Plain Words* (incorporating both *Plain Words* and *The ABC of Plain Words*, H.M.S.O., London, 1954).

Hirsch, E. D., *Validity in Interpretation* (Yale University Press, 1967).

Lewis, C. S., *Studies in Words* (Cambridge University Press, 1960).

McGinniss, Joe, *The Selling of the President 1968* (Trident Press, 1969; Pocket Books 1970).

McLuhan, Marshall, *The Gutenberg Galaxy: The Making of Typographic Man* (Routledge, 1962).

Understanding Media: The Extensions of Man (Routledge, 1964, Abacus 1973).

The Medium is the Massage: An Inventory of Effects, with Quentin Fiore (Penguin, 1967).

Miller, Jonathan, *McLuhan* in the 'Fontana Modern Masters' series (Collins, 1971).

Muggeridge, Malcolm, *Christ and the Media*, the 1976 London Lectures in Contemporary Christianity (Hodder & Stoughton, 1977; Eerdmans, 1978).

Packard, Vance, *The Hidden Persuaders*, an introduction to the techniques of mass-persuasion through the unconscious (David McKay, 1957, Penguin 1960).

Reid, Gavin, *The Gagging of God*, the failure of the church to communicate in the television age (Hodder & Stoughton, 1969).

Screen Violence and Film Censorship, Home Office Research Study No. 40, (H.M.S.O., London, 1977).

Solzhenitsyn, Alexander, *One Word of Truth*, the 1970 Nobel Speech on Literature (Bodley Head, 1972; Farrer, Strausz & Giroux, 1970).

Thiselton, Anthony, *Two Horizons* (Paternoster, 1980; Eerdmans, 1980).

The Willowbank Report on Gospel and Culture, Lausanne Occasional Paper No. 2 (1978), also published in *Explaining the Gospel in Today's World* (Scripture Union 1979).

Winn, Marie, *The Plug-In Drug*, television, children and the family (Viking Press, New York, 1977).

3. Historical, Biographical and Autobiographical

Bainton, Roland H., *Erasmus of Christendom* (1969; Collins, 1970).

Here I Stand, a Life of Martin Luther (Hodder & Stoughton, 1951; New American Library, 1957).

Barbour, G. F., *The Life of Alexander Whyte* (Hodder & Stoughton, 1923).

Beavan, Peter, *Klemperisms* (Cock Robin Press, 1974).

Bosanquet, Mary, *The Life and Death of Dietrich Bonhoeffer* (Hodder & Stoughton, 1968).

Cadier, Jean, *The Man God Mastered*, a brief biography of John Calvin, translated by O. R. Johnston (Inter-Varsity Fellowship, 1960).

Carlyle, Thomas, *Heroes and Hero-Worship* (1841; third edition, London, 1846).

Carus, William (ed.), *Memoirs of the Rev. Charles Simeon*, (Hatchard, 1847).

Chorley, E. Clowes, *Men and Movements in the American Episcopal Church*, the Hale Lectures (Scribner, New York, 1946).

Colquhoun, Frank, *Haringay Story* (Hodder & Stoughton, 1955).

Day, Richard Elsworth, *The Shadow of the Broad Brim*, the life-story of Charles Haddon Spurgeon (Judson Press, 1934).

Dillistone, F. W., *Charles Raven* (Hodder & Stoughton, 1975).

Dwight, S. E., *The Life of President Edwards* (Carvill, New York, 1830), being Vol. 1 of *The Works of President Edwards* in 10 Vols.

Gammie, Alexander, *Preachers I Have Heard* (Pickering & Inglis, 1945).

Haller, William, *The Rise of Puritanism* (Columbia University Press, New York, 1938).

Harford, J. B., and MacDonald, F. C., *Bishop Handley Moule* (Hodder & Stoughton, 1922).

Haslam, W., *From Death into Life* (Marshall, Morgan & Scott, 1880).

Hennell, Michael, *John Venn and the Clapham Sect* (Lutterworth, 1958).

Henson, H. Hensley, *Robertson of Brighton 1816–1853* (Smith, Elder, 1916).

 Retrospect of an Unimportant Life (O.U.P., Vol. 1, 1942, Vol. 2 1943, Vol. 3 1950).

Hopkins, Hugh Evan, *Charles Simeon of Cambridge* (Hodder & Stoughton, 1977).

Inge, W. R., *Diary of a Dean*, St. Paul's 1911–34 (Hutchinson, 1949).

Jones, Edgar De Witt, *American Preachers of Today*, intimate appraisals of thirty-two leaders (Bobbs-Merrill, 1933).

Keefe, Carolyn, (ed.), *C. S. Lewis, Speaker and Teacher*, a symposium (Zondervan, 1971, Hodder & Stoughton, 1974).

King, Coretta Scott, *My Life with Martin Luther King, Jr.* (Hodder & Stoughton, 1970; Holt, Rinehart, and Winston, 1969).

Moorman, J. R. H., *A History of the Church of England* (A. & C. Black, 1953).

Morgan, Irvonwy, *The Godly Preachers of the Elizabethan Church* (Epworth, 1965).

Muggeridge, Malcolm, *Chronicles of Wasted Time*: Part 1 *The Green Stick* (Collins, 1972).

Nicoll, W. Robertson, *Princes of the Church* (Hodder & Stoughton, 1921).

Paget, Elma K., *Henry Luke Paget, Portrait and Frame* (Longman, 1939).

Pollock, John C., *George Whitefield and the Great Awakening* (Hodder & Stoughton, 1973).
    Wilberforce (Constable, 1977, Lion paperback, 1978).
    Amazing Grace (Hodder & Stoughton, 1981).

Rupp, Ernest Gordon, *Luther's Progress to the Diet of Worms 1521* (S.C.M., 1951).

Ryle, J. C., *The Christian Leaders of the Last Century* or *England a Hundred Years Ago* (Thynne, 1868. New edition).
    Light from Old Times (Thynne & Jarvis, 1924).

Sangster, Paul, *Doctor Sangster* (Epworth, 1962).

Simpson, J. G., *Preachers and Teachers* (Edward Arnold, 1910).

Smyth, Charles, *Cyril Forster Garbett*, Archbishop of York (Hodder & Stoughton, 1959).

Warren, M. A. C., *Crowded Canvas* (Hodder & Stoughton, 1974).

Wesley, John, *Journal,* abridged by Nehemiah Curnock (Epworth, 1949).

White, Paul, *Alias Jungle Doctor*, An Autobiography (Paternoster, 1977).

Whitley, Elizabeth, *Plain Mr. Knox* (Scottish Reformation Society, 1960).

Wiersbe, Warren, *Walking with the Giant*, a minister's guide to good reading and great preaching (Baker 1976).

Williams, W., *Personal Reminscences of Charles Haddon Spurgeon* (Religious Tract Society, 1895).

Woodforde, James, *The Diary of a Country Parson* 1758–1802. Edited by John Beresford in 5 Vols. (O.U.P. 1926–31).

4. Miscellaneous

Abbott, Walter M. (ed.), *The Documents of Vatican II* (Geoffrey Chapman, 1967).

Barth, Karl, *The Word of God and the Word of Man*, a collection of addresses first published in German in 1928. (Hodder & Stoughton, 1935; Peter Smith, 1958).

Baxter, Richard, *Poetical Fragments* (1681; Gregg International Publishers, 1971).

Berger, Peter L., *Facing up to Modernity* (Basic Books, New York, 1977).

Blamires, Harry, *The Christian Mind* (S.P.C.K., 1963).

Bounds, E. M., *Power through Prayer* (Marshall, Morgan & Scott, 1912).

Calvin, John, *Institutes of the Christian Religion*, first published 1536; completed 1959. (translated by F. L. Battler, in The Library of Christian Classics, Vols. 20 and 21, S.C.M. and Westminster, 1960).

Chrysostom: *Works of St. Chrysostom*. In *Post-Nicene Fathers*, Vol. X (Eerdmans, 1975).

Coggan, Donald, *Convictions* (Hodder & Stoughton, 1975; paperback 1978).

The Didache. In *Ante-Nicene Fathers*, Vol. VII (1886. Eerdmans 1975).

Eliot, George, *Scenes of Clerical Life* (1858; Penguin 1973).

Eusebius, *Ecclesiastical History* (S.P.C.K., 1928).

Golding, William, *Free Fall* (Faber, 1959; Harcourt Brace, 1962).

Fant, Clyde E., and Pinson, William M., (eds.), *Twenty Centuries of Great Preaching*, 13 Vols. (Word Books, 1971).

Glover T. R., *The Jesus of History* (S.C.M. 1917; Hodder & Stoughton, 1965).

Green, E. M. B., *The Truth of God Incarnate* (Hodder & Stoughton, 1977).

Grubb, Kenneth G., *A Layman Looks at the Church* (Hodder & Stoughton, 1964).

Henson, Hensley H., *Church and Parson in England* (Hodder & Stoughton, 1927).

Hernandez, José, *The Gaucho* (Part 1 1872, Part 2 1879. English translation by Walter Owen 1935; bilingual edition Editorial Pampa 1967).

Irenaeus, *Adversus Haereses*, Book IV, Ch. 26 (circa A.D. 200). In *Ante-Nicene Fathers*, Vol. 1 (1886; Eerdmans, 1962).

Justin Martyr, *The First Apology*, (circa. A.D. 150). In *Ante-Nicene Fathers*, Vol. 1 (1886; Eerdmans, 1962).

Knox, Ronald, *Essays in Satire* (Sheed & Ward, 1928; new edition 1954).

Latimer: *Select Sermons and Letters of Dr. Hugh Latimer* (R.T.S. und.)
  Works of Hugh Latimer (Parker Society Edition, Vol. 1, C.U.P., 1844).

Leacock, Stephen, *Sunshine Sketches of a Little Town* (McLelland & Stewart, 1948).

Lehmann, Helmut T. (ed.), *Luther's Works* (Fortress Press, 1965).

Lewis, W. H. (ed.), *Letters of C. S. Lewis* (Geoffrey Bles, 1966).

Luther's Table-Talk, 1566 (Captain Henry Bell, 1886).

Luther's Works (Concordia Publishing House, St. Louis, 1956).

Manning, Bernard L., *A Layman in the Ministry* (Independent Press, 1942).

Maugham, Somerset, *The Moon and Sixpence* (Penguin, 1919).

Melville, Herman, *Moby Dick* or *The Whale* (1851; Penguin, 1972).

Parker, J. H. (ed.), *A Library of Fathers of the Holy Catholic Church* (O.U.P., 1843).

Portable Mark Twain, The (Viking Press, New York, 1958).

Ramsey, Arthur Michael, and Suenens, Leon-Joseph, *The Future of the Christian Church* (S.C.M., 1971).

Schaff, Philip (ed.), *The Nicene and Post-Nicene Fathers* (1892, Eerdmans 1975).

Simeon, Charles, *Horae Homileticae*, or Discourses (in the form of skeletons) upon the whole Scriptures, in 11 Vols., 1819–20. Also An Appendix to the Horae Homileticae in 6 Vols., 1828. (Richard Watts, 1819–28).

  Let Wisdom Judge, University Addresses and Sermon Outlines, ed. Arthur Pollard (Inter-Varsity Fellowship, 1959).

Spurgeon, C. H., *Twelve Sermons on the Holy Spirit* (Marshall, Morgan & Scott, 1937; Baker, 1973).

Stewart, James S., *A Man in Christ* (Hodder & Stoughton, 1935; revised edition 1972; Baker, 1975).

Tertullian, *The Apology* (circa A.D. 200). In *Ante-Nicene Fathers*, Vol. 3 (1885; Eerdmans, 1973).

Toffler, Alvin, *Future Shock* (Bodley Head, 1970; Random, 1970).

Trollope, Anthony, *Barchester Towers* (1857; J. M. Dent, Everyman's Library, 1906).

Trueblood, Elton, *The Humour of Christ* (Harper & Row, 1964; Darton, Longman & Todd, 1965).

Twain, Mark, *The Adventures of Tom Sawyer* (1876; Pan Books 1965).

Walsh, Chad, *Campus Gods on Trial* (Macmillan 1962).

Welsby, Paul A. (ed.), *Sermons and Society*, an Anglican Anthology (Penguin, 1970).

Wesley, John, *Sermons on Several Occasions*, published in 4 Vols. 1746–60 (Epworth, 1944).